**THE STANLEY THORNES
TEACHING PRIMARY ENGLISH S**

SERIES EDITOR
JENI RILEY

Teaching
Reading

at Key Stage 2

NICHOLAS BIELBY

STANLEY THORNES (PUBLISHERS) LTD

First published in 1999 by:
Stanley Thornes (Publishers) Ltd
Ellenborough House
Wellington Street
CHELTENHAM
GL50 1YW
UK

A catalogue record for this book is available from the British Library.

ISBN 0 7487 4040 6

99 00 01 02 03 / 10 9 8 7 6 5 4 3 2 1

The author and publishers would like to thank the MIT Press for permission to reproduce the figure on page viii; and A.P. Watt Ltd on behalf of The Royal Literary Fund for permission to reproduce the poem 'The Donkey' by G.K. Chesterton on pages 115–116.

Typeset by The Florence Group, Stoodleigh, Devon

Printed and bound in Great Britain by Martins the Printers Ltd, Berwick upon Tweed

Contents

The Teaching Primary English series

The importance of literacy for individuals and society cannot be over-stated. This series of six complementary volumes supports the Government's initiatives to raise standards in reading and writing. At the individual level, literacy determines personal growth, quality of life, self-image and the ability to function in the world. Being literate opens up opportunities, in an increasingly information-rich world, to access knowledge, to make choices and to achieve self-fulfilment. At national level, the smooth functioning and economic prosperity of a society depends upon a well-educated, flexible and highly skilled workforce.

> Literacy is fundamental to thinking, to formal education, and to life-long learning. The link between high levels of literacy and academic success occurs, initially, through allowing individuals access to the curriculum, and secondly, through enabling them to achieve success educationally.

(McGaw, Long, Morgan and Rosier, 1989)

THE NEED FOR HIGHER LEVELS OF LITERACY

Schools continually strive to maintain literacy standards, but with higher and higher levels of literacy required by modern society, more is demanded of them. Reading and writing have become even more crucial with the increased use of information and communications technology, although the production and form of texts are changing with the advent of fax, e-mail and the Internet. More has to be done to enable teachers to meet the greater demands placed upon them.

THE IMPORTANCE OF PRIMARY EDUCATION IN IMPROVING STANDARDS OF LITERACY

Primary schools and, in particular, the early years of education, are key to the success of any literacy drive. There is a body of research evidence that supports the claim that the foundations of literacy are laid in the first two years of school. I have argued elsewhere that a positive early start to school benefits pupils for the whole of their school careers (Riley, 1996). Furthermore, researchers in Australia suggest that efforts to correct literacy difficulties after the third Grade (Year) are largely unsuccessful:

> Students who fail to make progress in literacy during the first two years of school rarely catch up with their peers and are at risk of becoming low achievers who are alienated with school and drop out at the earliest opportunity.
>
> (Kennedy, Birman and Demaline, 1986)

Conversely, there is empirical evidence that supports the view that it is possible for all children, except a very small percentage, to be successfully taught to read and write (Piluski, 1994). This encouraging evidence comes from the evaluations of the effectiveness of whole school programmes such as *Success for All* (Slavin *et al.*, 1996) and an intervention programme, *Reading Recovery* (Hurry, 1995).

HOW ARE LITERACY STANDARDS TO BE RAISED?

It is clear from the American and Australian experience that class teachers cannot raise literacy standards alone and simply by working harder (Crevola and Hill, 1998). However, dramatic improvements can be achieved with comprehensive programmes that embrace 'system and school-wide commitment and co-ordination' (op. cit.)

The principles that underpin comprehensive initiatives to raise standards of literacy are that (Crevola and Hill, 1998):

- there needs to be an attitude shift. High expectations and a belief that all children can be successful is the essential first step
- there is a need for a detailed, systematic and on-going record of progress to be kept on every pupil. This information guides decision-making regarding identification of, and intervention relating to, children 'at risk' and monitoring the teaching and learning of all
- good targeted teaching needs to occur. Such a requirement demands teachers who are well trained and who understand the literacy process; additional in-service opportunities are needed to support class teachers in their development of new modes of pedagogy and co-ordinating the programme across the school
- intervention programmes need to be available for the children who, despite effective teaching, fail to make progress
- strong links need to be in place between schools and their pupils' homes and communities.

Concern was identified by the Labour Party's Literacy Task Force in 1996 and the National Literacy Strategy, with the above characteristics, was planned and introduced in the United Kingdom in September 1998. As well as the introduction of this programme, Initial Teacher Education received increasingly prescriptive directives on how the country's primary teachers should be trained (DfEE Circulars 10/97 and 4/98).

THE SERIES

The underlying principle

> ... that almost all children will become literate more easily and fully if they are given systematic help which is based on a good understanding of the nature of the enterprise but which never fails to respect them as individual learners.

(Donaldson, 1993, p. 57)

This series of six complementary and inter-connecting volumes re-affirms a wide and balanced ideological base for teaching language and literacy in primary schools and one that builds on existing successful provision. Such a view of the teaching and learning of English is informed by research evidence and established educational principles. The books aim to provide primary teacher educators, primary teachers and students with the knowledge, understanding and skills that are required to teach English effectively and imaginatively in primary classrooms. The intention is also to view reading in a wide frame of reference. The series dovetails reading with writing into literacy and sees them as integral with and inseparable from speaking and listening.

Previous influences on the teaching of English

Concern about literacy standards in primary schools has been the driving force for the Government initiatives referred to earlier. The teaching of English has been the source of much debate, and the recipient of fruitful and abundant research. Important initiatives such as the National Curriculum, the National Writing Project, the National Oracy Project and the LINC (Language in the National Curriculum) Project have contributed to the advancement of thinking to its present position regarding the teaching and learning of speaking and listening, reading and writing. There is a great deal to be understood by primary teachers to enable them to teach English well; and the support of literacy particularly in the early years of school requires great skill and a rich knowledge base of the theory which informs understanding and underpins practice.

The DfEE Circulars and the National Literacy Strategy

This series readily acknowledges the need for DfEE Circulars 10/97 and 4/98 and the value of the introduction of the National Literacy Strategy. For the first time in history all teacher education institutions will be designing courses of Initial Teacher Education that have the same starting points for English, Mathematics and Science. All students will be taught how to teach the Core Subjects of the National Curriculum from the same viewpoints with the same emphases and using the same content. No longer is there room for personal preferences, ideologies or flights of fancy. The National Literacy Strategy provides in considerable detail the content to be covered by teachers at different stages of the primary school, stipulating when and how it is to be addressed. This unification and prescription of the English curriculum and how it is to be taught will have an immense effect on primary teachers and their professional functioning. Whilst some will mourn the loss of the greater autonomy of the past, many will find the framework and the structure supportive and enabling. Pupils remaining in the same school, or moving from school to school, will benefit from the consistency of approach, and the clearly thought-out progression of teaching.

The above introduction might seem to render unnecessary a series of books on the teaching and learning of language and literacy. The authors would like to argue exactly the reverse; we consider that these government initiatives require a series of volumes to expand on the documents, to explain them from a theoretical standpoint and to provide an academic rationale for the practice suggested. I have suggested elsewhere (Riley, 1996) that teachers have to be extraordinarily knowledgeable about the processes involved, if they are to enable their pupils to become effective users of spoken and written language.

Teachers are not technicians, they are professionals making complex and finely tuned judgements that inform their teaching. Primary teachers cannot be given the equivalent of a painting-by-numbers kit and told to teach it. This is as unthinkable as a surgeon being given a step-by-step guide on how to conduct a heart operation. Both require a thorough and deep understanding of what is involved, the processes at work and sound direction regarding proven successful practice. These volumes aim to flesh out the theoretical references that underpin the thinking, to fill in the gaps in the explanations so that teachers are better able to implement the National Literacy Strategy with confidence and genuine understanding.

PSYCHOLOGICAL PROCESSES AT WORK WHEN READING

The view of literacy held by this series is one based firmly on the evidence of psychological research.

The starting point for these volumes is that literacy is an inter-related process and needs to be taught in a balanced way: that is a way that takes into account the different aspects of the processing. This perspective is the one adopted by the Government initiatives. Teachers, we believe, in order to teach reading effectively, need to have an understanding of the processing which takes place in order for an individual to be able to read.

Any methods of teaching reading that aim to be comprehensive need to look for an explanation of the literacy process that accounts for its complexity. Figure I.1 demonstrates the inter-relatedness of the different processes involved.

Figure I.1
The inter-relatedness of the reading process

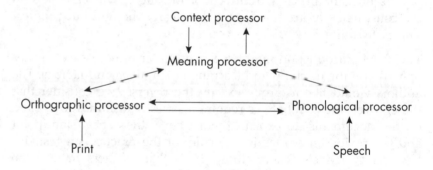

(Adams, 1990, p. 158)

This diagram shows how the two main strategies of reading work together to help the reader make sense of the text. The two strategies are the so-called 'top-down' processing and the 'bottom-up' processing of text.

Top-down processing skills
It can be seen from the Adams diagram that at the centre of the act of reading lies meaning-making which fulfils the whole purpose of the activity. The context of the grammar and the meaning allows the reader to be supported in the task of decoding by being primed to expect what words might come next. The use of context is described as the top-down processing and is in turn supported by the child's knowledge of the world, the story as a whole, the cover, the illustrations and the format of the book.

Bottom-up processing skills: sound awareness and print awareness

In order to read text, readers have to realise that there is a connection between the sounds that are spoken and the written marks on the page. Very crudely and simply this is the understanding that there is written code (the alphabet) that represents the sounds of speech. There are various stages of progress as readers work towards this understanding.

On the way to learning to read, the child has to be able to hear and distinguish between the different words and then to discriminate between the constituent sounds in words (phonemic segmentation). These are then decoded from the letters and groups of letters on the printed page. The child who has this ability is said to understand grapheme–phoneme (letter–sound) correspondence. This aspect of reading is shown clearly in the diagram. An appreciation of both the visual aspects of print (orthographic processing) and the identification of the aural sounds of spoken language (phonological processing) develop side by side, and the inter-relationship ensures that each complements the other. This processing is referred to as the bottom-up or de-coding skills.

Both top-down and bottom-up processing strategies have to be functioning if children are to learn to read successfully and speedily. Teachers need to know how to teach reading so that the whole processing system is developed and can operate effectively. This is the important principle that underpins the series and the two books on the teaching of reading in particular (*Teaching Reading at Key Stage 1 and Before* and *Teaching Reading at Key Stage 2*).

The authors of the volumes re-affirm their belief that:

> Means must be found to ensure that all children's first experiences of reading and writing are purposeful and enjoyable. Only in this way will they be drawn into applying their meaning-making strategies to the task of making sense of written language. Only in this way will they learn to exploit the full symbolic potential of language and so become fully literate.
>
> (Wells, 1987, p. 162)

Jeni Riley, Series Editor
January 1999

Introduction

READING AT KEY STAGE 2: A PROBLEM AREA

Teaching reading at Key Stage 2 is a problem area. Both the teaching of reading in schools and the teaching of students about reading in initial teacher training courses have been identified as problems by OFSTED. Knowing what to do about teaching reading is a problem to the Key Stage 2 teacher – what exactly is there to do, apart from encouraging reading and remedial teaching? Knowing what to do about the teaching of student teachers for Key Stage 2 is a problem to the lecturer – the focus is not as clear as it is in the early stages of Key Stage 1.

The teaching of reading seems to fall between the two stools of the initial teaching of decoding skills on the one hand and literary studies on the other. Lecturers, students and teachers find problems in conceptualising the task and find it comforting to believe that, at this stage at least, children 'learn to read by reading'. It was into this context that the *National Literacy Strategy Framework for Teaching* (DfEE, 1998) impinged, with its emphasis on specifying detailed objectives and teaching activities.

THE NOTION OF LITERACY INFORMING THIS BOOK

This book is concerned with relating a relevant concept of literacy with the current context of teaching. It will, perhaps, be helpful from the start to indicate the concept of literacy, relevant to the demands of Key Stage 2, that informs this book, before we turn to a more detailed discussion of the context within which it has been written.

Beyond the notion of functional literacy – what we need in order to survive as participants in the social and economic order and not as its victims – is a more liberal notion of literacy: a literacy that not only *enables* us to read, but *motivates* us to read with reflective pleasure and *empowers* us to read with critical attention. A central element in developing reading in Key Stage 2 is to develop not only skills and motivation but also curiosity, imaginative response and self-confidence in the face of different types of texts.

THE CONTEXT OF THIS BOOK

In the situation of uncertainty outlined in the first two paragraphs above, the teacher may feel most secure adhering religiously to the requirements of the National Curriculum and the National Literacy Strategy. After all, there is more than enough there, in the *Framework for Teaching*, to keep a teacher busy for years! It was put together with the idea of saving the teacher the trouble of having to work out *what* to teach, leaving the teacher simply with the task of *how* to teach it. However, the effect has largely been to overwhelm teachers with yet more to get their heads round, yet more to feel they haven't time to tackle adequately!

In 1995, the slimmed-down National Curriculum was presented to the profession by Sir Ron Dearing with the injunction, 'Use your loaf!' By this he meant that it is there, in all its generality, for teachers to interpret as they see fit. The aim was to restore professional responsibility to teachers. On the other hand, the National Literacy Strategy (DfEE, 1998) seems to be prescriptive in every detail. Nevertheless, teachers will still need to use their loaves to make coherent sense of the *Framework for Teaching*. After all, the objectives are not entirely coherent on their own (see Jeni Riley's introduction to the Teaching Primary English series on page vii).

The National Literacy Strategy

The problem with the objectives is to do with the way the *Framework for Teaching* aims to provide a comprehensive, systematic and linear design to teaching objectives, and thereby to teaching:

- In dealing with objectives, it deals predominantly with the overtly measurable – though occasionally, realising the limitations of an 'objectives' approach, it inconsistently suggests other goals.
- In aiming to be comprehensive, it succeeds only in touching on and hinting at certain important issues, so that it is written in a code only initiates can understand.
- In aiming to be systematic, it throws its word-level, sentence-level and text-level graticule across the territory as a way of mapping it: but as with any such convention or system of co-ordinates, like Mercator's projection, it creates distortions at the same time as providing a chart that permits navigation.
- In being linear, it suggests development is linear, not recursive. And in any event, its lines are full of holes. In so far as it also aims to accommodate 'the spiral curriculum' by revisiting certain elements at a higher level, it gives the impression of vain repetition in certain areas, since it doesn't indicate how later visits are at a higher level than earlier visits. The areas chosen for

revisiting seem arbitrarily selected, since other areas could just as easily be seen to deserve similar recursive treatment.

Overall, the *Framework for Teaching* represents a brave attempt to systematise teaching objectives, but it deserves to be treated as a basis for critical discussion, development and exploitation, and not as a Bible for fundamentalists!

Comprehending the requirements

For the teacher, comprehending the Curriculum and the Strategy raises the general issue about comprehension: you can only make sense of something if you already have a coherent body of prior knowledge to fit it into, to interpret it in terms of, and to mould or modify in the light of your new comprehension. With comprehension comes confidence, and the teacher needs confidence in her own understanding to be able to make best use of the National Curriculum and the *Framework for Teaching* objectives.

Part of the aim of this book, and this series, is to provide a coherent body of 'prior knowledge' so that you may understand the National Curriculum and the *Framework* better and have the confidence to 'use your loaf' in order to work in the spirit, and not the dead letter, of the legal requirements.

THINKING ABOUT THE PLACE OF READING IN KEY STAGE 2

A part of the problem of thinking about reading is to do with conceptualising the nature of the development we are looking for in Key Stage 2. If we think of Key Stage 1 as having the primary responsibility for teaching children to embark on the reading process, Key Stage 2 may be seen primarily as being to do with consolidating the initial learning, developing speed, fluency and accuracy. Beyond this, it is to do with 'reading to learn' and developing comprehension skills. And alongside this, it is to do with developing habits of reading for pleasure, leisure and interest. At the same time, reading clearly is a tool used in nearly every curriculum activity in Key Stage 2. At least half the difficulties children have with mathematical problems are to do with understanding the words, not the numbers!

It is too readily assumed that reading, once initial fluency is achieved in Key Stage 1, will develop both in terms of process and of function all by itself, as long as it is being exercised. However, there is compelling evidence that one in five of the population, educated at any time from the 1930s to the 1990s, has not spontaneously developed functional literacy simply by being immersed in an educational system and social order that assumes it.

Where reading is already used as a tool to other curriculum ends, it is easy to overlook the degree to which functional skills need deliberate development. We must never under-estimate children's capacity for concealing their ignorance, muddling through and getting by, without really making the skills and knowledge we are trying to inculcate their own!

If 'reading to learn' has the wide application that we ascribed to it in the notion of literacy given at the beginning of this Introduction – from reading a train timetable or a textbook, by way of taking issue with an opinion or picking holes in an argument, to empathising with and evaluating the feelings of a Hamlet or a Treehorn – we must not forget that 'learning to read' is still a contin-uing (though partly covert) development during Key Stage 2. And not only for the less able readers. The actual processing of print is still developing, alongside the processing of more complex grammar and meanings and alongside the development of response.

The aim of this book

The aim of this book is to address the issues both of 'learning to read' and 'reading to learn'. The notion of reading that informs it encompasses state-of-the-art knowledge about the processing of print together with psycho-linguistic and literary perceptions. These things come together in a rich conception of comprehension.

In its concern with comprehension, this book deals not only with reading processes but also with the nature and requirements of the texts that are to be read. Different approaches and skills are involved in reading different kinds of texts for different purposes. For example, in relation to literature, comprehension has not only cogni-tive but emotional and moral dimensions; and not only does it involve paying attention to meaning, but also to the language that conveys meaning. On the other hand, with an information text, the language ideally is transparent, but its hierarchies of organisational structure demand attention – as finding your way round a train timetable, or even this book, demonstrates!

The structure of this book

The book is divided into seven chapters, the first three of which deal with general issues to do with children's development, the dynamics of the reading process and factors contributing to compre-hension. These are followed by three chapters, each of which focuses on one of the major genres, stories, poetry and information texts. The final chapter looks again at more general issues, this time to do with assessment and its place in implementing a teaching programme.

In each chapter, theoretical discussion is supported by detailed illustration. The genre-focused chapters will include discussion of the peculiar nature of the particular genre and the demands it makes upon the reader through the study of short passages of text, before moving on to consider practical approaches and activities that interpret and fulfil the requirements of the National Curriculum and the *National Literacy Strategy Framework for Teaching*. Examples of approaches and activities are looked at in the light of *Framework for Teaching* objectives and the specifications of the Literacy Hour, among other criteria. In this way, the book hopes to ensure that students gain an understanding they can use in practice.

The place of this book within the series

The conceptualisation of literacy development that informs this book seamlessly continues the themes of *Teaching Reading at Key Stage 1 and Before*. It is underpinned in part by perceptions and concepts about language developed in *Understanding the English Language* and complements the books about writing, particularly in its recognition of the interactive developments of writing and reading skills, its concern with re-presentation and imitation as aspects of comprehension and with the development of imagination.

Children and the reading process **1**

When you have read this chapter, you should begin to be able to:

- understand the nature of the reading process and its development during the primary years

- interpret and evaluate approaches to teaching reading

- intepret children's reading strategies in the light of your understanding of the reading process.

The aim of this chapter is to provide an introduction to the reading process and a framework for understanding how children are taught to read in Key Stage 1 and for understanding the development of the reading process that continues through Key Stage 2.

THE READING PROCESS

By 'the **reading process**', we mean the way we make sense of print, translating the black marks on the page into meaning. But the way we make sense of print as adults is the sophisticated end-product of a long and complex learning process that began before we entered school and continued beyond the primary years. Nevertheless, it is during the primary years that the main stages of learning to read are developed.

reading process
the psychological processes of perceiving print and translating it into words, sentences and meanings

How children learn to read is a result of the interaction between the ways they are taught and their own innate drive to make sense of the world as they experience it. Both the abilities and problems with reading that children bring with them from Key Stage 1 to Key Stage 2 are the product of this interaction. One aim of this chapter is to help you think in an informed way about the motivation and reading strategies that children exhibit in Key Stage 2, so that you will be in a good position to be able to encourage and help them.

What children bring with them from Key Stage 1

For many Key Stage 2 teachers the questions of how children learn to read and how to teach initial reading remain mysterious. Many junior schools have no idea not only of what approach and methods their contributing infants schools employ but even of which reading schemes have been used. Children simply arrive, reading at whatever level they have attained.

Traditionally, as far as teaching reading goes, the Key Stage 2 teacher has seen her task as being largely a matter of giving the children a lot of practice, listening to readers and handing over problem cases to remedial teachers. Traditionally, teacher training institutions, wedded to **'language experience' approaches** (see Brooks *et al.*, 1992), have encouraged Key Stage 2 student-teachers to believe that children 'learn to read by reading', as if that were the end of the matter, and have spent more time on discussing children's literature (and, more recently, information skills) than on considering the reading process as such.

Clearly, it would be helpful if the Key Stage 2 teacher knew something of how the children she receives have been taught to read. And clearly, the teacher would be in a better position to understand her task if she were equipped with some psychological model of the reading process and how children learn to read. After all, even the good readers at 7 years old haven't acquired all the skills of processing print. There are processes that go on developing throughout the junior years and beyond.

First, then, let us consider the **sources of information** that readers have available when reading, and then sketch out some of the ways children may have been taught in Key Stage 1. After that, we shall look at the development of the reading process itself and some of the factors that influence reading performance in Key Stage 2.

Sources of information when reading

Reading is a complex process. It is not just about identifying words but is also about understanding them. The process is not a one-way street – first we decode (translate the print into) the words, then we make sense of them. It is interactive. The sense of what we are reading sometimes helps us with the **decoding** – we anticipate words. The sense of the overall text determines what meaning it is appropriate to ascribe to a particular printed word. For example:

They signed the contract.

As it cools, the mercury will contract.

To read, we need to get information from the print on the page, but we also need to take information from the **context** into account

'language experience' approaches
approaches to the teaching of reading that emphasise the importance of motivation, contextual meaning, prediction and supportive adult help in shared reading, while devaluing decoding skills

sources of information
the reader has three ways of helping to identify the words in a text: (a) graphophonics, including sight recognition and decoding the print; (b) using semantic information to prime graphophonic perception, predict wording and check for meaningfulness; and (c) using syntactic information for priming, prediction and guiding semantic processes

decoding
the process of identifying words by using alphabetic information to determine pronunciations

context
the surrounding situation of meaning

in order to interpret the words. So powerful is our drive to make sense of what we read that we would pause if we came across the following sentences:

They signed the contrast.

As it cools, the mercury will contrast.

We might try to imagine a possible context for each of these sentences in which it could conceivably make sense or, alternatively, we might decide there was a misprint!

Contextual information can be subdivided into semantic information and syntactic information. Semantic information is about meaning: in the first of our sentences, the verb 'signed' suggests which meaning to ascribe to 'contract'; in the second, the words 'cools' and 'mercury' suggest which meaning of 'contract' is going to make most sense.

At the same time, syntactic information is at work. Your sense of the grammar of the sentence leads you to anticipate a noun in the first sentence and a verb in the second. You even hear the words differently in your head as you read them – '*con*tract' and 'con*tract*'. So unconscious is this processing that, if you came across these sentences in another context, you probably wouldn't even notice that the word 'contract', in isolation, is ambiguous.

Although context is such a powerful factor in reading, text has priority. Even if the reading process is not a one-way street, most of the traffic goes one way – from the printed text upwards. The print on the page is where we start from, and is what all processes defer to. So these three remain: **semantic context**, **syntactic context** and text. But the greatest of these is text.

Top-down and bottom-up processes

Approaches to teaching reading can generally be distinguished according to whether they primarily emphasise getting information from the print on the page or primarily emphasise getting information from the context about what meanings and words are likely to come next.

Getting information from the printed text, the black marks on the page, is sometimes called '**bottom-up processing**'. And using the context of meaning (semantic and syntactic) to provide **cues** (clues) is called '**top-down processing**'. Successful reading involves using and co-ordinating both bottom-up and top-down sources of

semantic context
the context of meaning

syntactic context
the grammatical situation of a word within a phrase or sentence which specifies the part of speech or agreement that is required

bottom-up processing
the aspect of the reading process concerned with identifying the words on the page

cues
the clues a reader uses in identifying words and determining meanings

top-down processing
aspect of the reading process concerned with identifying and checking word recognition using information from semantic and syntactic contexts

information. Yet many approaches and schemes, sadly, tend to develop one emphasis at the expense of the other.

Top-down anticipation

Top-down contextual processes promote **guessing** or '**prediction**'. The context primes the child to expect certain meanings or even specific words and the child anticipates the text. The expression

> Once upon a Tuesday

is funny (funny-peculiar, if not funny-haha) because we expect it to say 'time'. Such anticipation may operate at a number of levels. One level is a generalised or '**global**' priming, derived from the overall context, about the sort of words that might be expected. For example, Nabila (Year 5), in a story called *The Rocket*, reads the word 'collect' as 'clocket'. It seems she is expecting the word 'rocket' to come somewhere and consequently reassembles the letter sounds within the word 'collect' in an approximation towards that expectation.

At a more local and specific level, the context of meaning and the grammar may suggest words towards the end of a sentence or phrase. For example, Anne-Marie (Year 3) reads

> 'Can I play with you?' he said

where the text actually says

> 'Can I play with her?' he asked.

For children, the top-down processes of anticipation often operate more swiftly than the bottom-up processes of decoding or **sight-word recognition**. Thus, Anne-Marie anticipates words that were not there, making up her own sense.

Note, however, that Nabila's attempt in the example given above, makes no sense at all. What she produces is not a real word, but she lets it stand. It is the product of some bottom-up information from the page and a certain top-down expectation, but neither the bottom-up processing of the print, nor the top-down anticipation is working as it should, to make sense. The sounds are not being processed properly in sequence and the word produced is not being checked for meaningfulness.

Cross-checking and self-correction

For the adult reader, unlike the child, processing the print is generally swifter than anticipating the meaning, and the adult reader

guessing or **prediction**
the use of context to anticipate what a word should be, without actually reading the word

global context
the wide context of overall meanings in a text, not restricted to the immediate phrase or sentence

priming
the effect of context in facilitating predictions

sight-word learning/ recognition
learning to identify words on sight, without having to work them out. Some such learning is logographic, with the words learned by rote. But later on, words that have been fully worked out a number of times also come to be recognised instantly as sight words

tends to read the actual wording of the text. It is only if the meaning starts to go awry that the adult reader needs to go back and check whether he has read the text correctly, and self-correct as necessary. For the adult reader, meaning acts, in the words of the National Curriculum, 'as a checking device'. Thus, top-down and bottom-up processes work in harmony, with bottom-up processes taking the leading role.

The child needs to learn to use both bottom-up and top-down processes and habitually cross-check between them. Such **cross-checking** takes a while to develop, and is a strategy that the teacher needs to encourage. One key indication of whether the child is doing so is her tendency to self-correct. If the child, in reading a piece of continuous text, makes a mistake (**miscue**) and then corrects herself, this suggests that she is learning to cross-check between, and co-ordinate, top-down and bottom-up information. This attentiveness enables her to learn from her mistakes. **Self-correction** thus constitutes a **self-tutoring** mechanism.

Self-corrections can occur in two situations. One is where the child's predictions have leaped ahead of her processing of the text, and she then notices that the word on the page does not correspond with what she has just said, so she self-corrects. We can tell that this is what is happening because the substitution, (a), makes (some sort of) sense in context and, (b), does not in any way depend upon bottom-up **graphophonic** cues from the text. By 'graphophonic' I mean cues that relate spellings to the sounds that constitute words.

To return to the example of Anne-Marie, given above, and to tell the whole story, this is just what Anne-Marie does with both words:

'Can I play with you . . . her?' he said . . . asked.

She anticipates what the word is going to say, but then checks against the print, finds her expectation was wrong and so self-corrects using the graphophonic cues.

The other situation is where the child half-decodes a word and guesses the rest, then decides that it either, (a), does not make sense or, (b), that it does not correspond with the complete printed word, and so self-corrects. For example, Nabila reads:

'Fast . . . first of all . . . He dregs . . . drags them . . .'

It would be interesting to know whether it was the anomaly with meaning (for example, 'dregs' is not a verb, and so doesn't

cross-checking
the process of ensuring the different sources of information agree

miscue
an error or mistake in reading a word, resulting from processing or taking into account only a part of the information available

self-correction
spontaneously correcting a miscue or mistake in reading as a result of reviewing the contextual or graphophonic information available

self-tutoring
the autodidactic learning of the better identification of words as the result of self-correction

graphophonics
the whole range of ways in which spelling-sound correspondences can be used to identify words, including phonics and rime analogy

make sense) or with graphophonics that prompted Nabila's self-corrections here. The teacher could ask her – and doing so would tend to do three valuable things: it would draw Nabila's attention to the three possible sources of information, the semantic, the syntactic and the graphophonic; it would encourage her to be reflective about her own processing; and it would reward and encourage self-correction by giving it attention and approval.

Alternatively, a child may not notice the mismatch between what he has read and the word on the page. So long as the meaning seems to flow, he is happy, even if he is making up his own text! For example, Daniel (Year 5) reads:

The funnel stops the petrol from splitting ... spitting out

where the text actually says:

The funnel stops the petrol from spilling out.

At his first attempt, Daniel seems only to process the graphophonics of the beginning and the end of the word, leaving the middle to guesswork. He registers that 'splitting' will not do (though how far this is a matter of its not corresponding with the written text or its not making sense is unclear) and so offers 'spitting'. This word does make reasonable sense in context and the decoding of the **onset** is more satisfactory: he lets the word stand. He has not fully cross-checked with the word on the page.

onset
the consonant sounds that precede the vowel sound in a syllable

Without full cross-checking and self-correction, he does not have a satisfactory self-tutoring mechanism in place. Reading will remain a frustrating experience for him if he does not refine his sight-recognition skills through thorough-going self-correction, and he will continually find himself stumbling over words and meanings.

self-monitoring
the alertness to meaning and graphophonic information that permits and triggers self-correction

Specific help for Daniel might involve encouraging reflective **self-monitoring** and greater attention to the full spelling of words for checking purposes by, for example, stopping at the bottom of the page and saying, 'I liked the way you corrected yourself just now, when you said "splitting". What was wrong with "splitting"? Did it make sense? Was that why you changed it? You then said "spitting". Does that make more sense? Yes, petrol could spit out, couldn't it? But look at it again. Are you happy with "spitting"?'

The primacy of print
Of course, the black marks on the page are the final arbiter of what should be read. The meaning of the text inheres in its specific wording, not in some other approximate wording the child may

invent by guessing. Even if we tolerate some meaningful miscues in a child's reading for the sake of keeping the story going, ultimately we are aiming to inculcate accuracy. Self-correction, which indicates the growing co-ordination between top-down and bottom-up processes, is for this reason a major step towards accuracy.

Another indicator of positive development is when, after an interruption or pause to work out the decoding of a word, a child spontaneously re-reads a phrase or sentence accurately to establish the flow of meaning. The child shows herself to be concerned both with accuracy and establishing the meaning of the phrase or sentence. The swift, accurate reading enables her to process the passage of text for coherent meaning. She is getting her reading-for-meaning under the control of the text.

If, however, the child produces miscues without self-correcting, then the child is not co-ordinating the sources of information. In the examples given above, Nabila's 'clocket' for 'collect' was nonsense for two reasons: it is a non-word, meaning nothing, and it was an approximation towards 'rocket', a noun, where grammatically a verb was required. This suggests that she wasn't checking against either meaning or **syntax**.

What using meaning or syntax as a checking device should do is send the child back to revise her attempted decoding. More often than not, in simple, predictable texts, if the child is alert to the context, even partial decoding is enough to prompt an accurate guess. However, when Daniel revised his reading from 'splitting', which made no sense in context, to 'spitting', which does, partial decoding was not enough to ensure accuracy!

Progressively, as texts use a wider vocabulary and become less predictable, prompted guessing becomes less successful as a strategy. This is why we need to encourage full, accurate decoding. However, at the same time, we want children to be alert to context cues and to use them to facilitate word identification. We want children, in the learning stages, to use decoding to check guesses just as habitually as to use meaning 'as a checking device' to ensure accurate decoding.

Marie Clay (1991) suggests that if a child is self-correcting one in three miscues, then she is on her way to becoming self-tutoring. But if she never self-corrects, she is very badly at risk. The Key Stage 2 teacher will need to be alert to how far children use information from the print on the page, and how far they use information and expectation derived from the context of meaning. Alertness to children's self-corrections is vital in assessing how far they are co-ordinating this information, bringing their reading under the control of print.

syntax
the grammatical rules governing word order and agreements in constructing well-formed phrases and sentences, e.g. 'a red cart', not 'cart a red'

APPROACHES TO TEACHING READING IN KEY STAGE 1

The way that children are taught to read should develop both top-down and bottom-up processing skills. And in fact, this is the implicit goal of the eclectic approach that most Key Stage 1 teachers claim to use – doing a bit of sight-vocabulary teaching, a bit of 'language experience' **shared reading**, a bit of **phonics**, etc. Even those most wedded to the **'apprenticeship'** approach of shared reading, approximating as closely as possible to learning to read at mother's knee (discussed more fully below), tend to teach some phonics. The question of approach is likely to be more one of initial emphasis than of absolute distinctions. However, differences in emphasis can make major differences in the ways children tackle reading.

Different reading schemes encourage and give practice in different approaches – and provide children with different levels of motivation. Some schemes are intrinsically more interesting to children than others. Not only, then, do children arrive in Key Stage 2 having been taught differently, but they also arrive with different experiences of reading itself: some will have enjoyed their reading books, while others will have been put off reading by dismal texts. It is not surprising that Key Stage 1 teachers, selecting new reading materials, tend to be more concerned about whether they think their children will enjoy them than about which theory of teaching reading underpins them!

Initial teaching approaches

Top-down and bottom-up processes need to be co-ordinated, checked against each other. They are both necessary. However, different approaches to teaching initial skills and the different emphases teachers follow affect the ways that children learn to put the skills together. Different approaches can create their own specific kinds of problems for children learning to co-ordinate their developing skills. We will start by considering two bottom-up approaches and then look at top-down approaches before considering their possible effects upon children's strategies and propensities in Key Stage 2.

Whole-word sight-learning

Whole-word sight-learning is an approach that builds on children's spontaneous capacity to sight-learn words that they encounter in the world around them. Children readily learn to recognise their own names, the names of supermarkets, and so on – all the things that constitute '**environmental print**', the print in the world around them.

shared reading
the procedure of an adult and child(ren) reading a text together, with the child progressively, over a number of readings of a particular text, taking over the reading from the adult

phonics
whether for reading or writing, the exploitation of letter–sound correspondences for working words out

'apprenticeship'
a 'language experience' approach to teaching, emphasising the close relationship between teacher and child in shared reading

environmental print
words in the environment (labels, shop names, road signs, etc.) that children learn to recognise spontaneously even before attending school

Of course, children have to be told what the word says before they can recognise it again. The fact that they may identify any word that starts with the right initial capital letter, or has some letter features in common, or even recognise the logo rather than the letters as saying a word they know, doesn't diminish the fact that they are learning that specific printed symbols 'say' specific words.

Few teachers nowadays will claim to teach by **look-and-say** methods, though in fact most will do so to some extent. The *Framework for Teaching* (DfEE, 1998) lists 'sight recognition' words that children are expected to recognise both in context and out of context, i.e. both within a text and as isolated items. Even if the teacher does not use flash-cards for the initial teaching of these words, she will still probably use **flash cards** to reinforce their learning. Most children, during the Reception year, will have been sent home with a box of word-cards to learn.

Whole-word teaching, then, depends upon children's spontaneous ability to learn whole words they are told the meaning of and recognise them subsequently as sight-words. Teaching them the words to be found in the first books of their reading scheme can help children to achieve a quick experience of success in reading simple texts. And teaching the high frequency words, for example, the dozen type words that constitute a quarter of all the **token word**s we encounter in print, is an economical and effective way of helping children with access to text in general.

The limitations of early 'sight-learning'

However, *how* children learn such words does not necessarily help further or future development. They aren't learning transferable **word-attack skills**. They don't even learn to recognise the word as a spelling sequence, because the chances are that they don't yet know the alphabet nor know that letters are sequenced left-to-right in writing. They pick on arbitrary details – whatever happens to strike them – to remember the word by, and this may lead to confusions when other words share the same details. For example, one boy, having learned the word 'black', identified any word with a 'k' in it as saying 'black' (Seymour and Elder, 1985).

Children who have been taught sight-words tend to distinguish between 'their' words which they have learned and other words which they feel no responsibility to attempt. And indeed, they have no strategy for attempting words they have not been taught. Such children may simply stop reading, ask, or wait to be told the word. If they guess, they do so without showing any evidence of being

look-and-say
an approach to the initial teaching of reading that emphasises the rote learning of a sight-word vocabulary to ensure successful reading of early texts

flash cards
single-word cards used to teach sight recognition of words by rote, characteristic of look-and-say approaches

whole-word teaching
teaching sight-word recognition without reference to the word's alphabetic composition

token word
'fish, fish, fish' constitutes three token-words, but only one **type word**

word-attack skills
graphophonic and other skills used for working out unknown words

alert to any phonic cues within the word. The Key Stage 2 teacher needs to be alert to such characteristics and recognise that grapho-phonic word-attack skills need to be developed.

Phonics

sounding-out routines
in phonic reading, the process of sounding out the letters and blending them into a pronunciation

All teachers will discuss with their children, at some point, the way letter sounds can be put together to synthesise word sounds. However, the expression 'teaching phonics' is generally used to designate the early and systematic teaching of letter sounds and **sounding-out routines** for decoding words. The child is taught to sound out the letters and then put the sounds together and listen to what they say. Thus, 'cat' sounds out as /cuh-a-tuh/ and the child, with a leap of phonological insight, hopefully (because it doesn't always work!) learns to hear these separate sounds as saying /cat/. This approach gives children a way of tackling new words and partly-familiar words. Hopefully, frequently encountered words tackled in this way quickly become sight-words, recognised instantly without the child needing to work them out afresh each time.

The limitations of phonics

The use of the word 'hopefully' a couple of times in the previous paragraph indicates two problem areas in phonics. Another problem with phonics is that many of the commonest words in English are not regular in their spelling, for example, 'was', 'have', 'he', 'of'. However thoroughly texts are restricted to regular words, the child will almost certainly have to learn some very common and basic irregular words as sight-words. However, Mona McNee, an ardent advocate of phonics, maintains that 'the' is the only word that needs to be taught as a sight-word (private communication).

stress
in pronunciation, the relative auditory prominence or accentuation of one syllable compared with adjacent syllables, creating rhythm in speech

In any event, the translation of letter-sounds into word-sounds is rarely without problems, especially with multi-syllabic words, where **stress** is an important factor in sound recognition. For example, a child, tackling 'carpet', might not necessarily recognise /ca-r-pet/ as saying /carpit/.

rime
that part of a syllable that includes the vowel and any subsequent consonant sounds; the part that potentially could rhyme

Further, children who have been taught to read by phonics may develop certain negative habits or characteristics as readers. Over-emphasis on training in sounding-out routines can discourage children from attempting to use context cues to help them with problem words. They may feel that they have to sound out each word as they go, mistrusting their sight-memory for words and feeling it is cheating simply to know them! When decoding, they tend to work letter-by-letter and not look for bigger, known spelling patterns within words, like **rimes**.

Further, since the emphasis in phonic reading is on word-by-word decoding, children may come to feel that reading is about decoding and not about getting meaning from a text. Mistrusting the context of meaning as a cue to word recognition, they may not understand that reading is about getting meaning from a text nor employ meaning as a checking device. These are clearly characteristic dangers that the Key Stage 2 teacher should be alert to, and she should have strategies for weaning children away from such limiting phonic dependency.

The value of phonics
On the other hand, the child who has worked out a word is likely to be able to work it out again – and more quickly. Even a partial phonic cue can act as a mnemonic for helping to remember a word. And the habit of looking at words as potentially grapho-phonic patterns focuses attention on sequenced spelling features, supporting future recognition. So, while phonic dependency can be limiting, phonics provides a positive way of tackling new words and can open up wider graphophonic skills. There is more future in it than in sight-learning dependency.

The contribution of bottom-up processes
To sum up, then, what we have said about the bottom-up processes. Sight recognition has a place as it comes naturally to children and it permits instant recognition of the relatively limited number of high-frequency words, whether they are regularly or irregularly spelled. Phonics has its place because it opens up the possibility of developing word-attack skills for working out new words and of learning to identify words from their spelling sequences at a more sophisticated level of sight recognition. In terms of future development, these two processes complement each other, and this is why they are both promoted by the National Literacy Strategy, running in parallel from the very beginning.

Language experience approaches
If phonics and sight-learning are both bottom-up approaches that depend upon children processing (however incompletely) the black marks upon the page, 'language experience' emphasises top-down strategies. Over the last couple of decades, 'language experience' was the most influential approach to teaching reading up until the advent of the National Literacy Strategy. It underpinned the most commercially successful reading scheme of recent years (now to become a television cartoon series!), the Oxford Reading Tree, and it underpinned the scheme most widely canvassed by teacher education institutions, Story Chest (Brooks *et al.*, 1992). The most

recommended book on teaching reading was Liz Waterland's *Read with Me: An Apprenticeship Approach to Reading* (1985). I will consider this booklet now as representative of 'language experience' approaches in general.

Waterland argues that if written language is made meaningful to the child, then the mechanics of reading will not present much of a stumbling block. She views 'the reading process as a continual interaction between the reader's language experience, under-standing of the world and strategies of decoding, and the text's meaningfulness, graphic clues, predictability and interest level' (p. 9). But from this point onwards in her argument, Waterland tends to forget the 'strategies of decoding' and the 'graphic clues', and concentrates upon the reader making 'informed guesses' based upon expectations derived from the context, not upon 'exact knowl-edge of every word on the page'.

She argues that learning to read is as natural as learning to speak, and therefore formal, sequenced teaching is not appropriate. It is not a matter of acquiring 'a series of small skills fluently used; it is a process of getting meaning . . .' (p. 11). The two crucial elements are the quality of the text and the way the adult acts as 'guiding friend'. The relationship with the guiding friend is variously likened to 'apprenticeship to a craftsman', '"sitting with Nellie"', and learning to speak at mother's knee. The model approach is shared reading:

> The adult first reads all the story while the child cannot read any, then the child will put in the words she or he knows while the adult reads the rest, then the child will take over the reading.

(Waterland, 1985, p. 13)

The teacher ensures that the child has sufficient prior knowledge of what she is expected to read to have a basis for making informed guesses. The child is deemed to have done well if her version of the text makes sense, and she self-corrects to make it make sense, whether it is accurate or not. Making sense is the criterion of success, not accuracy.

This approach raises two related issues. How does the child learn the words? Are no word-attack skills to be taught? In answer to the first question, presumably the child learns the words *in situ* as sight-words. But she can only do this if she has guessed their identities accurately in the first place. Whether she can readily transfer this learning to another context remains an open question, especially as the child has probably not looked at the spelling analytically.

With regard to the second question, reports suggest that 'some children still need a lot of help with word attack skills' (see Beard and Oakhill, 1994, who provide a balanced and scholarly critique of the apprenticeship approach). How you can 'get meaning' without using 'skills fluently' is not clear. Guessing has to be upon the basis of a context that the child has to acquire somehow – and if not from the actual words of the text, from where else?

Nevertheless, much of the 'language experience' approach is admirable. Waterland cites Vygotsky: 'What a child can do in co-operation today, he can do alone tomorrow.' The close support of shared reading is something that the National Literacy Strategy advocates strongly. The emphasis on meaning and natural, predictable language is important. Motivation, encouragement and the experience of success are invaluable. The good thing about 'language experience' approaches is that they are humane. The child learner is seen as a thinking person, not as an empty vessel to be filled with facts and programmed with procedures (see *Teaching Reading at Key Stage 1 and Before* in this series for more detailed discussion of these issues).

The National Literacy Strategy

The National Literacy Strategy, with its renewed emphasis on phonics, was conceived in part to counter the influences and effects of 'language experience' approaches. While it does not want to throw the baby out with the bathwater, it clearly aims, in the objectives, to provide the child with bottom-up alphabetic knowledge and graphophonic word-attack skills. It aims to balance top-down and bottom-up approaches. Underpinning both the National Curriculum and the National Literacy Strategy there is an implicit model of predominantly bottom-up reading development, based on up-to-date research findings. It is to this model we now turn.

A MODEL OF READING DEVELOPMENT

Teachers need a model of development in terms of which they can understand the skills, difficulties and needs of their children. Otherwise, they are working blind. They need a conceptual framework for assessing children's abilities and needs. They need a conceptual framework in terms of which to identify individual strategies and how they may be related to individual differences or different teaching approaches. They need an idea of the ways their children have been taught in order to judge how far to build on these approaches and how far they need to use other approaches to ensure **balanced development**. They need also to be alert to

balanced development
combining bottom-up and top-down processes in reading, with bottom-up processes taking the leading role

individual interest and motivation, which may relate in part to teaching approaches, in part to individual, socio-cultural and gender differences.

A phase model of development

First, in discussing the developmental models of Frith and Ehri (below), we will hope to establish a general map of qualitative development over time, and then we will consider the nature of the reading process in more detail.

Uta Frith (1985) and Linnea Ehri (1995) both offer staged or phased models of reading development (see Figure 1.1).

Figure 1.1
Two models of reading development

Age	Frith (1985)	Ehri (1995)
3–5 (?) years	logographic phase	pre-alphabetic phase partial alphabetic phase
5–7 (?) years	**alphabetic** phase	full alphabetic phase
7–9 (?) years	**orthographic phase**	**consolidated alphabetic** phase

alphabetic reading
decoding using alphabetic knowledge

consolidated alphabetic reading
the orthographic phase of reading in which spelling patterns are chunked as recognition units

Frith developed her model so that she could compare the development of dyslexics with normal development patterns. She also included writing in her model (not shown here), being interested in the way reading and writing develop slightly out of step, but in interaction, with each other.

Ehri developed her model in relation to the contribution of alphabetic skills to the development and changing nature of sight-word recognition.

While their terminologies and some of their interests and interpretations are different, their accounts are reasonably congruent. They both start with recognising logographic/pre-alphabetic sight learning and show how, through developing alphabetic/graphophonic processes, letter-by-letter decoding is superseded by a more sophisticated form of sight-recognition in which words are perceived in terms of known spelling patterns (hence the term 'orthographic' – to do with spelling).

For both of them, the term 'phase' is perhaps preferable to 'stage', because development is seen as fuzzy-edged and cumulative, not leaving earlier processes behind, but incorporating and modifying them in more complex processes, while also retaining some of the earlier processes as a 'fall back'.

I shall tend to use the terms 'logographic', and 'pre-alphabetic' fairly interchangeably. I will use the term 'partial alphabetic' because it is usefully self-descriptive and the term 'orthographic' because it more manageable and more self-explanatory than 'consolidated alphabetic'. The sequence of phases is as follows:

- *Pre-alphabetic phase* learning covers the sight-learning of words from environmental print and from word cards, etc., identified from visual memory, without the assistance of alphabetic knowledge.
- *Partial alphabetic reading* uses alphabetic knowledge, but only involves the use of some of the letters in a word, as when Nabila read 'first' as 'fast'.
- *Full alphabetic reading* involves the sequenced use of all the letters to work out or identify a word, for example, as in phonics.
- *Orthographic reading* involves the sight-recognition of words in ways that take all the letters into account exploiting known spelling sequences, recognised as units.

pre-alphabetic reading
reading dependent on the sight recognition of words from some aspect of their appearance prior to the learning of the alphabet – also called 'logographic reading'

partial alphabetic reading
identifying words by decoding only a few of the letters and guessing the rest

orthographic reading
reading by identifying words from fully processed recognition units (whole word or part word spelling chunks)

The reading process

The reading process is the whole process of translating print into meaning. This process is very complex – it involves elements ranging from visual perception and the control of eye-movements to judgements about meaning, relevance and significance which involve long-term memory and relating new information with existing mental schemas. The process is an interactive one in which top-down and bottom-up processes play complementary roles. But, as we have argued, the bottom-up processes of word identification have priority.

The essential element in the overall process is learning to recognise words – that is, learning to relate patterns of print with known words. This is not the whole of reading, but it is where reading starts from and it is very largely the focus of attention in the early years.

The alphabet and decoding

As we saw when discussing teaching approaches, children can learn to recognise words as sight-words before learning about the alphabet. But learning about letters and their sounds opens up a new world of word recognition. Instead of having to learn each word as a one-off, the child can use letter-knowledge in two inter-linked ways: with letter recognition, the word takes on a more meaningful structure as a sequence of recognisable units; and the child begins to learn how to translate the letters and digraphs into the **phonemes** of the language, thus allowing the child to attempt a pronunciation. Ehri (1995) notes that children can use the letters

phonemes
the minimal units of sound within words that are significant for distinguishing one word from another, e.g. 'fax' has four phonemes, but 'facts' has five

they know to help with word identification, even before they've learned the whole alphabet.

Translating print graphophonically into pronunciations is called 'decoding'. In an alphabetic language like English, the pronunciation of spoken words is coded in writing, and a key step in learning to read is learning to decode written spellings into pronunciations. Subsequently, learning to perceive words as pronounceable alphabetic sequences, and thus identify them at sight, is a key element in learning to read.

Spoken language and reading

Learning to read is parasitic on speech. It is parasitic in two ways.

- The child's knowledge of language is speech-based, and reading is, in the first instance, a matter of translating the black mark on the page back into speech in order to understand them. Comprehension operates on the spoken version of the text.
- The black marks on the page are alphabetic – that is, they represent, individually and in combinations, the speech sounds of the language. So the process of learning to read is, at least in part, a matter of learning the correspondences between spellings and sounds, and thus learning to decode print into pronunciations.

This second point is not intuitively obvious to children. They construct many theories about how print relates to speech. For example, the child may think that the word 'ant' is smaller than 'elephant' because ants are, or that an 's' is added to the letters of a word to make it plural because there are more of them. If a child writes 'c' to represent 'cat', the child may write 'ccc' for 'three cats'. In general, pre-readers tend to think that written symbols represent semantic and not phonological properties of words. They don't tend to leap to the realisation that the letters constitute a **phonological code** without considerable assistance. Byrne (1998), providing a fuller discussion of these issues, concludes:

phonological code
the way printed letters represent the sounds of words

> [C]hildren need to discover that print does not represent meaning in a direct way, only by mediation through the structures of speech.

(Byrne, 1998, p. 44)

phonological awareness
alertness to the component sounds within words, identified by research as significant in facilitating learning to read

Realising that writing constitutes a phonological code is crucial to learning to read. This is perhaps why, in the earliest stages of reading, letter knowledge and **phonological awareness** are better predictors of reading success than intelligence. By the later stages of Key Stage 2, however, as phonological processes are replaced by orthographic processes and as reading for meaning becomes the predominant requirement, intelligence becomes the better predictor.

Children can acquire an initial sight vocabulary before they learn to apply phonological and alphabetical knowledge to their reading, but the sight vocabulary of the skilled reader is based on a thorough graphophonic processing of spellings. We will approach the stages of reading development by considering the development of a sight vocabulary. In doing this, we will expand on the developmental models of Frith and Ehri, outlined above.

The development of a sight vocabulary

The notion of a sight vocabulary is complex. As we have seen in discussing the logographic or pre-alphabetic phases, children can learn to recognise certain words 'at sight' from arbitrarily selected details before they learn the alphabet. They can learn to read words as visual symbols in much the same way that, as adults, we read the ampersand (&) as saying /and/ (and the French learn to read it as saying /et/). That is, by learning the words by rote, without using any links between individual letters and individual sounds within the words.

Later, they will know many words 'at sight', using the mnemonic support of their alphabetic knowledge about spellings and by recognising various frequently encountered word-parts as spelling chunks. As adults, we recognise most words at sight, having thoroughly processed their spellings at sometime in the past. Though sight recognition is the goal in adult reading, sight recognition of words at some earlier stages does *not* necessarily mean knowing the word thoroughly and understanding its spelling.

For children to be able to move on from pre-alphabetic sight learning based on the recognition of some visual detail to becoming able to work words out from their spellings, they have to become thoroughly familiar with the alphabet – instantly and accurately recognising the *shapes* of the letters as well as knowing the (various) *sounds* they can represent. Such knowledge is best mediated through a thorough knowledge of the *names* of the letters – which is perhaps why letter-name knowledge is the best predictor of future reading success with pre-reading children (see *Teaching Reading at Key Stage 1 and Before* for further discussion of this point).

Phonological awareness

The ability to work words out depends not only on alphabetic knowledge but also upon phonological awareness – alertness to the sounds that constitute a word. Clearly, the early spelling of words

segmenting
the reverse of blending:
the separating out of a
pronunciation into smaller
units, e.g. syllables, onset
and rimes, phonemes

depends on the child distinguishing (**segmenting**) the individual
sounds (phonemes) in their sequence in order then to represent
them in writing. Reading, however, is rather differently dependent
upon phonological awareness in ways that are not always clear.
It would seem, on the face of it, that the phonic translation of the
letters of regular words should simply permit the synthesis of the
pronunciation of a word without the help of phonological segmentation skills.

However, phonological awareness is more than segmentation skills
and it facilitates graphophonics in at least three ways: in the
auditory memory
the ability of the short-term
working memory to retain
sound images

auditory memory and synthesis needed to 'hear' the string of
sounded-out phonemes as a recognisable word; in the unitisation
of such worked-out words to facilitate their transfer to the sight
vocabulary; and in the interconnections between writing (phonetic
spelling) and reading.

Children with reading problems in the early and middle years of
Key Stage 2 are predominantly characterised by phonological weaknesses – the inability to distinguish the sounds within words in their
sequence (Bryant and Bradley, 1985). For such children spellings
remain strange, arbitrary patterns, not held together as phonological patterns, and as such, they are difficult to learn.

For children with good phonological awareness and letter knowledge, spellings start to cohere as meaningful letter sequences. At
first this may only mean sounding the initial letter as a prompt to
guessing or recalling the word. But frequent encounters with words
soon enable more of the letters in their spellings to act as mnemonics
for remembering the word. At the same time, writing words,
working out their spellings, starts to focus children's attention on
the sequence of sounds and letters in them.

Chunking and rime analogy

Alphabetic knowledge and phonological awareness combine in
working out words in two major ways. One way is in the sequenced
translation of letter-sounds, as in traditional phonics. This develops
and exploits letter–sound (or grapheme–phoneme) correspondences. As a strategy, this is very largely dependent on its having
been taught as a procedure. While children will readily sound the
first letter and guess, they do not commonly resort to a full letter-
by-letter sounding out unless they have been trained in phonics
(Clay, 1991). And, in practice, attempts to do so are often not very
successful (Bussis, 1985).

The other way of using spelling–sound correspondences is in
enabling the child to see certain spelling sequences as chunks,

corresponding reliably with certain sound sequences in words, for example, '-tion'. This is a more spontaneous process, more native to the fuzzy logic of the way the human mind and perceptions work than the linear logic of **synthetic phonics**.

Certain heard phonological sequences are perceptually prominent, in particular, **syllables** and rimes (the potentially rhyming last part of a syllable). The spellings of these phonological chunks tend to be more trustworthy guides to pronunciation than are the individual letters that compose them. For example, 'rain' always says /rain/ and '-ain' always says /ain/, while the letters 'r', 'a', 'i' and 'n', taken individually, can say different things in other contexts (for example, as in /or/, /man/, /sit/ and /song/). Taken together, however, the perceptual prominence of the phonological chunk and the reliability of the spelling sequence, '-ain', enable the sound and spelling chunks to be readily mapped one on to the other, supporting learning. We saw earlier, for example, the way Daniel (Year 5), while having difficulty with 'spilling', had no problems with the unitised rime, '-ing'.

Phonological chunks, like syllables and rimes, begin to help unitise spelling sequences. Thus, monosyllables which are both read and written frequently come to be learned as unified sequences. And in relation to rimes, Usha Goswami (1993, 1994) has shown that children can become self-tutoring by making analogies for themselves between words they know and new words.

Recognising the homographic spelling of frequently encountered rimes (for example, '-ain' as in 'rain', 'drain', 'gain') begins to enable the child to use the known chunks to make analogies from known to unknown word. Goswami shows how children transfer their knowledge of a word like 'peak', using the rhyming of the rimes as the analogical link, to decode a new word like 'beak'.

They can, though less effectively, make analogies using the alliteration of onsets as the link. Indeed, it is perhaps their alertness to onsets that helps them learn the graphophonic significance of single consonants when they appear as single consonant onsets (for example, 'cat' → 'cup'), and this is perhaps one reason why initial single consonants are such salient features in early word identification.

Children also, though to a lesser degree, make analogies using the onset and vowel as a an analogical chunk (for example, 'beak' → 'bean', 'for' → 'fork'). Slightly later, children go on to develop vowel digraph analogies (for example, 'beak' → 'seam'). In this kind of way, through **chunking**, children work out ever-more-refined graphophonic word-attack strategies for themselves. This is what Dombey and Moustafa (1998) call 'whole-to-part' phonics.

synthetic phonics
reading by phonic procedures, synthesising the word sound from the letter sounds by blending

syllable
that phonological unit in a word that centres on a vowel sound, together with its associated consonants

chunking
the process of consolidating separate items into a single perceptual unit for recognition purposes, e.g. as you perceive MALT, but not LTMA, as a single unit

affix
the generic term for prefixes and suffixes

prefixes
bolt-on word parts at the beginning of a word, e.g. **un**clear, **pre**pare, **re**peat

suffix
a word-part added after the stem of a complex word, determining meaning and part of speech of a word, e.g. creat**ion**, comfort**able**, sing**ing**

stem
the morphemic core of a word (often a free morpheme) which may then have bound morphemes of various kinds added to it to develop the word's meaning and syntactic status, e.g. **love** → **lov**able → un**lov**able → un**lov**ably.

morphemes, bound and free
the minimal units in language that carry an element of meaning. A bound morpheme is one that cannot stand on its own, but has to be part of another word, e.g. '-ed', as in 'walked' and 'talked'

graphic knowledge
the ability to identify grammatically and semantically significant part-word units like prefixes, suffixes and inflections

Morphological chunks

Children are also spontaneously alert to another kind of spelling chunk. During Key Stage 1, certain frequently encountered **affixes** begin to be recognised, for example, the **prefixes** 'pre-' and 'un-', the past tense suffix '-ed', the pluralising **suffix** '-s'. These affixes are semantically and grammatically meaningful units. Bussis *et al.* (1985) suggest that children begin to acquire a vocabulary of such part-words in a way analogous to the way they acquired a vocabulary of sight-words at an earlier stage of development. For example, they might perceive 'unhappily' as consisting of the chunks 'un-happ(y)-ly'. 'Un-' and '-ly' are units that they will have encountered elsewhere attached to a variety of different word **stems**, but always with the same grammatical and semantic significance (for example, 'unkind', 'quickly').

Morphemes

Such units of meaning are called 'bound **morphemes**'. Morphemes are the minimal units of meaning in a language, and these morphemes are 'bound' because they have to be attached to a stem, they can't stand on their own like 'free morphemes' such as 'kind'. The National Curriculum refers to this alertness to morphemic chunks as '**graphic knowledge**'.

We have already observed that children are implicitly sensitive to grammar in their substitutions, and this includes being sensitive to the morphemes that distinguish the grammatical functions of words within sentences. Byrne (1998) cites evidence that pre-literate 4½-year-olds, in a training programme that involved distinguishing between written words, were more inclined to interpret the pluralising '-s' at the end of a word as a morphemic/semantic marker indicating the plural meaning, than as indicating anything to do with pronunciation. Children seem, then, to have some spontaneous inclination to look for morphemic significance in spellings even when they do not spontaneously interpret spellings as having graphophonic significance.

Morpho-syntactic awareness

Bryant and Nunes (1998), in relation to spelling, call this sensitivity to semantic/syntactic regularities '**morpho-syntactic awareness**', and they see this as a separate stage or phase in development from phonological or graphophonic awareness. They comment:

> Just as the earlier learning about letter-sound relationships may depend to a large extent on the children's awareness of phonological distinctions . . ., so this later learning could depend on their sensitivity to grammatical distinctions . . .

By the time children are using alphabetic skills in reading, of course, such morphemic spelling chunks are also pronounceable. As the child learns to decode, these spelling chunks begin to cohere as **recognition units** because they both are pronounceable and are units of meaning. Phonological and morpho-syntactic awarenesses work together, for example, in unitising the '-ing' suffix.

Chunking, whether based only on phonological units or also on morphological units, provides an efficient part-word system of constructing pronunciations and thus identifying complex words by subdividing the spelling into manageable (manage-able) and meaningful (mean-ing-ful) units. Where there is a morpho-syntactic suffix involved, this helps with clarifying the grammatical structure of the sentence as well as the pronunciation of the complex word ('meaningful' has the adjectival '-ful' suffix). We still employ phonological and morpho-syntactic chunking systems in our processing as adults.

Phonological or alphabetic reading

Reading at the top end of Key Stage 1 and the lower end of Key Stage 2 tends to be primarily a matter of translating the spellings (some of which are now chunked into recognition units) into pronunciations, and listening (even if only in the 'mind's ear') to what the text says. The better readers at this stage are not dependent solely on whole-word learning, but use phonic cues readily even with new words, as success in reading **pseudo-words** like 'cef' and 'cal' indicates.

Words and meanings are still generally recognised from how they sound, even if the child is reading silently and only pronouncing the words in her head. Thus, a child at this stage is likely to deem a sentence like 'I have know time' as meaningful because it is phonologically identical to the meaningful sentence 'I have no time' (Harris and Coltheart, 1986).

Orthographic reading

The ultimate phase of reading development begins to assume dominance during the later years of Key Stage 2. Frith's term 'orthographic' means 'to do with spelling', and many spelling sequences are now so thoroughly over-learned as a result of frequency of encounter and analysis that they are recognised as a cohesive pattern or chunk as quickly as a single letter may be – 'the' is read as instantly as 'a'. This stage in reading development, which children are still consolidating at the top end of the primary school, is characterised by two related elements: an ever-increasing and ever-increasingly fully-processed sight vocabulary; and access to

morpho-syntactic awareness
the awareness associated with graphic knowledge and the morphemic and syntactic significance of certain spelling chunks, e.g. in distinguishing the occasions when the final 's' on a word is part of the stem (e.g. is), a plural marker (e.g. tins), a possessive (e.g. Tony's) or a third person singular verb (e.g. fills).

recognition units
spelling sequences, whole or part words, that are perceived and identified as complete units

pseudo-words
invented meaningless 'words' to test graphophonic or morphological skills, e.g. **gluph**; one **wug**, two ___?

meaning directly from spelling without the need to pronounce the word.

There is a tendency for any sub-word chunking to operate in terms of morphology, i.e. in terms of spelling sequences that convey meaning. Thus, 'know' and 'knowledge' are seen as sharing a crucial morpheme, even though the morpheme is pronounced differently in each word. The meaning is accessed directly from the spelling, without recourse to the pronunciation. Thus the child may never confuse 'too' and 'two', and may not even notice that they sound the same. At the top end of Key Stage 2, since meaning can now be accessed from spellings, few children will say that sentences like 'I have know time' make sense.

The dual route model of reading

Nevertheless, complex, infrequently-encountered or new words are still processed phonologically as well as orthographically, and regularly spelled words are identified measurably faster than equally frequently encountered irregular words. This kind of evidence has led to the concept of a '**dual route**' in reading. We identify words both from their spellings and from their internalised pronunciations. We still hear the words we read in our 'mind's ear', but we also have a guide to their meanings from the spelling. Children's delight in puns during the Junior years may derive from playing with the dual routes – we access one meaning from the spelling and another, contradictory, meaning from the **phonological route**. For example, consider the children's joke:

Why was 6 scared of 7? Because 7 8 9!

This joke would be incomprehensible if we didn't hear the pronunciation in our mind's ear. And it would also be incomprehensible of we didn't know that 8 doesn't really mean 'ate'!

A review of the development processes in Key Stage 2

The phonological (graphophonic) route, then, develops the raw capacity for sight-recognition by making spellings meaningful. The identification of sight-words now comes to depend not upon partial and freakish cues, but upon the instant recognition of spelling patterns that have become organised under the tutelage of the graphophonic processes and, later, of morpho-syntactic awareness. This is the main line of reading development that is going on in children under the surface and unbeknownst to the children themselves (and to most teachers!) during Key Stage 2.

dual route
the two routes that operate in parallel in orthographic readers to identify words: directly from the spelling; and from the internalised pronunciation

phonological route
the processing path that identifies a printed word by translating it into an (internalised) pronunciation

IMPLICATIONS FOR PRACTICE

This chapter has been rather more theoretical than later chapters will be, and so the implications for practice here tend to be general, rather than specific. The crucial issues for teacher are to:

- maintain a balance between bottom-up and top-down processes
- develop both sight-learning and phonics systematically, together with analogical and chunking skills, within a broad conception of graphophonics
- help children develop their word-attack and self-correction skills
- guide children towards orthographic reading skills, by alerting them to spelling patterns, first by drawing attention to regularities between spelling and pronunciation units, for example, rimes, and later, to morphological patterns
- enable children to perceive complex spelling sequences as organising themselves into chunks or part-word recognition units.

Summary

The reading process is the way we translate printed text into meaning. Because the written code is alphabetic, with spellings representing pronunciations, we need to learn to translate print into pronunciations in order to identify the words. Development in reading is largely to do with the developing efficiency of this process. This is, in great measure, a development from rote whole-word learning via letter-by-letter translation to ways of identifying whole words or significant part-words like prefixes, suffixes and other morphemes as unitised spelling patterns.

Phonological processes play a large part in reading development since sounds need to be perceived as discrete units in order to be mapped on to letters and spellings, and larger scale phonological units like rimes and syllables help in the unitising of spelling patterns as recognition units. Skilled reading involves the virtually instant sight-recognition of virtually all words encountered.

- The written code is alphabetic – that is, spellings represent pronunciations; and decoding is the process of identifying pronunciations from spellings.

- The bottom-up process of decoding print and the top-down processing of context make complementary and interactive contributions to successful reading.

- Reading development depends on the cross-checking between top-down and bottom-up processes, which reveals itself in self-correction which operates as a selt-tutoring mechanism.

● Graphophonic decoding goes through stages of development in which one causal factor is the influence of phonology, not least because of the help it gives in developing the perceptual chunking of spelling patterns as recognition units.

● Skilled reading involves the virtually instant identification of most words or part-words at sight, because the spelling patterns of these words have been previously established as recognition units under the aegis of phonological and morphemic constraints.

Further reading

Adams, Marilyn Jager (1990) *Beginning to Read: Thinking and Learning about Print*, MIT
This is a highly influential and authoritative text, commissioned by Congress in the USA, to look at phonics and the teaching of reading. A very substantial modern classic.

Bielby, Nicholas (1994) *Making Sense of Reading: The New Phonics and its Practical Implications*, Scholastic
A clear and comparatively brief account of what we now know about the reading process, written for students and teachers.

Ellis, Andrew W. (1993) *Reading, Writing and Dyslexia: A Cognitive Analysis*, 2nd Edition, Lawrence Erlbaum Associates
A clear, succinct account of what we know about the reading process, writing and dyslexia. Not classroom orientated.

Riley, Jeni (1999) *Teaching Reading at Key Stage 1 and Before*, Stanley Thornes
An up-to-date account of the early years of reading, the background to Key Stage 2, written for students and teachers.

Children and their reading 2

When you have read this chapter, you should:

- have a generalised picture of the development of children's reading characteristics through Key Stage 2

- have an overview of various social and individual factors that influence development

- be able to begin to interpret children's reading behaviours diagnostically in relation both to general influencing factors and to specific skill deficits

- be able to plan for classroom activities to extend and support the development of children's reading processes.

Introduction

This chapter begins by considering the general array of reading skills and characteristics that children may be expected to have when they move up from Key Stage 1 and the stages of development they move through during Key Stage 2. It then looks at some of socio-cultural, gender and individual differences that may affect children's reading and cause problems, and at some effects that different approaches to teaching reading may have on children's reading development. The aim of this discussion is to provide a conceptual framework for the teacher to use in thinking about individual children's reading characteristics and needs. Since the general trend of development during this phase is the progression from alpha-betic to orthographic reading skills, teaching strategies that help with this development are also discussed.

CHILDREN'S READING CHARACTERISTICS

Children enter Key Stage 2 with very different levels of ability in reading, and it is part of the teacher's role to identify these abili-ties and act accordingly. The teacher's task is to help children take the next step from where they are in the direction they should be going. This, of course, means the teacher needs to assess the child's reading and to know what the next step ought to be. This is why the teacher needs to have a clear model of the processes and problems of reading development and of the goal to be aimed at.

The (mythical) average child

Let us first sketch an average, generalised picture of the reader entering Key Stage 2 and trace her development, after which we will look at specific influences and difficulties individuals exhibit.

Word identification

The average child enters Key Stage 2 as a silent reader who pauses to mouth tricky words *sotto voce*. She has a sight-vocabulary of frequently encountered words, including most of the **function words** of the language – articles, prepositions, pronouns, verbal auxiliaries, and so on. This sight vocabulary may not be fully processed and automatic: it may still depend upon initial letter cues to some extent, so that the child may still stumble over discriminating between 'for' and 'from', 'when' and 'where' and so on. She will also have begun to acquire a sight vocabulary of part-words, both phonological units like syllables and rimes, and prefixes, suffixes and **inflections** which she can identify irrespective of the stem to which they are attached. Thus she has started to acquire some skills in orthographic chunking – that is, perceiving familiar letter sequences, for example, 'the', '-ing', as recognition units.

The alphabetic principle

As well as having a sight vocabulary, the child will have some grasp of the alphabetic principle that letters and their combinations represent the sounds of the language, and will have some level of graphophonic processing in operation, however shaky and incomplete it may be. The child may have some grasp of phonics. She may only use first and last letter phonic cues. Her vocabulary of part-word chunks together with her alphabetic knowledge help her to begin to organise her perception of spelling sequences as chunks, as discussed above.

Making sense

The child expects what she is reading to make sense and she will have a self-correction mechanism in operation that picks up a fair proportion of her miscues and helps secure word identifications by marrying graphophonic information from the page with semantic and syntactic context cues, even if the graphophonic processing is still only partially effective and the context cues are incomplete. Stumblings over basic words will generally be self-corrected, and she will pause, if necessary, to work out a difficult and unfamiliar word.

function words
words without much meaning in themselves but which qualify or indicate the relationships between content words in a sentence, e.g. articles, prepositions, conjunctions, etc., as in '**The** cat sat **on the** mat'

inflection
the morphemic modification of word endings to indicate their meanings and grammatical agreements in a sentence, e.g. he sit**s**, a dog**'s** breakfast, it br**oke**

Teachers, working with children at this stage, need to give the child time to work things out and not intervene too early. They need to praise the child for her efforts and help make explicit for the child how she worked things out, for example, 'I liked the way you took your time with that word, and sounded out "grab". And then you realised the whole word must say "grabbed" to fit the sentence and make sense.'

The child is operating at the phonological stage in which words have to be translated into pronunciations in order to be identified. She accesses meaning largely from such pronunciations – even if those pronunciations go on in her head and not aloud. The level of her reading skills, involving a sight-vocabulary and graphophonic decoding, at this stage are still more closely related to her alphabetic and phonological skills than to intelligence.

Orthographic chunking

As time goes on during Key Stage 2, more and more words become established in her sight vocabulary and they become established more and more in terms of organised and recognised spelling patterns. Patterns of spellings cohere as recognition units, so that the identifications of individual letters in their sequential relationships with each other mutually support each other's identification. While initially such frequently encountered spelling chunks came to be unitised according to the phonological units that the child was spontaneously alert to, for example, syllables and rimes, progressively the unitising principle tends to include grammatical and morphological factors. This is first seen in the way children begin to acquire a sight vocabulary of common part-words such as prefixes, suffixes and inflections which they encounter as sub-units in many different words they meet. For example, the Year 3 boy who read 'friends' as 'friend' and then self-corrected to 'friends', shows that in his processing he is perceptually dividing the word into two chunks, the known syllable 'friend' and the known inflection '-s'.

These spelling patterns come more and more to permit access to meaning directly, without recourse to internalised pronunciations. Nevertheless, graphophonics remains an available strategy, when needed, for dealing with new and difficult words; and internalised pronunciation persists, permitting the use of auditory memory to support retention of phrases and sentences for processing in the working memory.

Contextual support

At the same time, the child's growing experience of reading and of life helps her to develop the contextual support that enables her to

homographs
different words, spelled the same, but possibly pronounced differently, e.g. sow (noun), sow (verb)

anticipate the text and to select the appropriate meanings of words, as is shown in the appropriate reading of **homographs**, like 'row' and 'row', which are pronounced differently according to their required meanings, as in

They had a row on the lake

They had a row on the lake, so she pushed him in

Those processes of cross-checking between sources of information that initiated the development of self-correction become so habitual and rapid that overt self-correction may tend to disappear – but only because it has become more and more internalised and auto-mated, showing itself overtly, perhaps, only in hesitations.

Reading and intelligence

The child's level of reading ability progressively becomes more closely related to intelligence than to phonological awareness and alphabetic knowledge, since this ability is now more closely related to orthographic skills, to the ability to extract information from a text, to make relevant **inferences** and to integrate what she reads with what she already knows in a coherent act of comprehension. Intelligence is not a major factor in the initial acquisition of reading skills (after all, even children with disabilities like Down's Syndrome can learn to read), but it becomes a major factor in reading devel-opment during the junior years.

inferences
meanings, not explicit in a text, but derivable from it

PROBLEMS CHILDREN MAY HAVE

'normal' distribution
a statistical concept referring to the equal distribution of scores about a mode, producing a bell-shaped graph

skewed distribution
a statistical concept, where the distribution curve is asymmetical

One would expect children in a statistically **'normal' distribution** of population to differ in their performance, even without any partic-ular problems or causes. There is naturally a spread of abilities. However, there are reasons to think that there are some specific influences that relate to reading differences and reading backward-ness. After all, for various reasons, populations of real children usually tend to have a **skewed distribution**, with a longer tail at the lower end. Differences can result from differing tendencies among children to favour particular reading strategies. Differences can result from differences in linguistic and processing skills and differ-ences in motivation and interest. Problems with reading that children may exhibit can result from any one, or a combination, of five causes:

- issues relating to background, socio-cultural and linguistic experience

- issues and attitudes related to gender differences
- not being secure in basic knowledge and skills
- individual perceptual and processing preferences and difficulties
- having learned limiting habits from the way they have been taught.

It is not, in practice, always easy to make clear distinctions between these causes, but it is important for the teacher, in her diagnostic role, to consider all the different possibilities and not jump to conclusions. For example, marginal hearing impairment (for example, **glue ear**) or undiagnosed short-sightedness, though much less glamorous than **dyslexia**, can easily be overlooked as causes for reading backwardness!

glue ear
a common medical condition, impairing hearing, but readily treatable by the insertion of a grommet to drain fluid from the inner ear

dyslexia
a developmental processing impairment generally related to a phonological deficit

Socio-economic and cultural background

Children from some backgrounds will have had massively more experience of being read to and of sharing and enjoying books with a parent or carer in the pre-school years than other children. Some children will come from homes where there are no books and where reading is no significant part of the way of life that they have been brought up in. Such children will be unclear about the point of books and will be unskilled in listening and in comprehending stories. Further, they will not have begun to grasp some of the basic knowledge about written texts – things like which way up books go, the way the pages go, the direction of print, and even that print represents language and a printed word represents a spoken word. Such background deficits can affect the acquisition of skills, motivation and ultimately self-esteem, with long-term, even life-time, consequences.

More fundamentally still, some children's experience of language, and of the kinds of meaning that language can have, is severely restricted. If conversation and explanation and story-telling, language-play and sharing of nursery-rhymes is no part of their experience, then the experience of spoken language as a conveyor of conceptual meanings and as an object of phonological awareness, upon which reading is parasitic, may well be shaky. Such children can learn to decode satisfactorily but may only do so in order to get by, to get teachers off their backs, without their having any real interest in books and the meaning of texts.

Other problems can arise, not so much from linguistic inadequacies, but because of the social gap between the culture of the home and the middle-class culture and language of the school. As Wells (1987), for example, argues, working-class children may not be dumb, but may be rendered dumb by the school environment. Similarly, children coming from ethnic minority backgrounds may be rendered dumb by both language and cultural considerations. Children clam up in hostile or threatening situations, do not identify with the aims and aspirations of the school and are perceived and treated as less able.

Gender differences

There is a lot of concern today about the possibility that boys may be falling behind girls in their education. Maybe this has always been the case, at least during the primary years. At the time of the 11+ examinations, girls had to score very much more highly than boys to get to grammar schools – not only because there were fewer places for girls, but because their average marks were so much better than boys'. This meant that they had to do better to compete success-fully against each other. Boys' marks were adjusted upwards to give the impression of parity.

Biddulph (1998) argues that:

> boys develop neurologically at a much slower pace than girls ... At age five there is a six months to one-year gap between the motor skills of boys and those of girls. Yet they are the skills needed for sit-down schooling. No wonder boys fall behind so quickly.

He argues that since boys have 25 per cent more red blood cells and 30 per cent more muscle than girls, girls are built for sit-down education and boys need action. He cites experiments in Australia where starting the day with 20 minutes of physical activity has led to marked improvements in boys' behaviour. He goes on to argue that boys should not start school at the same age as girls. They should be at least a year behind. It takes them until 19 years old to catch up (though, of course, some people would argue that they never do!).

SATs
Standard Assessment Tests – government-sponsored tests for accountability purposes

Boys tend more to the extremes than girls, at both ends of the scale, and they do not seem to achieve as well as girls in Key Stage 1 **SATs**. Certainly, as far as reading goes, boys appear to present more problems, though there is some doubt as to whether this is because they are differentially worse at reading or whether they draw more attention to themselves and their problems! What is certainly clear is that, differentially, they come to choose not to read as much as girls.

It is no part of my intentions here to enter the nature–nurture debate, though it seems to me that since every cell in the body is sex-coded and that there are physiological differences between the sexes even in the brain (though not so much in the young brain), it is not inconceivable that there are innate differences. However, what we can more easily identify, and perhaps more readily do something about, are the differences in nurture.

Effects of nurture

There are a number of factors that may contribute to this effect. Girls' language development is faster than boys', perhaps in part because they tend to spend more time conversing with their mothers and sharing their mothers' interests and concerns (Wells, 1987). Certainly girls tend to come to school scoring better on the Concepts About Print test (Byrne, 1998) which suggests that they have had more, or gained more from, experience of sharing books with adults. Boys, however, tend to be able to identify more environmental print. But beyond these points, there appear to be few significant differences (for example, in phonological awareness and letter knowledge) between the sexes at this stage.

Primary teachers tend predominantly to be women. In 1998, in primary schools only one teacher in a hundred under 25 was a man, and it has been suggested that a female culture prevails in schools and boys' interests are not catered for. Biddulph (1998) says that schools have become 'feminised'. If girls become more interested in human relations as a result of their conversational closeness to their mothers, while boys are more interested in activity, science and sport, then the emphasis in reading materials on everyday stories, rather than on facts, fantasy and football, may privilege girls.

At the same time, it has been suggested that male macho culture militates against reading. Real men are seen as Action-Men and not as readers. Boys, who may be deprived of male role-models at home as a result of broken marriages and partnerships, may well also lack male role-models at school and feel education is a female activity. While girls enjoy teachers' approval, boys can feel quite ambivalent about it, feeling they may lose credibility among their peers.

Additionally, many teachers report that there are some boys, at the top end of primary school, who appear to have been socialised by their family or culture to have a low opinion of females and activities they regard as feminine, such as reading. Progressively during the primary years and puberty, the time such boys give to voluntary reading tends to diminish.

Millard (1996) suggests that there is something *aversive* to boys in the experience of reading at the top end of primary school and beyond, resulting in boredom and patterns of avoidance. She found that the factors that contributed to boys' negative attitudes included:

genre
kind or category of written text, e.g. novel, biography, etc.

- the focus on narrative
- the limited choice of **genres** available and the exclusion of certain kinds of literature deemed to be 'unsuitable' (for example, junior horror stories, computer games related materials)
- the lack of teacher intervention to help boys find books that relate to their interests
- the way reading tends to be 'sold' as a leisure activity and not as being useful for getting a job
- the use of reading as a time-filler in the classroom
- the tendency for children to be presented with information in pre-digested worksheets, rather than being presented with the challenge of researching topics for themselves.

Compared with girls, boys are 'differently literate' (Millard, 1997). We tend not to cater for the differences in school.

Browne (1996) suggests strategies to foster a gender-fair reading curriculum by:

- ensuring a better balance between fiction and information books
- teaching in single-sex groups, using appropriate materials
- recording books read in order to review choices and make appropriate future provision
- 'selling' images of men as readers and involving older boys and men in classroom reading activities, for example, inviting male storytellers into school
- exploiting interest in computers
- addressing gender issues with parents, enrolling the help of fathers with boys' reading.

Insecurity in basic knowledge and skills

One thing that is aversive about any activity is a feeling of inadequacy. For a variety of reasons, for example, home experience, starting formal schooling at barely 4 years old, illness and absence, phonological deficits or minor physical impairments, children may fall behind their peers in the acquisition of early reading skills and consequently develop both emotional and intellectual problems with reading. Children work hard at and are quite good at concealing their ignorance – up to a point. Shyness and quietness in the classroom and failing to volunteer answers may result as much from insecurities in knowledge as from social insecurities. And further exacerbating the problem, the quiet non-reader tends to get ignored whilst the teacher deals with more demanding children.

Alphabetic knowledge and the alphabetic principle

The alphabetic principle that children need to grasp is that the written forms of words represent, through letters and their combinations, the sounds within words. The application of this principle in reading is *graphophonics* which, as a term, covers all the kinds of ways that spellings can be translated into pronunciations. Children can have problems with graphophonics if:

- they have poor phonological awareness
- they have never been taught about the alphabetic principle or what they have been taught is patchy
- they have problems with identifying letters instantly
- they are uncertain about what sound(s) a letter or digraph represents
- they are uncertain about other letter combinations and spelling sequences
- they have problems with **blending** the sounds and identifying a word from the blend.

blending
fluently combining individual phonemes into the sound of a word

For successful reading, letter identification needs to be instant and accurate. Yet it is possible for children to slip through the early years of reading largely using pre-alphabetic whole-word learning and context cues, supported by partial alphabetic cues, and remain slow and shaky on their alphabetic knowledge. Their problems with decoding new words may result as much from not recognising the letters accurately or quickly enough, as not being secure in their phonological translation.

Children's miscues and their attempts at tackling a word can indicate where problems lie. A child may guess on the basis of the first, first and last, or some other letter(s) in a word, showing she is operating in a partial alphabetic way. She may sound the letters but have problems with holding them in memory or in their right sequence long enough to try blending them. She may blend them, but not recognise the pronunciation that the blended effort is an approximation of. She may try pronouncing a word letter-by-letter when she might operate in larger spelling chunks, for example, recognising that the spelling of the rime of 'right' is a more reliable guide to pronunciation than letter-by-letter decoding. In each case, the teacher should be alert to what immediate prompts and supportive instruction would be appropriate.

Individual differences
Some individual differences may result from specific problems or deficits, some may result from more general traits. For example, one general trait might be a readiness or unwillingness to take risks. It is fairly clear that guessing or predicting words, based upon context cues, is a more risky undertaking than working a word out by phonics. The taught procedures of synthetic phonics, although

laborious, can provide a sense of security. The child can do *something*, even if she doesn't finally achieve success.

For many children, as for many adults, it feels safer to say nothing than to risk being wrong. For a child who is averse to risk-taking, language-experience approaches to teaching reading may be less appropriate than an approach the provides the prop of a clear procedure of word-attack. Perhaps this is why phonics often works better than language experience approaches with working-class children, second-language learners and special educational needs children like those who have Down's Syndrome. On the other hand, some children, including some dyslexics, find contextual prediction easier to cope with than phonic procedures and use intelligent guessing to compensate for poor graphophonic skills.

The balance between sight-reading and graphophonic decoding

Even when children have undergone very much the same pattern of instruction in reading, maybe a quarter of readers tend to be overly dependent on a sight vocabulary, with a corresponding weakness in decoding skills, while another quarter tend to rely more on decoding, with a corresponding limited sight-vocabulary (Byrne, 1998).

These differences can be seen as relating to the two elements of the dual-route model of skilled reading in which whole-word learning and phonological decoding are distinguished. The dual route model of skilled reading accounts for the fact that we can readily read irregular words like 'laugh' and 'aisle' *and* readily read regularly spelled psuedo-words like 'winsup' and 'pilk' (which is, of course, the same skill as is required for reading unknown *real* words). Some children, however, are better at operating one of the routes rather than the other: some have more difficulties with irregular words and others with decoding unfamiliar words. These differences relate interestingly, but not perfectly, with the differences between phonological and surface dyslexia among adults who have become dyslexic as a result of brain damage (acquired dyslexia) – a finding that is consistent with the two routes being located in different areas of the brain. Such differing tendencies in children may result from differing innate characteristics.

The longer-term benefits of graphophonic decoding

Byrne (1998) confirms the suggestion made in Chapter 1 that, as children enter the junior age range, graphophonic ways of looking at words tend to organise (or *unitise*, to use Ehri's (1991) expression) the perception of spellings so that words can become new sight-words. That is, the sight vocabulary is progressively constructed through the graphophonic processes. Development depends upon graphophonic processes consigning more and more processed (unitised) spellings to the sight vocabulary.

At about 7 years old, Byrne found, a reasonable vocabulary of sight words is sufficient for reasonable reading proficiency, even if the child is not a good decoder. On the other hand, good decoding skills without a stock of sight words produces slow readers with below average reading comprehension.

However, a year later, at about 8 years old, things are different. The good decoders with a poor sight vocabulary, though still rather slow readers, are above average at comprehension and better than the children who had a good sight vocabulary but poor decoding skills. Overall, the results of Byrne's study showed that satisfactory decoding skills at 7 years old produced better readers at 8, both in comprehension and word identification. Poor decoding skills at 7 give rise to problems at 8.

Why there should be a reversal in the reading comprehension performance of good decoders/poor sight readers between 7 and 8 years old is not clear. It is possible that their slowness of reading at 7 affected their comprehension, but that, a year later, even though they were still *relatively* slow readers, their reading was fast enough to allow reasonable comprehension. This is not an issue Byrne examines.

A follow-up study (Byrne, 1998) found the same pattern continuing between 8 and 9. The children who were better at decoding improved both absolutely and relatively to the poorer decoders with a better sight vocabulary. Overall, the results confirmed that, although a relative weakness in decoding at seven does not seem to be a great disadvantage as long as a good sight-vocabulary is in place, the longer term consequences are bad. Children who are ill-equipped, through a poor grasp and application of the alphabetic principle and graphophonics, to cope with the rapidly expanding vocabulary they encounter in print during their junior years face an uphill struggle.

The effects of phonological weaknesses

A similar area of difference between different 'normal' readers is in the relative balance between top-down and bottom-up processes they habitually employ. An extreme case of context-dependence is found in developmental dyslexia. While there are different forms of dyslexia (for example, the forms that relate to problems with visual perception), the most prevalent form relates to phonological deficits leading to problems with mapping phonemes on to **graphemes** and

graphemes
the written equivalent of a phoneme, e.g. a, ee, igh, eigh, p, ph

graphophonic decoding. Such children may compensate by developing contextual prediction strategies to a high degree (Snowling, 1987). But prediction tends to fall down when more wide-ranging, less predictable texts are encountered at the top end of primary or the beginning of secondary school.

At a less extreme level, differences in phonological sensitivity have an effect on reading. The usual indicator of phonological awareness among pre-school children is their sensitivity to rhyme. At the earliest stages of learning to read, rhyme sensitivity has an enabling function in relation to phonemic awareness, perhaps by directing attention to the sounds within words rather than their meanings. At later stages, rhyme sensitivity may contribute to the development of orthographic knowledge, particularly in relation to irregular spellings, by drawing attention to spelling chunks like '-ight', '-tion' and '-ought'.

Bryant and Bradley (1985) found both that rhyme sensitivity was a strong predictor of future reading success with younger children and that weakness in rhyme sensitivity was very marked among backward readers in the middle junior years as compared with younger children with the same reading age. This finding suggests that poor phonological awareness is a significant cause of reading backwardness. However, on a more positive note, they conclude that training in phonological awareness is possible and that children can also be helped to use the skills that they do possess more effectively. Training that relates phonology with spelling is particularly effective (see also Hatcher *et al.*, 1995).

Influences of teaching methods

Children do not, in general, discover the crucially important alphabetic principle for themselves; they have to be taught about it (Goswami and Bryant, 1990; Byrne, 1998). Yet one of the key differences between different approaches to teaching reading is the emphasis laid upon alphabetic instruction and procedures. Language experience approaches, emphasising context, will tend to encourage children to concentrate on contextual cues and sight-learning at the expense of alphabetic (i.e. graphophonic) cues.

Such approaches refer to miscues which don't change the meaning, or which make sense in their own terms, as 'good' miscues. If teachers are happy to let 'good' miscues go without correction, children are not going to be primarily concerned with accuracy and will not tend to develop self-correction mechanisms so readily. They are not being trained to check their predictions against the graphophonic information from the page.

Approaches that emphasise the alphabetic principle may encourage children to concentrate on phonic translation at the expense of using context cues at all. Traditional phonics can produce such decoding automata who don't notice what they are reading; and it may sap children's confidence for attempting other strategies. They may well feel reluctant – may well feel it is cheating – to try to identify words by any other means. It can be difficult to wean a child away from letter-by-letter processing to looking at wider spelling patterns in words or to get them to attempt a contextually-inspired guess. Considering the context as a source of information may not feature in their concept of what reading is all about.

On the other hand, children who have been taught exclusively by 'language experience' approaches may too readily accept their own guesses without cross-checking with the text. Their problems are going to be more to do with accuracy than speed and concern with meaning. Clay (1991) notes that *slowing down* in response is often a sign of developing new skills, especially when it comes to cross-checking between the different sources of information to ensure accuracy. Teachers should, as a consequence, encourage children to cross-check and allow children time to work words out.

It will be noted that the effects of teaching approaches parallel quite closely the differences in predisposition that Byrne (1998) identified in half the 7-year-olds he tested. We can speculate about possible effects where teaching approaches either confirm a child in her predisposition or run totally counter to it. Presumably children will either feel at home under one approach and succeed within its parameters, or will feel alienated by it. Unfortunately, we know very little about the effects of this kind of match or mismatch between individuals and methods. Perhaps a child will tend to fail under one approach where she might flourish under another. But one thing we do know is that, overall, children do less well in schools that concentrate on one approach at the expense of others (HMI, 1990).

Teachers receiving children into Key Stage 2 should, then, be alert to the different strategies that children favour and to the effectiveness of their self-corrections. They should be ready to try different approaches to match the needs of different children. In particular, amongst strategies, they should be concerned to develop flexible graphophonic strategies to encourage the development of orthographic processes.

PRACTICAL IMPLICATIONS FOR THE CLASSROOM

The developments in reading processing are not as overtly obvious in Key Stage 2 as they are in Key Stage 1. Similarly, the causes of problems and potential problems are not so obvious. So it behoves the Key Stage 2 teacher to be particularly alert to the strategies (including avoidance strategies!) that children are employing in relation to reading. In particular, what the teacher needs to give diagnostic attention to is the pattern of the child's miscues, which indicate the child's predilections and weaknesses in the skills she brings to bear in reading (discussed more fully below).

The teacher who has a conceptual model of reading development is in a stronger position to be able to help children effectively. She will be in a better position to diagnose difficulties and will have a better idea of what to do about them.

The two key things for her to bear in mind are that:

- children can develop different strategies to enable them to get by early on, but that the use of graphophonic strategies, leading to orthographic reading skills, is the key to successful longer-term development
- at the same time, reading has to become a search for meaning, not simply a task of decoding, so the quality of texts and the engagement of children's motivating interest are vital. Matching the text to the child demands consideration of both textual difficulty and content interest.

In the classroom, there are two major divisions of teaching to be considered: there is the ongoing help that can be given to the child during the process of continuous reading, and there are the activities that develop contributory skills and knowledge that feed into the individual's reading processes and repertoire of strategies. In terms of organisation, this will tend to mean that there is help given in individualised reading sessions (and maybe at home by parents); and there are class and group activities focusing on the explicit teaching of skills and processes, and these activities will tend to take place in the Literacy Hour.

Listening to readers

Listening to readers is a time-consuming activity that is difficult to fit into the normal classroom day. Yet it is not something that can be totally delegated to parents and helpers. The reason for this is that it is an occasion for diagnostic listening and specific instructional interventions. As **miscue analysis** and **running reading**

miscue analysis
a procedure for recording miscues verbatim and then interpreting them to determine what reading strategies are being attempted

running reading records
a procedure not unlike miscue analysis, designed by Marie Clay for use in the early years

records demonstrate, if children make mistakes, there is always a reason for it. And it is the teacher's task peculiarly to interpret the miscues (you can't expect parents and helpers to do this). It may not be possible or desirable to keep the silent reading periods that are scheduled into the timetable entirely sacrosanct (even if they survive at all, under the time pressure created by the National Literacy Strategy!). Not all children are ready to profit by them without some external support. You may need to listen to readers during this time.

Listening to readers may involve listening to children read or listening to children talk about what they have read. Both aspects are important, but the balance between them will tend to be different for different children. And the balance will tend to change over time. When the child has become well established in self-monitoring and self-correction, longer periods of sustained silent reading become valuable since the child is now self-tutoring. Discussion about what she has been reading becomes more important both for your monitoring of the child's comprehension and to enhance the child's motivation through adult interest, attention and shared enjoyment. At this point, however, I want to concentrate on listening to reading and intervention.

Listening and intervening

As we saw in the first chapter, miscues result from the child attempting, not wholly successfully, to use one, or some combination, of the contextual and graphophonic sources of information to enable her to read the word. By definition, since there is a miscue, the child hasn't used the information as well as she might. The teacher's job is to identify what source(s) of information the child is attempting to use and to understand the nature of the child's inadequacies of strategic performance. It may be a matter of the child not having used one of the sources at all, for example, when the child is guessing from context and doesn't use the graphophonic information at all. Or it may be that she isn't using the source as fully as she might, for example, when the child attempts a word by guess and by first-letter sound. The aim of the teacher is to inculcate a balanced and co-ordinated use of the three sources of information, with the graphophonic progressively coming to take the leading role.

As we have seen, self-correction is a crucial element in learning to read. It depends upon the child monitoring her own reading for sense and for accuracy and reviewing her reading if any anomalies occur. She will only be aware of anomalies if she:

- is alert to meaning – both the meaning of the sentence itself and its meaning in the wider context of the passage
- is attentive to the print on the page
- cross-checks between them.

So it behoves the teacher not to correct the child when she produces a miscue but, first, to allow her time to correct herself; and if she does not, to draw her attention to the anomaly, thus encouraging her to correct herself. The teacher's skill lies in her ability to prompt the child into self-monitoring and self-correction.

How might the teacher draw the reader's attention to an anomaly in what she has produced as a reading? With younger or weaker readers, the teacher may need to stop immediately after the word and say, 'Does that make sense? No. Well, try that again' or 'Look again at the first letter? What does it say?' or some such prompt, adapted both to the particular situation in the text and to the teacher's judgement about what help is appropriate to that particular child. Once the word has been established accurately, the whole sentence will need to be read again to establish the continuity of meaning.

With an older child or better reader, it may be better to wait for a natural break (maybe the end of the page), and make a comment like, 'You read that well. Except there was just one problem. What was it? Did you notice...?' In this sort of way, the teacher puts the onus of reflective self-monitoring on to the child. If the child isn't sure, it may be appropriate to say something like, 'Look again at the sentence beginning "The witch ..." What did you say? Did that make sense?' In doing this, you are trying to establish the use of meaning, in the words of the National Curriculum, 'as a checking device'.

It may be that the teacher finds that the child is lacking in certain basic skills or knowledge. Clearly, the teacher must address this deficiency, though, depending upon its nature, it may be more than can be dealt with during the on-going reading session. The teacher may have to devise some individual remedial work for the child or, if she suspects more than one child has the problem, she may need to devise a group instruction or practice session. It could be, for example, that certain children are not secure on the alphabet or have no word-building strategies available.

Classwork to develop processing skills

The Literacy Hour is time allocated specifically for developing literacy skills through direct teaching and directed activities, in the case of reading, starting from a shared text. But rather than looking immediately at the prescribed objectives, let us first consider, in relation to what we know about reading development, what kinds of work are going to be appropriate to help children to develop relevant processing skills.

The processing skills we are concerned with during Key Stage 2 are primarily graphophonic and orthographic skills, because reading is primarily about getting meaning by identifying words from the black marks on the page. At the beginning of Key Stage 2, children are still largely identifying words and getting the meaning by translating the print on the page into pronunciations, and this is done by a mix of means. In any one sentence, different words may be read by different processes. For example, in the following sentence:

> Get me some bread, or I'll hit you with my bommy-knocker

> (from *The Hungry Giant*, Story Chest)

certain irregular words may be recognised as logographic sight-words, certain words may be sight-words that have been fully processed, others may require some partial alphabetic reminder along with contextual cues; some may need to be deliberately partially processed by phonics before a contextual guess selects a reading, while others (like the invented word 'bommy') may need a full phonic translation. But the direction we are hoping to take the children is one of developing graphophonic recognition skills so that phonic translation is largely superseded by sight-recognition of words as coherent spelling sequences. Our aim is that what we do in Word Level work will help push graphophonic skills towards orthographic reading. Looked at in this light, the *Framework for Teaching* (DfEE, 1998) objectives make reasonable sense.

At the same time, developing the contextual skills relating to syntax and **semantics** as they feed into word recognition and as they contribute to comprehension are important. Since comprehension is what reading is ultimately all about, we must view all the work to do with reading at the Sentence and Text Levels in this light.

semantics
the study of meanings

Word level work
Initially, the *Framework for Teaching* objectives emphasise phonics and graphophonics in ways that lead on to orthographic sight-word recognition. They begin with revision and consolidation of work done in Key Stage 1. This includes work on identifying, blending and segmenting phonemes for reading and spelling. And this objective goes on reappearing, with little variation in wording, throughout Years 3 and 4. Hopefully, what you teach will have a bit more variation and development in it! Additionally, work

continues on high-frequency words which initially were learned as sight-words, but which now, in part through the emphasis on spelling, come to be more fully processed as recognition units.

Children will have been taught some phonics during the early years – they will know the sound values of the letters and some of the digraphs, and will have some skills in synthesising word-sounds. How extensive these skills are will be variable, depending on the approaches taken in the early years. The children may have learned some of the context-sensitive rules, like the 'magic *e*' and the soft '*c*' and '*g*' when followed by an '*e*' or an '*i*'.

Nevertheless, despite any teaching, it remains more likely that the child who can read 'giant' correctly has learned it as a one-off sight-word rather than as an instance of the soft '*g*' rule! But again, if knowing 'giant' helps her read 'gigantic', maybe she has transferred some phonic understanding from one word to the other – possibly with the help of both meaning and the commonality of letters. Such 'reading by analogy' is dependent on alphabetic strategies but not directly on phonics procedures. Children learn to use alphabetic information on their own account.

Children are likely to arrive from the early years with partial-alphabetic skills – to use graphophonic cues, if not a full graphophonic translation. This is a skill which they tend to develop spontaneously, as well as being supported in it by teacherly prompts. But however intensively or minimally children have been taught phonics in Key Stage 1, not all the possible 'phonic rules' will have been taught because there are too many of them! What the Year 3 teacher will be looking for is a certain flexibility of approach – a readiness to use graphophonic information to help solve a problem word, but also a readiness to use other sources of information as well.

Partial alphabetic skills are a clear example of this. The child may use the partial alphabetic information available to her to support her logographic sight-reading, or she may use it as a sound-prompt for a contextual guess, or she may use it to check that a guess is not inconsistent with the alphabetic information she has available to her. In all these cases, she is learning that reading involves making links and checking between parallel processes.

What specific phonic skills should the teacher ensure children have? They should be able to name and sound the letters instantly – and know that certain letters can represent more than one sound, and that certain letters work in combination to produce a new sound. They need to be able to sound and blend the letters in a word, but not so mechanically that they can't make a guess at a word from the uncertain pronunciation they are producing. For example, Chew (1997) cites the example of children sounding out 'school' and coming up with the correct reading, despite the some-what misleading sounds a phonic rendering initially produces!

Children should also be secure in phonic analysis in ways that enable them to produce accurate spellings of regular words and attempt reasonable spellings of other words. Of course, in Key Stage 2, we would not be happy with *merely* phonic attempts at spellings. We expect children also to develop a visual memory for words – in the kind of way that prompts us as adults to write out a spelling to see if looks right.

So what we are saying is that we must teach the application of phonics for reading and writing both on phonically regular words (where it works flawlessly) and on irregular words (where the child has to develop more flexibility of approach). Not only does this demonstrate the uses and limitations of phonics, but phonics also develops useful letter-sequencing habits of looking at words that are useful for further developments. Children will begin to learn impli-citly for themselves some of those hundreds of context-dependent spelling rules that we can never hope to teach explicitly. For example, a child may read the word 'cell' as /sell/ without being able to say why it should not be /kell/.

Graphophonic chunking

If phonics has been concerned with synthesising word sounds from letter sounds, graphophonics has a wider remit, which includes but extends beyond phonics. Graphophonics is concerned with *all* the possible ways that alphabetic knowledge and spelling patterns can be used to identify a word from its pronunciation.

The child entering Key Stage 2 will probably already know some sight-words in a fully-processed orthographic way – words like 'the', 'are' and 'have' which she will have written and read a thousand times and will recognise instantly. It is perhaps difficult to know when such words move on from being known logographically, when they are recognised in a partial-alphabetic way and when they are known orthographically. But what seems certain is that writing has a lot to do with establishing them as orthographic words, because writing requires them to be written as an alphabetic sequence which, with repetition, becomes overlearned and automatic. Words known in this way certainly constitute 'graphophonic chunks' or recogni-tion units. Such words tend to be high frequency monosyllables – though being high-frequency is more decisive than their being monosyllables.

Whole words and part words

Graphophonic chunks are not necessarily whole words, but they do tend to have to be pronounceable phonological chunks. For example, the part-word affixes (for example, 'un-', '-ful') that Bussis *et al.* (1985) observed children acquiring like a sight-vocabulary, are unitised as pronunciations. The critical factor is that a high-frequency sequence of letters is perceived as a chunk or recognition unit when it represents a phonological unit.

For example, the sequence '-ing' represents the phonological unit, the rime, of many words, for example, 'king', 'ring', 'sing'. It also represents the phonological unit, the suffix of many words, such as 'walking', 'talking', etc. The graphophonic chunk represents the marriage of a reliable pronunciation with a reliable spelling. Such units are not built up from letters as in phonics, but become unitised because they represent phonological units. However, such chunking is dependent on pre-existing letter and sequencing knowledge for the spelling pattern to become identifiable.

Part of learning to see if a spelling 'looks right', as discussed above, involves applying knowledge about common stems and affixes. For example, while an early years child may be showing phonic intelligence in writing 'craen' for 'crying', by the time the child is in Year 3 we would expect her to know the '-ing' ending and to have a sense of where grammatically it is appropriate.

Unitising spelling chunks

Such chunking results from applying alphabetic knowledge, paying letter patterns attention, encountering them frequently and being attentive to their pronunciation. In the first instance, the unitising element tends to be phonological awareness – a given sequence of letters always says a given word-sound chunk. Typically such sequences are whole syllables or rimes, but they can also be other familiar letter combinations. For example, the letter combination 'wor-' never says /war/, it almost invariably says /were/. We learn this implicitly from words like word, work, world, worm, worse, worst, worship and worth. So we know how to pronounce less frequently encountered words like wort and even whortleberry, and we tend to mispronounce 'worsted', which is properly pronounced /woosted/.

Rime spellings

Rime spellings are one of the most significant kinds of graphophonic chunk. This is because rime spellings represent perceptually salient auditory units. Frith (1985) notes that children more readily read 'nght' than 'nite' as saying /night/. Even an incomplete, though still very distinctive, graphophonic chunk is more readily identified than a regular, but novel, homophonic spelling. In children's experience, the '-ght' combination probably occurs most frequently in the rime '-ight', and '-ight' is a graphophonic chunk showing 'rime stability' (Goswami, 1995), i.e. pronunciational reliability.

Rimes and rime spellings play a significant part in developing ortho-graphic word recognition.

As discussed in Chapter 1, and in a way not dissimilar to the 'giant/gigantic' and the 'wor-' analogising discussed above, children spontaneously exploit rime analogies between given and new words. Such analogies can be deliberately developed through explicit teaching by:

- presenting clue words and new words, for example, 'If "peak" says /peek/, what will "wreak" say?', and encouraging children to invent similar questions for themselves
- showing how words can be changed by substituting new onsets or rimes and how different combinations of common onsets and rimes can produce different words (both real and nonsense words), for example, with rime-and-onset domino cards.

Curiously, despite an emphasis on learning about rhymes throughout the early years, after the Reception Year the *Framework for Teaching* does not specifically mention rimes and analogy for reading purposes. In Year 1, children are expected to relate rhymes and spelling patterns, and the National Curriculum says, 'Pupils should be shown how to use their sight vocabulary to help them read words that have similar features', which requirements could be a rather obscure gesture in the direction of rime and other analo-gies. One might have expected the term 'graphic knowledge' to have covered such issues, but it seems to be restricted to the area of affixes and stems. During Key Stage 2, analogy is only mentioned in connection with spelling. Though, of course, spelling feeds indi-rectly into reading skills.

Morphological chunking

Morphological chunking is very much what the National Curriculum and the *Framework for Teaching* mean by 'graphic knowledge'. 'Graphic knowledge' is the ability to recognise stems (wrongly called '**roots**'), prefixes, suffixes, inflections and so on as graphophonic chunks. Morphological chunking comes naturally to children as a result of both phonological and syntactic–semantic factors: chunks become unitised as a result of their frequency of encounter, their pronounceability and their part-word meaning-fulness.

root
the etymological origin of a word, or (sometimes) the stem of a word

However, even what comes naturally needs cognitive and reflective support. For example, a child may recognise the suffix '-ly' as a unit and have an intuitive grasp of how it affects or relates to the grammar of sentences, marking variously, as it does, adjectives and adverbs (for example, lovely, quickly). Whether '-ly' marks an adjective or an adverb seems to depend upon the grammatical part of speech of the stem ('love' is a noun and 'quick' an adjective). Discussion about the use of '-ly' words and how to make and use them will reinforce and generalise children's powers of recognition and understanding, and develop their appreciation of how words work together in sentences (though there is a danger that children may come to think that only words ending in '-ly' can be adverbs – but note, for example, 'He did *well*', 'She ran *fast*'). Thus, for example, Year 4, Term 3 work will build on Year 2, Term 3 work – though sticking rigidly to the programme of objectives may prevent your exploiting teaching opportunities as they occur.

Exploring words and their morphology

Imagine, for example, that a child stumbles, in reading an adult information text, over the word 'neonate'. The *Oxford Primary School Dictionary* only gives 'neon' – which, in the event, is not very helpful. The meaning doesn't fit and the spelling suggests that the word should perhaps be syllabised as 'neon-ate' – a possibility, since 'neon' is a word and '-ate' is a frequently-met-with rime. Since nothing to do with 'neon' makes any sense in context, we might suggest that the child finds another dictionary.

An old edition of the *Concise Oxford* doesn't give 'neonate', but it gives a lot of words beginning 'neo-', including, as a head-word, 'neo-', a prefix meaning 'new'. So could our target word be syllabised 'neo-nate'? So we try 'nate', and find 'nation', 'native', 'nativity' and 'natural' with their associates in the *School Dictionary*. The *Concise* gives more words – including 'natal' (of, from, one's birth), 'natation' (swimming) and 'nates' (buttocks).

It is time to look at context again – or a bigger dictionary. However, the *Shorter Oxford* (1973) doesn't give 'neonate' at all. But the context does provide cues:

> Birth allows the brain to go on growing, since otherwise the head would soon become too big for the birth canal of the mother. At birth, the human head is roughly the same size as a chimpanzee. . .The development of the brain in both the fetus and the neonate is a gradual process. . .

(Greenfield, 1997)

The context is about the brain before and after birth, so neither 'new-country', 'new-nature', 'new-swim' nor 'new-buttocks' make much sense, but 'new-birth' looks a possibility. So, paralleled as it is by 'fetus', let's guess that it means 'new-born baby'. (At last, this meaning is confirmed by *Chambers 20th Century Dictionary*!)

Such a process of exploration of a word raises questions about morphology, word construction, etymology and word-families based on common morphemes and roots. It will widen the child's sense of geography and history if she finds out why Natal Province in South Africa got its name. She will not only discover that 'nativity' is linked to 'neonate', but that 'nation' and 'native' are also linked through the Latin. It will add to her repertoire of part-words with their meanings, in terms of which she can tackle and interpret new words she meets. And doing all this meets a whole raft of Word Level objectives in the *Framework for Teaching*, for example, for Year 5, Terms 1, 2 and 3; Year 6, Term 1.

Developing morphological awareness

Further word explorations might include inventing neologisms (there's a nice word to work at!) using prefixes, suffixes, and discovering etymologies and roots (Year 6, Term 3). Nunes (1998) argues that children learn a framework for thinking about language when they master morphological spellings in this kind of way. She cites the examples of children inventing new dinosaur names and operating with other kinds of psuedo-words (for example, 'unclimb') that use standard rules about how morphemes go together to compose words.

The spelling system can itself become an object of thought. For example, in spoken language the past tense of 'weak' verbs may be marked either by /t/ or /d/ (for example, /kissed/, /killed/). But in the written form the spelling for both is '-ed'. Likewise, the relationship between, for example, 'know' and 'knowledge', 'medical' and 'medicine', and 'sign', 'signal' and 'signature' are much more evident in the written forms of the words than in the spoken forms. The spelling system makes meaningful patterns (morphological units) available for thinking about.

Nunes, Bryant and Bindman (1997) carried out a three-year longitudinal study on children's awareness of morphology, looking, among other things, at spellings that reflect morphology. One thing that became clear was that children's spelling of morphemes at an early stage predicted their awareness of morphemes at a later age.

These findings cast an enriching light on Uta Frith's (1985) suggestion that, as reading develops into the orthographic phase, 'the orthographic (recognition) units ideally coincide with morphemes'. Work done on morphological awareness should feed into the development of orthographic reading.

Summary

The teacher has to be alert to the different strategies and problems that children face in developing their reading processes during Key Stage 2. To do this effectively, she needs to have a mental model of reading development in terms of which she can both interpret reading difficulties and devise strategies to help her pupils. And she also has to be alert to the kinds of differences and difficulties that children may exhibit, resulting from individual, socio-cultural and gender differences, and differences resulting from previous educational experiences. Since the development of processing during Key Stage 2 is largely a matter of developing and moving on from alphabetic to orthographic processes by developing graphophonic and morphological chunking skills, activities that focus on spelling patterns and structures and on the morphological composition of complex words are going to be particularly valuable.

- Children enter Key Stage 2 with different levels of reading attainment, but they generally come with some alphabetic word-attack skills and some partial-alphabetic sight-word dependency.

- Individual differences between children may depend upon socio-cultural, gender or individual factors, or upon the ways children have previously been taught.

- The teacher needs to be able to diagnose individual reading characteristics and needs in order best to be able to help with children's reading development.

- Among the important developments that the teacher is aiming to promote are developing self-tutoring abilities and the graphophonic skills of perceiving spelling patterns as recognition units.

- Word-level work in the classroom that explores spelling patterns and the morphemic composition of words will be helpful in this development.

Bielby, Nicholas (1998) *How To Teach Reading: A Balanced Approach,*
Scholastic
This book gives a theoretically balanced view of the teaching of
reading, with the theory itself balanced by detailed practical teaching
strategies and suggestions.

Bryant, P. and Bradley, L. (1985) *Children's Reading Problems,* Blackwell
This is a highly influential book which, almost single-handedly,
introduced the notion of the important of phonological awareness to
educational discussion and which remains illuminating and relevant.

Further reading

3 Children construing meaning

Objectives

When you have read this chapter, you should be able to:

- discuss the relationship between decoding skills and comprehension

- understand the way that prior knowledge and the new knowledge derived from reading a text combine with each other in comprehension

- distinguish between the different levels of comprehension, for example, the literal level, inferences and elaboration, evaluation and exploitation

- develop classroom strategies for assessing and promoting comprehension.

Introduction

We read in order to understand what has been written, and this chapter is concerned with the process of understanding, that is, with comprehension. It discusses what we mean by comprehension at different levels, from literal comprehension to integrating new information with pre-existing knowledge, inference-making and evaluation. It considers some of the ways texts are constructed to make sense; what kinds of sense children should be making from different sorts of texts; and some of the problems children have, for example with grammar and expression, in making sense of texts. In conclusion, it considers general classroom strategies for developing comprehension.

'READING TO LEARN' AND 'LEARNING TO READ'

A distinction is sometimes drawn between children 'learning to read' at Key Stage 1 and 'reading to learn' at Key Stage 2. This over-simple distinction ignores the fact that children are still developing their processing skills throughout Key Stage 2, and that children at Key Stage 1 are not learning to read properly if they aren't, at the same time, understanding and learning from what they read. Yet this simplistic distinction does highlight an important emphasis.

The emphasis in Key Stage 2 now falls on reading for a purpose, not so much on decoding as an end in itself. Children are expected to read longer and more sustained texts, and cope with a wider range of vocabulary and genres. Children are expected to follow written instructions and to read more non-narrative texts and are expected to make their own selection, searching for suitable books. They are expected to know how to search for and retrieve information. They are expected to be able to report on their reading, making analytical and critical comments, and to select information relevant to a given purpose and to put the ideas into their own words. In a word, the emphasis falls less on decoding and more on comprehension.

A MODEL OF READING COMPREHENSION

Comprehension involves a number of factors, and the model presented in Figure 3.1 highlights some key features.

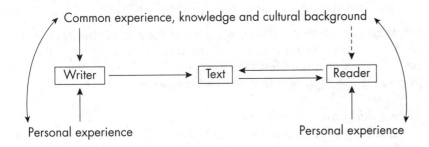

Figure 3.1
A model of reading comprehension

Shared knowledge
The writer and the reader share not only a language but also some background knowledge of life – without this shared background of reference, much in any text would be unintelligible. The reason the arrow coming down to the reader is broken is that the reader (especially if a child) may not share all the background with the writer. For example, consider:

> ...John had a
> Great big
> Waterproof
> Mackintosh...

For many young children nowadays coming across *When We Were Very Young* (A.A. Milne) for the first time, the term 'mackintosh' might well be meaningless.

The writer assumes a certain background in the reader. For a child, registering and responding to the background assumptions is sometimes the way she acquires common knowledge and vicariously learns about the world. It is possible that the context and the illustrations might help to make the word 'mackintosh' intelligible!

Textual meaning

In the middle of the model stands the text. This embodies the meanings that the writer put into it. The meanings that the reader derives from it depend both on what the writer put into it and on what the reader brings to it in terms of both background common knowledge and personal experience. If the sense that the reader makes of the text is limited, this will probably be the result of the limitations of the reader and her background knowledge and of some sort of mismatch between the text and the reader.

The model indicates that there is:

- meaning inherent in the text
- personal meaning-making, within constraints, going on within the reader, melding prior knowledge, including personal experience, and the new information from the text.

In discussing comprehension, we need to keep both the role of the reader and the meaningfulness of the text in mind. While much of our subsequent discussion will focus on the role of the reader, it is important not to forget that the text has some authority too!

Literal and implicit meanings

In discussing the meanings inherent in the text, we sometimes distinguish between the literal meaning and – well, lots of other different kinds of meanings, for example:

- the implied meaning – as with 'the piggy-bank felt heavy', meaning there's money in it; or as with sarcasm, when 'Oh, you *are* clever!' means the opposite of the literal meaning
- the literary-conventional meaning – where 'Once upon a time...' means 'Here comes a particular kind of story. Expect magic, etc.'; and where, in *Tess*, Alec D'Urbeville's 'full lips, badly-moulded' means he has a sensual badly-moulded moral character, but Tess's 'mobile peony mouth' means she is sensitive and has the purity, beauty, sexual ripeness and vulnerability of a flower.

Rather than trying to categorise all the kinds of implicit meanings here, I simply want to make two general points.

- Literal meanings are the least of our worries – though still presenting a challenge to children.

- Understanding other sorts of meaning depends upon the knowledge and experience we bring, as readers, to the text – knowledge and experience of life and of texts.

Perhaps there is never a totally clear boundary between 'literal meanings' and more implicit meanings. Meaning is always more than the simple addition sum of the lexical meanings of each word in a sentence. Even to understand something 'literally' the reader may have to understand the meaning in terms of a pictured situation – for example, when 'the cat sat on the mat' it was clearly doing something different from (and more peaceful than) when 'the cat sat on the rat'.

The challenges of comprehension

Comprehension is what reading is all about. We read in order to understand what has been written. Avid readers at Key Stage 2 are motivated by curiosity about the possibilities of the world and of experiences beyond their own. This hunger to stock their imaginations impels their interest in non-fiction as well as fiction. And it doesn't necessarily matter too much that they don't always understand everything that they read, as long as they are gaining a sense that there is an inviting world out there awaiting to be experienced and understood.

Even as adults we don't always understand what we are reading – as when we are trying to follow the instructions with a new video recorder, understand the small print in an insurance policy or read up about personal computers in a computer magazine. In each case, the problem may well be different – understanding the application of instructions, following internal references backwards and forwards in the document, or lack of knowledge both about things and about technical terms.

Children, of course, have all these problems – in spades! Their attention and short-term memory spans are limited, they don't have experience of all the complexities of English grammar nor a comprehensive knowledge of English vocabulary, and they don't have all the background knowledge and information about the physical and social world that might help them make sense of what they are reading. And additionally, they may not be able to read all the words!

The reason we have children's books is to temper the challenge to comprehension by writing in short, simple sentences and familiar language; and to make novel information accessible by mediating it through familiar themes. For example, we tend to write about history in terms of common experiences of everyday life with which children can empathise, not in terms of politics and economics. And we use a lot of illustrations to help provide a context of information to help the anticipation and interpretation of the text.

The challenge of non-narrative texts

Even so, we are not always aware of the challenge to comprehension that children's texts provide. Let us consider a passage from a non-narrative text written for 9–10-year-olds and look at some of the potential problems it presents:

> **Mammals evolve**
> Mammals evolved from reptiles into very different creatures. They are generally covered with fur or hair, the mothers produce milk in their bodies to feed their young and they are warm-blooded. Humans, elephants and whales are all mammals, although the first mammals were very small.

> (from *The Age of the Dinosaurs*, Collins Pathways)

Vocabulary

The term 'reptile' should be clear since it has been discussed earlier in the chapter, and one aim of this passage is to provide an explanation of the word 'mammal'. It does this by providing three defining characteristics and three examples of mammals with which the child will be familiar (the classic 'rule of three' in action!). Nevertheless, not all children will be able to tell you what a mammal is after reading the passage – just as Sissy Jupe in Dickens's *Hard Times* cannot define a horse, although she has lived with them all her life! Maybe a better test of comprehension here would be to ask for further examples of mammals and get the children to tell you why they think they are.

The word 'evolved' is probably the only word here that might be totally new to children. It is used a number of times in the chapter, but never explained. The context is one where other 'creatures had developed from the first life forms' and where amphibians 'arrive', reptiles 'arrive' and 'evolve', and mammals 'evolve'. Whatever sense the child makes of this word, it will not carry all the intellectual baggage of the theory of evolution that it will for the adult reader. It may convey something like 'changed' or 'developed' – or even, 'came from somewhere else'!

And, of course, the word may not mean anything to them. It is characteristic of children's learning that they learn the form of words relatively quickly, but if the words are not explained, the meaning that goes with them only develops slowly with more knowledge and more encounters in varied situations. The child may ascribe or induce some sort of meaning, however vague, to a new word from its context, or may simply set it mentally to one side to tackle at a later date – or the child may simply ignore it. In the normal course of events, children ignore a lot that doesn't make sense to them: this is a self-defence mechanism to avoid being overwhelmed by confusion and insecurity. And this mechanism may well be at work in those children, predominantly boys, who go through the motions of reading without trying to make it make sense.

Grammar

The grammar is reasonably straightforward. The second sentence is compound, listing three parallel main clauses. Only the last sentence is complex, tailed by a subordinate adverbial clause of concession beginning with 'although'. This word signals that the reader should look for some kind of contrast. Making sense of this concession depends upon the reader implicitly categorising humans, elephants and whales as 'large' and 'later', so that there is a contrast with the explicit 'first' and 'small'. It is perhaps only through understanding the implication of 'although' that the child might learn that humans, elephants and whales were not among the first mammals.

Questions of grammar don't just deal with issues like **parts of speech** and clauses, but with all the ways that word order works to make meaning, and a lot of these ways are idiomatic. Such usages can only be learned from exposure and experience. For example, the expression 'very different creatures' could raise a problem about what is different from what. Here, mammals are different from reptiles, but a very similar phrase, 'many different creatures' would suggest different kinds of mammals. Only careful questioning would establish whether children have understood that it meant mammals were very different from reptiles and not that there are many different kinds of mammals.

parts of speech
categories of word function in a sentence, e.g. noun, verb, preposition, etc.

Cohesion

'**Cohesion**' refers to the way links of meaning are embodied in word-links in a passage, knitting it all together. The verbal rivets (to change the metaphor again!) operate by internal references backward (anaphorically) or forward (cataphorically) within the passage. The word 'although', discussed above, is such a marker of cohesion, showing how meanings should be seen in relation to each other.

cohesion
the effect of verbal links of meaning within and between sentences, e.g. in 'She got up and went shopping. Buying new clothes on a bright Spring morning always made her feel good', 'buying' relates back to 'shopping' and 'morning' relates back to 'got up', connecting up the meanings coherently within the text

Markers of cohesion: pronouns

One of the simplest cohesive devices is the use of pronouns, to refer to something mentioned elsewhere in the text, for example:

- anaphoric reference: 'When Mike and Midge went to France, *they* bought a house.'

- cataphoric reference: 'When *they* went to France, Mike and Midge bought a house.'

Anaphoric references, back to something already mentioned, are the more common. Thus, to return to the 'Mammals' passage, the initial 'They' in the second sentence of the passage refers anaphorically back to the previous sentence.

proximity rule
the tendency to try to relate the things that are nearest at hand

But what does it refer back to? Is it to 'mammals' or to 'creatures'? According to the **proximity rule** (a rule of thumb), you might expect it to be 'creatures', but what the sentence seems to be doing is providing a definition for mammals, so it probably refers back to 'mammals'. Since the mammals *are* the creatures, it doesn't matter too much.

referent
that which is referred to

But this does raise the point that pronouns can be ambiguous. And children find identifying the **referent** of pronouns surprisingly tricky. They can get lost with pronouns – perhaps because pronouns require the reader to carry verbal information over from sentence to sentence and to use meaning as well as syntax and proximity to establish the referent.

Another tricky pronoun is the second 'they' in the second sentence. According to the proximity rule, it should refer back to either the 'young' or further back to 'mothers', following the trail of the preceding 'their's:

> ... their bodies to feed their young and they ...

If children only have a limited short-term working memory capacity, they may well only refer back a short way to find an antecedent. Perhaps we, as adults, only know it has to refer further back because we already know that warm-bloodedness is part of the generic definition of mammals, not only of mammalian mothers. But will the child realise this and refer back 28 words to find the antecedent, 'mammals'?

The process of maximising meaning often helps determine the antecedent reference. A tricky task – to use the meaning of the sentence to determine the meaning of the words that determine the meaning of the sentence! But this is a task that children accomplish all the time to some degree in listening and reading. Word meanings in context and sentence meaning (which is the context) are negotiated in the working memory as part of the reading process. But only up to the limits of the working memory!

Other markers of cohesion

Another marker of cohesion in this passage is the word 'the' in the phrase 'the mothers'. Why does the sentence need the word 'the' at all? The word 'the' (as distinct from 'a', or in the case of plurals, no article at all) often indicates that we, the readers, already know what is being referred to, it is a 'given'. Thus, 'a dog . . .' is any old dog, but 'the dog . . .' is a specific dog about which we already know something, for example:

A dog ran out into the road. The dog got run over.

'The mothers' are specifically the mothers that belong to the category 'mammals'. Such markers of 'giveness' act upon us, as readers, implicitly. It would not be surprising if such implicit links were not always taken on board by child readers.

The caveat or concession expressed in the term 'generally' is unlikely to mean much to the child reader. Its significance relates forward cataphorically to the fact that the three examples given, humans, elephants and whales, are largely devoid of fur and hair! Not many children will notice this (I didn't, at first. Did you?). But if you ask children to look for something peculiar about choosing humans, elephants and whales as examples of furry or hairy, warm-blooded milk-providers, they may spot it. Children can be prompted into reading with critical attention and spotting anomalies.

Inference

A great deal of what we take from any passage is not explicit in the text but is implicit. To make sense of the text we make inferences based on our background knowledge and experience. We have already touched on a number of such examples, in interpreting the significance of 'although', in making sense of the pronouns, and so on.

Communication depends very largely on the willingness of the listeners or readers to try to understand what the communicators mean and to meet them half-way by filling in and filling out the meaning. This may mean 'reading between the lines' with regard to intentions, and making '**bridging inferences**' with regard to meaning. A 'bridging inference' is one where the reader uses prior knowledge to fill in a gap where something is left implicit. For example, consider the following:

She took the cake out when it was done and burned her fingers on the door.

bridging inferences
inferences that fill in gaps in a text by the application of common knowledge, e.g. in reading 'He got a cup but found the kettle was missing', we infer he wanted a hot drink

What did she take the cake out of? What door did she burn her fingers on? We infer an oven. Research suggests that if, in half an hour or so, I were to ask you about the sentence,

She burned her fingers on the oven door,

you would accept that you had read that sentence previously. We tend to remember the meanings we have made, not the exact words of the text.

To return to our original non-fiction passage, it does not require us to make much in the way of bridging inferences and inferences about intention. However, we could draw further, more logical, inferences from the text, for example, reptiles are not furry, don't produce milk and are cold-blooded. We might even, mistakenly, be inclined to infer that nowadays there are no small mammals!

Inference in stories

Information texts aim to be very explicit and stories tend to depend much more on readers implicitly making inferences and filling out or elaborating the story from their own experience. Some inferences, like the existence of the oven, are as necessary for understanding the story as the information that is made explicit. The following passage, from a story for 9–10-year-olds, proves a happy hunting ground for identifying inferences that need to be made before the text can be properly understood:

> Luckily Adil was in and by himself, adding new stamps to another page in his album. Members of his family lived all over the world and seemed to love writing letters and cards to each other. So Adil's collection grew and grew.
>
> (from *The Pantomime Cat*, Collins Pathways)

At the simplest level, we, as adults, infer from his name and the global dispersion of his family, that Adil is probably not of English origin. But would a child necessarily have the knowledge and experience to infer this? The story is not incomprehensible if she doesn't, but it is enriched if she does.

There are more complex and more essential levels of inference to be made, based upon details of wording and on the knowledge of the social and physical world we bring with us to the text.

The disjunct 'Luckily' seems to stand outside the rest of the first sentence – nothing was lucky for anyone or anything *within* the sentence. Adil's being in was lucky *for somebody else*, whom we have to infer. We also infer that, because it was lucky Adil was by himself, the business this 'somebody' wished to transact with Adil was to be confidential or secret.

The word 'stamps' and 'album' activate our social knowledge about stamp-collecting as a hobby. The term 'another page' implies previous pages are full. This inference is reinforced by the next sentence which implicitly explains how he gets all his stamps. But for us to understand this, we have to know that letters have stamps on them and we have to assume that Adil gets these stamps.

We are not told explicitly that the family members do write to each other, but the expression 'seemed to love writing' implies it – and even that they did it a lot. We assume that the evidence for this must have been the existence of lots of letters – or at least, lots of stamps! Further, the love of writing had to 'seem' to somebody – somebody looking in from outside the situation. We probably assume that it 'seemed' to the same person who was lucky. With this 'seemed', as with 'luckily', we see the situation from the particular viewpoint of another character who is only implicit in this paragraph.

Elaboration

If inference is a matter of 'filling in' what is implicit in the text, elaboration is the process of 'filling out' the text with one's own imagination. To take one example, we have referred above to the 'rule of three' when dealing with examples. Of course, it isn't a *rule* as such, simply a typical device used in writing, whether in fiction or information texts. The writer mentions three things to stand for, or represent, a wider array of similar or related things. In descriptions and explanations, the giving of three instances, invites us, as readers, to supply a generalising principle to the instances and fill out the picture from our own experience. For example, consider the following passage from the same story discussed above:

> [The cat] adored exploring the narrow alleyway behind them, nosing in and out of big cardboard cartons and aromatic bags and boxes.

'Cartons', 'bags' and 'boxes' combine in such a way that we can picture the alleyway, adding yet further squalid details from our own experience of rubbish-filled back streets. We may fill out the scene with over-flowing dustbins, tin cans and broken bottles. More than three instances seems excessive, but fewer than three doesn't, perhaps, create the same sense of 'fullness' of description.

Elaboration is the process whereby the reader fills out the scene by providing her own imagery, visualising the scene out of her own experience and imagination. When we are, for example, lost in a dungeons and dragons story, all sorts of images we have gathered from books, films, comics, video-games, nightmares, etc., are activated, creating a world in our imaginations. We share collaboratively with the writer in picturing the story. But to do so, we need, (a), an active imagination for story, and, (b), a repertoire of available images derived from previous experience.

empathy
feeling with someone else;
emotional imagination

Empathy

In fiction in particular, but also in biographies and history, **empathy** is an important aspect of comprehension. Empathy is the feeling into the situation and emotions of another person or character. It may involve feelings relating to the questions, What does he/she seem to feel? What would I feel in his/her situation? What would I do? It may involve feeling sorry or happy for the character – though this is more to do with sympathy than empathy. It involves imagining feelings and emotions – and even exploring possibilities of feelings we have never yet felt. Hence the fascination of stories that deal with extreme emotions of love, terror and fear – What would it be like? Could I cope?

Without empathy, characters would be simply black marks on the page, a collection of traits and characteristics, actions and speeches. Empathy is not only what allows us to talk of characters in stories as if they were real people, but it is what enables us to believe that, in real life, we inhabit a world of real people like ourselves, and not androids. All we know of other people is traits, characteristics, actions and speeches. At least stories can take us inside other people's heads. We have more privileged knowledge of book characters than of other people in real life!

Empathy is born in us, as the responsiveness of babies to other people's feelings and facial expressions testify. And the skills of empathy and character-reading we learn from fiction develop our empathetic and character-reading skills in real life. And beyond this, empathy is also the basis of our moral feelings, for example, in the sense of fairness that develops in children so powerfully during the Key Stage 2 years.

Empathy is one of the most important contributors to inference in stories, in that both feelings and motives are often only indicated indirectly through actions, descriptions and dialogue, and are not stated explicitly. For example, where the text says, 'He turned and ran so no-one could see his tears', we know he is heart-broken: we all know what it is like to need to hide away in grief. But quite commonly in children's stories, we are told explicitly about people's feelings as well as being shown them in their behaviour: 'He looked cross – then surprised – and then his eyes opened as wide as a window and his jaw dropped.'

Evaluations within the world of the story

We don't just empathise with characters and their situations. We judge them. In thinking what we might do in a situation, we may think the character is brave or foolish or wicked in what he does.

We can both get within the characters and stand *outside* them. In our response to the characters and to the situations, we are like spectators, seeing more of the game, but not being in the game; we are in a position to 'contemplate possibilities of experience' (Harding, 1962) and thus to refine our judgements, values and our desires. It is in this way that reading fiction is a moral education. As Iris Murdoch (1970) says:

> ... the most essential and fundamental aspect of culture is the study of literature, since this is an education in how to picture and understand human situations.

Evaluations of stories and other texts

Evaluation works at another level as well. We judge the story – is it good or bad, boring or enjoyable, well or badly written, life-enriching or with something of the night about it? And if we are reading an information text, we make judgements about whether it is interesting and clear, how well it presents and explains things, how fully it covers a topic and its relevance and usefulness for a particular purpose, and whether we have learned something new from it.

A further important aspect of making overall judgements is categorising the text – What kind of book is it, what is its genre? What other books is it like, and in what respects? Categorisation and comparison are among our most important critical tools.

Exploitation

If the most fundamental element in comprehension is constructing a coherent mental model, part of comprehension is being able to put that understanding to use. Indeed, you might argue that putting it to use itself helps to create understanding. This is certainly the case with imitation. One of the best ways for children to get to grips with and understand a poem is to try to imitate it – or, at least, to imitate some aspect of it. And with information, it is never your own until you have put it into your own words. This is why the National Curriculum sets such store by requiring children to 're-present' information they have read – translating the information into some other medium or mode of discourse. If you understand something, you can use it, shape its application to your own purposes, and in doing so you get to understand it better.

The reader's contribution to meaning

In dealing with inference, elaboration, empathy, evaluation *within* and *of* texts, and exploitation, we have been discussing the contribution that the reader makes to meaning. What is conveyed by a text depends not only on the text but also on the reader of the text. Meaning is something that happens between the reader and the text, and this depends upon the reader's knowledge, interest, orientation and **mental set**.

mental set
a readiness to operate in one kind of way, with a associated inflexibility with regard to a change of approach

Experimental evidence confirms this (Oakhill and Garnham, 1988). Two groups of readers were given the same text, describing a house and its contents, but one group was asked to read it as if they were prospective home-buyers, and the other group as if they were potential burglars. Not surprisingly, they tended to recall different things! Comprehension is influenced by the significance of the text to the reader. We take from a text what is relevant to us and our interests. We bring more with us to a text about a subject we enjoy, and we take more from it. Interest and motivation, as well as background information, play a role in the meaning we take.

Reading, then, involves a huge range of mental activities, from perception to response. It is not surprising that brain-scan studies show that, in reading, a remarkably degree of neurological activity is involved, spread wide throughout the brain!

DIFFERENT KINDS OF MEANING

Now let us turn to the meanings that the writer, intentionally or unintentionally, puts into the text. One kind of meaning is the content or message that a text conveys. Another is the purpose or aim of the text – what does the writer mean, or intend, to achieve by it?

Register, genre and tenor

register
language variety distinguished according to its use

What are the writer's designs upon the reader? These issues are sometimes discussed within the socio-linguistic concept of 'register' that concerns itself with how language varies according to its social use. Register can be sub-divided into:

- *field*: field of discourse – the subject area
- *mode*:
  - the physical medium of communication, for example, spoken (face-to-face, radio, telephone, lecture, etc.), written (poster, pamphlet, web-site, book)
  - genre, for example, novel, biography, textbook, letters, poetry, encyclopedia, etc.

tenor
that aspect of language style that indicates social function and purpose and expresses attitudes to the subject and the audience, e.g. in levels of formality

- *tenor*:
  - functional tenor, for example, expository, persuasive, commanding, narrative, etc. (the writer's purpose)
  - personal tenor (style), for example, formal, informal, sarcastic, ironic, genial, etc. (the writer's attitude towards subject and towards audience).

For our purposes, the concepts of genre and tenor are going to be the most useful.

Genre

'Genre' refers to *kinds* of texts: most basically, for example, fiction and non-fiction. School libraries are often categorised by genre – fiction, poetry, drama, history, etc. The term doesn't refer to subject matter (that would be 'field') but to the implicit rules and conventions by which the particular kind of writing operates. Thus, *Tarka, the Otter*, Ted Hughes' 'An Otter' and *Ring of Bright Water* (and, no doubt, some natural history monographs) share the field of otters, but in terms of genre, *Tarka* is a novel, 'An Otter' is a poem and *Ring of Bright Water* is autobiography.

When the National Curriculum discusses 'Range', it is talking about reading in different genres. And when it requires children to be able to distinguish between fiction and non-fiction, it is concerned with children being able to distinguish between genres. We can operate in terms of general genres – fiction, non-fiction, poetry, drama, etc. Or we can refine our categories – historical novels, time-warp novels, short stories, romances, science fiction, adventure, dungeons-and-dragons, etc. All of these genres have their own characteristics and styles of writing. As such, they all need to be read and evaluated in slightly different ways. We want children to understand that some stories are fiction and others are true; that fairy tales, novels, biography and history, while they all tell stories, are different things and work in different ways.

The reader needs to learn to read texts in different genres in different ways. We don't want to be like the eighteenth-century bishop who threw the newly-published *Gulliver's Travels* into the back of the fire, angrily shouting, 'It's a damn' pack of lies!' Of course fiction tells lies, but it also tells truths.

To make sense, a story or a poem has to be read right through from beginning to end. But that is not the way to read an encyclopedia or a dictionary. When you read a poem, you usually read it more than once, and you pay particular attention to the rhythm and how it sounds. You may even read it aloud. But if you read a textbook aloud, it is probably only to see if hearing it helps you concentrate and make more sense of it! You read different things for different purposes and use different skills in doing so. The significance of 'Range' in the National Curriculum is that range requires the development of different higher order reading skills.

autism
a condition characterised, among other things, by problems with empathy and with relating to other people

semantic–pragmatic disorder
a condition characterised, in part, by an inability to distinguish between semantic and pragmatic meanings (i.e. meanings related to people's intentions in situations, as distinguished from literal meanings), possibly related to autism and problems with empathy

pragmatics
the aspect of semantics concerned with meanings and communication within a particular shared situation

elaborated and restricted codes
styles of language use associated with differing patterns of social communication and control, marked by differing levels of explicitness

sub-text
the meanings and motives that underlie overt expression, as with 'Come upstairs and see my etchings'

Functional tenor

Where the National Curriculum requires children to be able to distinguish between fact and opinion, this is perhaps more to do with functional tenor than genre. 'Functional tenor' refers to the social purposes of communication. The straightforward presentation of facts is exposition, and its purpose is simply to inform. But the expression of opinion is usually designed to influence the reader's opinions or actions: its purpose is persuasive.

We want children to understand the difference between facts and opinions because this has survival value for them in the real world. For example, some statements in advertisements are simply informative (price, address to write to, etc.), while others may be designed to tempt or persuade children to spend their pocket money or to badger their parents! Part of our task is to help enable children to be aware of when and how people are trying to manipulate them.

Intentions as meaning

Part of understanding, then, is understanding the speaker's or writer's intentions. When the teacher asks a child, 'Would you like to show me your work?', the child will normally take this as a command. There is, however, an interesting condition, somewhat allied to **autism**, called '**semantic–pragmatic disorder**' in which the child is incapable of understanding such obliquely expressed commands. Incapable of irony, the child will take the question literally as a question, not an instruction. He (it is usually boys who suffer from this condition) understands the words but not the intentions. If he doesn't show you his work, he isn't being insolent: he just doesn't particularly want to show it you!

Such failures to understand intentions are not limited to special cases. Bernstein (1971) attributed such problems to the mismatch between the '**elaborated**' and the '**restricted**' **codes** which were (to oversimplify a complex and subtle argument) typically social-class related styles of linguistic exchange and meaning. Wells (1987) similarly cites examples of working-class children's problems with indirect commands, such as 'Would you like to tidy up now?'

Yet the whole of social life depends upon our understanding the intentions or '**sub-text**s' behind written or spoken words – otherwise, how would there be any civilisation – or romance? You remember the famous sequence in *Annie Hall* where sub-titles provide the sub-text to the spoken words? Or, for that matter, the much subtler probings and battles going on in the polite conversations between Elizabeth Bennet and Mr Darcy? Talk about 'sub-texts' is just another way of talking about implied meanings relating to emotions, attitudes and motivation.

All this, then, about meaning *before* we mention understanding the message! We don't just need to understand what the message is saying but also how it is trying to influence us in the real world.

Referential meaning and emotive meaning

Ogden and Richards, in *The Meaning of Meaning* (1923), say that statements can have both a **referential** and an **emotive meaning**. If I say

> The cat sat on the mat,

this is merely referential (or literal) – it refers to a (possible) situation. If I say, 'Hell!', this is merely emotive, the expression of feeling. But if I say,

> The bloody cat is sitting on my hat!

then this has both referential and emotive meaning. It both refers to a (possible) situation and expresses an attitude.

Indeed, it expresses a complex of attitudes: its tenor expresses an attitude to the cat and an attitude towards whoever is listening – maybe I wouldn't use quite those words if granny or the vicar were present! The language I use both symbolises references and exhibits signs of emotions, attitudes, desires, and so on. Ogden and Richards suggest these signs can exhibit:

- attitude to audience (whoever is receiving the message)
- attitude to the referent (whatever is being referred to)
- the intentions or effects to be promoted
- and indications of ease or difficulty of reference (how hard you find putting it into words).

(Note how closely these emotive categories relate to tenor.)

In the real world of face-to-face human interactions, statements are hardly ever 'plain'. They nearly always carry an edge of command, manipulation, exertion of power or emotive expression. Babies, learning to talk, do so not because they want to make disinterested statements, but because they want to influence the world around them, to establish warm human relations and to get what they want when they want it. 'Mummy, I want a drink of water!' is not simply a statement of fact but is manipulative, attention-seeking or a move in negotiating a different bedtime!

M.M. Lewis (1963, 1969) with his notions of '**conative**' and '**manip-ulative**' speech and Halliday (1969) with his notions of the

referential meaning
literal meaning, what is referred to

emotive meaning
meanings other than the literal, e.g. expressing feelings, attitudes and motives

conative
expressing desires and striving to satisfy them

instrumental, regulatory and interactional functions of language, point out that the drive to communication is largely self-interested, with a survival value. When we are motivated to speak, it is because we have intentions and intend our speaking to have an effect. Books are not entirely innocent of such levels of meaning, but seem more often to approach the plain symbolisation of reference, simple exposition or presentation.

Referential meaning
If understanding intentions and emotive meanings involves 'reading between the lines', referential meaning is gained by reading the lines. The referential meaning of a text is the literal meaning, the fact, idea or imagined situation to which the text refers. It is some sort of construct in conceptual space and this is symbolised in the words. The text is the attempt to convey this construct from one mind to another.

Comprehending a text at this level means building a schema, mental model or construct derived from the text. Such schemas or models are not static things, but dynamic, for two reasons. The first is that the text takes time to read and the construct is built up piece-meal over time – even if it is only the time to move on from one sentence to the next. Each sentence can be considered as consisting of the 'given' and the 'new', a distinction that is often congruent with the subject and predicate, thus:

> Mr Parkin was one of the teachers. He lived three miles away and walked to school every day.

What we learn about Mr Parkin builds up cumulatively from clause to clause.

The second reason is that the elements that compose the mental construct or picture are derived both from the text and from prior knowledge and experience, brought to bear upon the topic through the links, inferences and elaborations that the reader makes in the process of interpretation. We assume Mr Parkin walked to school in the morning in order to teach and that he didn't walk to school at weekends. And part of what we infer about Mr Parkin is that he was reasonably fit and hardy! Comprehension is, in this way, both constructive and integrating, making a coherent mental model or schema.

Meanings we might hope a child would take from a text
The different kinds of meaning, then, include things like the expression of feelings, attitudes and intentions as well as the symbolising

of reference, the plain making of statements about (possible) situations. Consider the following sentences from the book quoted above for 9–10-year-olds:

> I loved school, I really did. We went to the village school in
> Bretherton: it's still there. I first went when I was about
> four – 1905 it was.

(from *Millie's Story*, Collins Pathways)

What sort of meanings would we wish a child to comprehend from reading this? First, I think, we'd expect a child to learn a lot about Millie's feelings and personality, partly from the emphasis of what she says, the indications of ease and pleasure of reference, partly because the written style seems so closely to imitate informal speech. The mode is 'writing to be read as speech', with its emphatic repetitions, its broken structures. These features help to create the informal personal tenor. Functionally, the tenor simply seems to want to engage the reader sympathetically in pleasurable memories.

We also learn facts about Millie – her age and where she lived and so on. In terms of mere facts, we could paraphrase the passage:

> Millie loved going to Bretherton village school, which she first
> attended in 1905, when she was four. The school is still there.

This includes all the facts, but it lacks the life.

In terms of inference and elaboration, we hope the child reader would infer something about Millie's character, will work out her age, will infer that Bretherton is a village and will perhaps be able to construct from memory a composite image of a village school – and maybe elaborate the image with pictures of children going to school in appropriate dress.

We might also hope that, despite the title's using the word 'story', the child will assume that she is reading real-life personal memories, and not fiction. The main marker that this is a personal memoir rather than a made-up story is the way it discusses experiences, looking back at the past, rather than presenting them as if they were in the process of happening. The mode is retrospective, not presentational. The child who, at 7, has only ever read made-up stories might not immediately understand the nature of the genre, but by 9, one might hope the child could distinguish between the genres.

Then there is yet another level of comprehension that we might hope for. We might hope that the child will compare her own feelings and memories about school with Millie's. She might compare her own school starting age with Millie's. We might hope that she will bring her historical knowledge, such as it is, to bear on the situation, trying to relate Millie's life with other things she knows about (Might Millie's brothers, if any, have been in the First World War? Had bicycles, cars and aeroplanes been invented then?) and maybe wonder if Bretherton is still a village or whether it has grown into a town over the years.

We might also hope she decides she likes Millie and would like to meet her or would have been her friend if she had lived then. In this kind of way, she takes Millie's experience into her own, widening and adjusting her perceptions both of Millie and of herself accordingly. This is what empathy, elaboration and evaluation are all about.

A RICH CONCEPT OF COMPREHENSION

If all this discussion of snippets of text seems excessively complex and long, if not long-winded, think: the skilled child reader is picking this all up at the pace she is reading the texts, without having to think about it. Or at least, without having to think about it explicitly. But the less skilled reader misses out on a lot of this and, for him (usually him), the texts are impoverished in meaning and will not be so rewarding to read.

The limitations of 'comprehension test' comprehension

A rich concept of comprehension is not one that merely enables the child to answer traditional paper-and-pencil comprehension questions on a passage. Such questions tend to be literal, focus on isolated details and rarely probe inference-making and global interpretations, never mind **interrogation**, response and evaluation. The reader may simply need to identify the relevant sentence and reformulate the wording of the question, eked out with words from the sentence. It is a trick that doesn't require the reader to understand the text, though it does require some of the skills of comprehension. Consider the following sentence (cited in Oakhill and Garnham, 1988):

interrogation of text
seeking for answers in a text to questions the text has itself provoked, e.g. as with suspense, where we want to know what happens next

> All the rak ibnu lurmed and wabed elirly.

You could answer a number of comprehension questions about this sentence, without having a clue what it means: for example:

- How many of the rak ibnu lurmed and wabed?
- What did they do? How did they do it?
- Describe the ibnu.

What you notice about your ability to answer these questions is that it is based more on understanding the syntax than the content. You have understood the grammar of the sentence, and what the questions are asking is for you to rearrange the **content words** into another grammatical structure. Clearly, while understanding the syntax is essential to comprehension, it is not sufficient. It is like manipulating an algebraic equation without knowing what the various functions refer to. In itself, it tells you nothing about the world and possibilities of experience. You have gained no substantive meaning from the sentence.

content words
words that convey the substantive conceptual meanings in a sentence, e.g. nouns and verbs, adjectives and adverbs

If you think a nonsense sentence like the one cited above is an unfair test, try the following:

> Each time you store a piece of information, even if it is less than 1K in size, you use a full 32K space on a system partitioned with FAT16. Windows 95 OSR2 and Windows 98 use FAT32 to address clusters of more than 64K, providing cluster sizes of 4K on hard drives over 1Gb.
>
> Question 1   Why is a system partitioned with FAT16 not always very efficient for storing information?
> Question 2   Identify an advantage of systems using FAT32.

I think I can answer these questions although I have very little notion of what this passage is talking about. Clearly, comprehension is about more than being able to answer such questions. It is about having the background information available to make sense of it and fit it into a global picture.

Comprehension as enrichment

A rich concept of comprehension involves learning about the world and contemplating possibilities of experience. It involves being alert to both referential and emotive meanings. It involves experiencing things vicariously and reflecting on those experiences. It involves imagination, empathy, judgement and evaluation. The following chapters will deal with the different aspects of a rich comprehension relating to the different genres and with helping children to enrich their comprehension. In the rest of this chapter, I want to systematise the elements and related skills that go towards such comprehension.

PRECONDITIONS FOR COMPREHENSION

Identifying words

We have already touched upon certain aspects of comprehension in discussing the place of meaning and prediction in reading texts. We have touched upon context, semantics and grammar insofar as they help to identify words. Identifying the actual words of the text is, obviously, a precondition for making full sense of it – otherwise, what you are trying to make sense of wouldn't be the text, but something else!

Determining word meanings

Identifying words gives access to word meanings – though, as we have already argued, the context helps to determine which meaning, or what aspect of meaning, applies to a particular word in a sentence. In the passage from the story discussed earlier, we never questioned that the word 'album' referred to a book rather than a musical recording. This was, in part, because of the context (stamps and albums) and this interpretation was subsequently confirmed by 'page', etc. In part, this interpretation of 'album' was a default interpretation – this is the first interpretation we would think of unless there were contextual reasons for thinking otherwise.

Many, possibly most, common content words are ambiguous to some degree – consider 'common', 'content', 'words', 'degree' and 'sentence' in this sentence, for example. But we hardly ever notice this in the process of reading, so eager are we to make what we are reading make sense. In part, we are guided by grammar – for example, in the syntactic context, 'common' must be an adjective, not a noun. In the same context, 'content' is behaving like an adjective, but we don't read it as meaning 'reasonably happy' because it wouldn't make sense in the semantic context, although this is the default meaning of the adjective. It is the default meaning of the noun 'content' that is here behaving like an adjective. We unconsciously slot the most appropriate meanings together in order to maximise meaning.

But this is a skill that children are only learning to acquire. For one thing, they don't necessarily know all the meanings or uses of a word that they can read. For example, children between 7 and 8 are only beginning to learn that words like 'bright', 'hard' and 'sharp' can be applied not only to physical things but also metaphorically to character traits. It is through encountering known words in unexpected contexts that their meanings develop. Words with multiple meanings can be misunderstood well into the teenage years.

Another source of difficulty is that children have not necessarily acquired all the knowledge and experience that would guide them to appropriate or probable meanings. Children are well aware that they don't know everything and they tolerate not understanding – at best, in the hope that things will become clearer if they wait for further clues; at worst, with sullen indifference.

Speed of word identification

Speed of word identification is important not just as an index of reading skill, but as a precondition for comprehension. This is because of the nature of the short-term working memory. The child can probably only hold five to seven items at once in the short-term memory. It is on the items in the short-term memory that the processes of comprehension begin to work. However, not only do items get pushed out by the input of new items, but items in the memory decay quite rapidly. There is, then, an minimum speed of input that will ensure that the memory has enough material in it to work on – it has been calculated as being about 200 words a minute. Less than this, and comprehension is compromised. Further, if word recognition is a problem, not only does it slow down the input speed, but there will also be less attention available for working on the sense of a passage.

This is why, after a child has been struggling with a word or sentence, we encourage the child to go back and re-read the sentence, fluently. Only then will the child have a chance of putting it all together and making sense of it. However, speed of decoding does not ensure comprehension. Some children, reading fast, still read a word at a time without construing the grammar and linking the meaning up. We have to encourage joined-up reading, not simply speed-reading.

From wording to meaning

With the assistance of the **'articulatory loop'** or short-term auditory memory for internalised word pronunciations, phrases, clauses or whole sentences are held in the working memory while they are construed for grammar and meaning. As the phrase or sentence is processed, the meaning is consigned to memory and the wording slips from memory as the words of the next sentence take their place. But the meaning lingers, decaying as it does so, until the next sentence meaning becomes available. Each sentence in turn acts as the context for the next. Together, they may integrate into a coherent overall meaning that can be consigned into the long-term memory as something that makes sense. This is how it comes about that we are able to remember the meaning, but not the actual wording, of what we read. However, if the gap in time between sentence meanings is too great, the earlier meaning decays and links aren't made. The text is experienced as incoherent and therefore unmemorable.

'articulatory loop'
the mechanism for the retention of auditory memory

These preconditions for comprehension partly explain why it is that, in the earlier primary years, achieving a reasonable speed of accurate decoding is seen as the essential goal, while in the later primary years, if reasonable speed and accuracy have been attained, comprehension becomes the criterion of reading success.

The processes of comprehension

Processing sentences: the importance of syntax

Processing sentences swiftly and successfully depends upon three factors: length, grammatical structure and familiarity of the content. It is not surprising that longer sentences are generally harder to construe because of the limitations of short-term working memory and there being more to be taken into account. Additionally, longer sentences are likely to be syntactically more complex. In short sentences the grammatical structure is usually straightforward:

subject	*verb*	*(object/complement)*	*(adverbial)*
Sean	caught	some tadpoles	in the net
She	spoke		quickly
She	was	sorry	

The brackets indicate elements in a sentence that may or may not be present. But a sentence generally must have a subject and a verb. However, this basic structure can easily be obscured by additional elements providing additional information. For example, consider the following sentence:

> From break-time to lunch-time, the group of Year 3 children I was watching worked industriously on their History project.

The basic subject-verb structure of the sentence is 'The group worked'. Too much information in a sentence can confuse children by disguising the basic structure.

However, it is not necessarily the case that longer sentences are always more difficult than short ones. Sometimes they are easier if they make things explicit, when a shorter version, full of ellipses, may be harder. An ellipsis is an element left out in order to avoid repetition when it can be 'understood' from the previous context. For example, compare the following sentences:

> He said, 'Turn the handle', so I turned the handle.
> He said, 'Turn the handle', so I did.

The second sentence is shorter, but to understand it, the reader has to supply some of the information, has implicitly to answer the question, 'Did what?' Though often stylistically neater, sentences with ellipses can often be harder work for the inexperienced reader. This is why early reading texts try to be totally explicit, even if this sometimes makes them sound a bit stilted.

Ellipses are just one syntactic construction that causes difficulties. We have already discussed the way children can find problems with pronouns. They also find problems with syntactic constructions that don't correspond with their basic intuition about how sentences work. For example, they tend to assume that the grammatical subject of a sentence is always the 'doer'. Indeed, even teachers can have a problem! Sue Palmer (1998) cites a teacher insisting that in the sentence

The jam sandwich was eaten by the queen

'the queen' is the subject because she is doing the eating! Passive sentences like this are counter-intuitive. The grammatical subject here is not the doer, but the done-to.

If children can find difficulty disentangling the doer from the grammatical subject, doing so is a lot easier where, as in the case of the jam sandwich, it couldn't conceivably be the doer – sandwiches can't eat queens! Children have a predisposition to assume that only animate objects like queens can be doers. Sentences where the meaning doesn't give such support (for example, 'Darren was hit by Kim'), are harder for children. Syntactic interpretation is facilitated by semantics.

Similarly, children find complex constructions confusing if they aren't semanticaly unequivocal. For example,

The woman following the man was carrying a dog

tends to be interpreted by 7½-year-olds as if it were saying,

The woman was following the man. The man was carrying a dog.

This tendency could be accounted for in terms of limited working memory capacity and the 'proximity rule'. After all, the last six words do say 'the man was carrying a dog'!

Other confusions can arise because of the ways specific words work. Similar wordings can have very different meanings, for example:

She promised him to go.
She told him to go.

She asked him how to do it.
She told him how to do it.

There isn't space here to go into all the complexities of grammatical constructions. Suffice it to say that many of these difficulties arise:

- when there is processing overload
- and/or when the relationship between structure and meaning is counter-intuitive
- and/or when the structure is unfamiliar.

Such grammatical constructions tend to be more frequent in information texts, where the language is more formal and impersonal, than in stories. And the syntax may less easily be disambiguated by semantics in information texts where the subject matter is less familiar. It is during the primary years that children have to learn how to deal with these difficulties. It certainly behoves the teacher to be alert to grammar as a possible cause of children's comprehension difficulties. For more detailed accounts of language difficulties, see Perera (1984) and Oakhill and Garnham (1988).

The two important points to remember are that, (a), children are still learning the complexities of sophisticated grammar throughout the junior years and beyond; and (b), children progressively get better at understanding as they get older. Perera (1984) argues that one of the most important factors in early reading is the way that the language is simplified. However, it should not be simplified in such a way that children never encounter new or challenging grammatical constructions – if they don't, they will never learn. But it is helpful if the semantic context supports comprehension.

For this reason, children cope much better with complex grammar if they are at home with the material being discussed. However, information books, as we saw earlier in this chapter, tend to be written in a more complex and impersonal style than stories. So unfamiliar ideas and unfamiliar grammatical constructions tend to coincide in information books.

To help obviate such sources of difficulty, it can helpful if the teacher reads complex texts aloud to the children and discusses any difficult 'book language' with them. The language of information books is an issue we will return to in a later chapter.

The semantic context

In the discussion so far we have referred again and again to 'context'. We have said that 'context' covers both the semantic (meaning) and syntactic (grammatical) context. Children, from very early on, are alert to syntax, and very few of children's miscues, from half-way through their first year of reading, are syntactically inappropriate. Children have an intuitive sense of what part of speech is permissible for the next word in the sentence. For example, Thomas, a struggling reader (Year 5), reads 'into the rocket' for 'into his rocket', and 'he pulls the cap back on' for 'he puts the cap back on'. In each case the substitution is grammatically appropriate.

'Contextual meaning', as an expression, may include syntactic aware-ness, but more generally refers to semantic awareness, a sense of what meanings are probable. The two examples of syntactically acceptable substitutions just given are also examples of semantic plausibility – they make sense. Semantic context works both at the local level of predicting the next word in the sentence and at the wider level of relating the meaning of the text with the reader's wider knowledge and experience. This wider knowledge enables the child both to interpret what she is reading and provides expectancies that aid prediction.

As we saw in relation to our model of comprehension at the begin-ning of this chapter, the writer implicitly assumes that the reader will know and understand certain things, be familiar with certain cultural practices, and consequently will be able to fill out and elab-orate the text from his or her own cultural knowledge. Children, of course, don't necessarily have all the cultural knowledge that the writer assumes. Indeed, reading stories is one of the main ways that fluent readers acquire the background knowledge that is the common currency of a culture. Most of us learn more history from stories than from textbooks and more about romance from novels than life!

Self-monitoring one's own understanding

Children (like adults) are not inclined to volunteer the information that they don't understand something. But (unlike adults) some-times this is not so much that they don't want to admit not understanding, but that they don't realise they don't understand. Sometimes this is because they haven't really taken on board that they are supposed to understand what they are reading, sometimes because they don't have the skills to monitor their own compre-hension.

In tests that involved children reading texts including deliberate inconsistencies, good comprehenders reported the texts were more difficult to understand than normal texts, whereas poor compre-henders rated them equally. Poor readers reported texts with difficult individual words as more difficult than texts with easier words but with inconsistencies. This suggests that poor comprehenders don't try to integrate the whole meaning of a text. Consistently with this interpretation, they viewed reading as being a matter of getting the words correctly, not as being a matter of deriving meaning.

Among 9-year-olds, poor readers, tackling difficult or inconsistent texts, tended to self-correct less often, marked fewer parts of the text as puzzling, asked fewer questions and consulted the dictionary less often than better readers. Better readers seemed to work harder at trying to puzzle the meaning out, presumably because they both expected texts to make sense and were aware that this particular text was not making sense! Poor readers become habituated to texts not making sense.

'Only connect'

Constructing meaning, then, involves connecting information in a coherent way. The things to be connected are: the various elements of information *within* the text; and the textual information with antecedent information, the reader's prior knowledge about the world. In stories, joined-up meaning begins to produce an imagined world. Here is the opening of a children's novel:

> Taran wanted to make a sword; but Coll, charged with the practical side of his education, decided on horseshoes. And so it had been horseshoes all morning long. Taran's arms ached, soot blackened his face. At last he dropped the hammer and turned to Coll, who was watching him critically.
>
> 'Why?' Taran cried. 'Why must it be horseshoes? As if we had any horses!'
>
> Coll was stout and round and his great bald head glowed bright pink. 'Lucky for the horses,' was all he said, glancing at Taran's handiwork.
>
> (from Lloyd Alexander, *The Book of Three*)

At the word-level, we automatically take 'cried' to mean 'shouted', not 'wept', because Taran is frustrated rather than sad. And we know this because he wants to do one thing but is made to do another; because he is tired; and because he expostulates against horseshoes.

At another level altogether, any boy, reading this, will identify with Taran – with wanting to make a sword. But at another level again, adults, at least, will stand outside Taran's situation and see things from Coll's point of view, responding to the irony of his remark, 'Lucky for the horses.' Even the narrator seems to join in the irony at Taran's expense, calling what he has produced 'handiwork' when we have gathered that it is not very competent!

Every detail has significance – though sometimes details raise questions that are only answered later in the text. We seek an answer, interrogating the text, awaiting further information. We cannot be sure quite why Coll's head 'glowed bright pink'. Has he got high blood pressure from being overweight? Is he hot from the forge? Is he angry with Taran? Is he holding in his amusement at Taran? The subsequent irony suggests the latter.

Not only is an imagined world created, a world of swords and horses containing a blacksmith's forge and a young apprentice, but characters and their relationships begin to take form. And beyond this, our sympathies and attitudes towards the characters are being guided into shape.

At yet another level, we have expectations based on what we know about the nature of story: as Chekov nearly said, if a sword is mentioned in the first line, it will be used in the last act. We have an implicit promise of action, and all the suspense that this entails. The connections link meanings at all different levels into a coherent world into which we are hooked by empathy and anticipation.

This, at any rate, is the way stories work for the skilled reader. For various reasons, some children have difficulty with making these connections. These reasons include themes we are becoming familiar with: perceiving reading as a matter primarily of decoding words; paying attention to words one at a time, rather than linking them up into meaningful phrases and clauses; possessing a poor short-term memory capacity, which leads to an inability readily to make inferences and to integrate all the information in the text; limited knowledge and experience of the world and of literature; and the level of general intelligence.

Summary

A rich concept of comprehension involves the child not only in reading the words, but constructing a mental model based on the interaction between the text and her previous relevant knowledge. New information is integrated with previous information to make this model coherent. Such mental constructs depend not only on what is explicit in the text but upon the inferences that the reader makes, filling in and filling out the meaning. The reader is not a passive container for new information like a library shelf, but actively processes it, not only gaining new information, but adapting and reconstructing her own world view, possibly including her values, sympathies and perceptions of herself in the process.

Different genres of writing have different social functions or aims and require to be read in different ways. Part of comprehension is recognising what genre of writing a text represents, recognising the intentions behind the text and reading the text in an appropriate way. We will look at how, specifically, we can promote joined-up thinking, rich comprehension and response in relation to each of the three genres, stories, poems and information texts, in the next three chapters.

- Comprehension is not a passive reception of meaning, but an active integrating of the new information with pre-existing knowledge.

- Comprehension has many levels, from the literal through inference and elaboration to evaluation and exploitation.

- One of the critical comprehension skills is making inferences, i.e. filling in gaps in literal meaning from pre-existing knowledge and experience.

- Another important skill is to interpret the intentions behind a text – what does it aim to achieve?

- What we remember of a text is not the wording of the text itself, but the meaning we made of it, including the inferences we have made, in a single, integrated whole.

- Different kinds of texts, different genres written in different registers, require different skills and kinds of comprehension because of their different purposes.

Further reading

Oakhill, J. and Garnham, A. (1988) *Becoming a Skilled Reader*, Blackwell
Still one of the most authoritative and comprehensive books about comprehension, it views reading not simply as a decoding exercise but as a search for meaning.

Perera, K. (1984) *Children's Reading and Writing: Analysing Classroom Language*, Blackwell
Perera is one of the most respected writers about the difficulties children have with book-language and the notion of what constitutes a 'good book' for children.

Reading stories 4

When you have read this chapter, you should be able to:

- discuss the nature of story and of different kinds of stories

- discuss kinds of meaning as they are applicable to stories

- evaluate stories in relation to their value and appropriateness to children

- plan and implement different strategies for promoting story reading and comprehension among children.

Introduction

This chapter begins by considering the nature of story and how narrative is a fundamental way in which we represent our experience to ourselves in order to make sense of it. It goes on to discuss the way stories support children's emotional and personal development and the ways in which children engage with stories, from identifying with the main character to reflecting on their own and the different characters' behaviour, desires and values. The developmental stage of children during the Key Stage 2 years and the nature of story determine the ways in which it should be taught, and the chapter concludes by discussing effective classroom teaching strategies for motivating children and guiding them into personal responses and reflection.

NARRATIVE AND MAKING SENSE

Narrative is perhaps the most basic literary genre. Folk-tales, myths and legends, transmitting concepts of cultural identity and values through oral traditions, seem to be the oldest forms of linguistic art, and they still have life in them today. Stories grab children's attention from a very young age, and even nursery rhymes tend to tell stories, for example, *Jack and Jill* and *Humpty Dumpty*.

But narrative is basic in a yet more fundamental way. It is, according to Barbara Hardy (1977), a 'primary act of mind'. It is not 'an aesthetic invention used by artists to control, manipulate and order experience', but it is an act of mind 'transferred to art from life'. That is to say, narrative is invented by life: we experience life as narrative. Our life experience is a matter of our doing things and experiencing events in a serial order through time. By the expression 'primary act of mind', Hardy means that the initial way we get hold of our experiences is by organising our mental representations in memory in their temporal sequence, as a kind of inner story-telling. Explicit story-telling greatly assists this organisation by making it more objective.

Narrative as the basis of causal thinking

The temporal sequence is also the sequence of cause and effect. The story we tell implicitly expresses this causal chain, and for children, it seems to be through this sequencing in time that they first come to express causation. For example, consider the function of 'when' in the following sentence:

It went dark when I switched out the light

The word 'when' may simply expressed temporal order, but it is tantamount to saying 'because'. But children's ability to use the word 'because', except as the first word in an answer to a why-question, comes a good deal later in their development than their ability to use 'when' with a suggestion of causation.

In a story repetition task that included a number of sentences of the form, 'Because the man saved me/us, I/we will do so-and-so', children from 4.10 to 7.4 years old variously used the constructions:

while a, b*	*when* a, b
a, *so* b	a, *and then* b
a, b	*now* a, b
as a, b	

(*In Yorkshire dialect 'while' often means 'since'.)

None of them used the word 'because'. All the conjunctions they used were primarily related to time, though some of them, by extension, have acquired a logical connotation.

It is largely through the temporal sequence of narrative that children begin to grasp or, at least, express the concept of cause and effect – in part, perhaps, because cause and effect impinges on their consciousness first in relation to human motivation – 'When I feel hungry, I ask for something to eat'.

Narrative as a means of modelling and shaping experience

Narrative is a fundamental means of making sense, getting our heads round our experience, grasping how and why it happened as it did and reflecting on its significance. Which is why we gossip, why we tell each other about our experiences. We do this in order to objectify and clarify what happened and to sort out how we feel about it.

And in doing this, we are already ordering and manipulating experience, making a fiction of it in a self-justifying way. Just think of the way, over time, you have modified the story about when you bumped the car. I bet it's not your fault any more! And the court of law you may end up in is an arena of conflicting narratives – whose narrative will gain credence?

Narrative is native to language

Language lends itself naturally to narrative. It is sequenced, extended in time. The structure of the simplest form of sentence constitutes an atom of narrative: it is active, with a subject and predicate, for example, *somebody does something*. Sentences following one after the other constitute a temporal sequence of actions which, with a common subject, readily becomes narrative. Narrative is our primary way of organising our experience and constructing explicit meaning for ourselves.

Chronicle and story

In discussing narrative, we should distinguish between chronicle and story. Chronicle is just one damn' thing after another – 'The king died, and then the queen died'. In this sense, diaries are generally chronicles. But story is structured narrative, chronicle with a plot. E.M. Forster (1962) defines the notion of plot according to its emphasis on causality: he says that 'The king died, and then the queen died of grief' is a plot. While the causality in this example is a matter of individual emotion, causality also works at the levels of physical causality and, most particularly, personal motivation. Characters do things because of who they are, how they are situated and what they want.

The beginning, the middle and the end

While causality is essential to plot, there is more to plot than this. A story with a plot has, we like to say, a beginning, a middle and an end. The beginning establishes a situation into which some disruption impinges. Some character feels the force of this disruption and feels obliged to act in order to achieve some goal and restore stability. For example, in Robert Swindells' *The Ice Palace*

(1982), this is the situation when the evil genius of winter, Starjik, abducts Ivan's little brother, and Ivan sets off on his quest to rescue him.

The middle records the main character's actions attempting to achieve his goal. These attempts may fall into many episodes, where an action simply creates or reveals new problems to surmount, as in Ivan's eventful journey to Starjik's Ice Palace. Events culminate in the climax in which the major problem or conflict comes to a head (Ivan finally meets Starjik face to face). An unexpected turn of events takes place, and the problem or conflict is resolved (you had better read *The Ice Palace* for yourself!).

The end comes when the goal is achieved, and some sort of stability is re-established. The sense of an ending is achieved because, in some way, it balances or answers the beginning (Starjik still visits children's houses in the dead of night, in the dead of winter, but instead of stealing children, he brings presents).

The need for intelligence and memory

As far as the audience is concerned, a plot, Forster says, demands intelligence and memory – 'for unless we remember, we cannot understand'. What we need to be able to remember is the beginning and the end and how what came between came about. We need to be able to remember the motivation and development of actions and characters. Intelligence enables us to relate and integrate these events so as to understand them.

The *Framework for Teaching* (DfEE, 1998) objectives for Year 4, Term 1 require children 'to explore narrative order: identify and map out the main stages of story: introductions → build-ups → climaxes or conflicts → resolutions'. The terminology of 'introductions' and 'build-ups' is not necessarily the best for discussing story structure, but it will do. It is perhaps useful, however, to add two further elements: first, the disruption, challenge or problem that irrupts into the initial situation in the 'introduction' and sets the action going; secondly, the surprising turn of events or discovery (what Aristotle calls '**peripety**') that is an aspect of the climax. The peripety in *The Ice Palace* brought tears to my eyes when I first read it.

peripety
from Aristotle: the unexpected turn of events or discovery at the climax of a story

Introductions and resolutions

To understand 'resolutions', we need to consider beginnings as well as endings. You can ask the children to draw up a table, for example:

Cinderella

Beginning	Ending
Initial situation	*Final situation*
happy family (before mother's death and father's re-marriage)	happy new family with prince
Disruption/problem	*Resolution*
(mother's death) not allowed to go to the ball poor, single and sad bullied by sisters and stepmother	goes to the Ball rich, married and happy more powerful than sisters and stepmother

Three Billy Goats Gruff

Beginning	Ending
Initial situation	*Final situation*
happy family (presumably)	happy family restored
Disruption/problem	*Resolution*
hungry wrong side of river troll	eating right side of river no troll

Build-ups

Looking at the stories in terms of 'build-ups':

	Build-up
Cinderella	the appearance of Fairy Godmother and going to the ball and needing to flee at midnight
Three Billy Goats Gruff	Little and Middle-Sized Billy Goats Gruff arguing their way successfully over the bridge

Climaxes or conflicts

Climaxes or conflicts are the final moment when the build-up results in the problem coming to the critical point when, through some action, it may or may not be resolved:

	Conflict	Climax
Cinderella	competition from the sisters	the slipper fits, recognition by the prince
Three Billy Goats Gruff	the challenge from the Troll	butting it into the river

In the first instance, you can ask children to look at well-known tales. But when they are clear enough about these patterns, you could ask them to look at more elaborated stories and at novels in these same terms. Even if the resulting discussion comes to no final conclusions, it will have clarified some reflective thinking about the story structure.

Why do children like stories?

Children seem to be hungry for stories. Chukovsky (1963) tells us that children in the USSR, deprived of fairy stories, spontaneously invented their own fantasy worlds, peopled with fantasy characters. What these fantasies lacked, apparently, was story structure. In disaster relief, what workers have found is that, after basic food and shelter, what children need most is teddy bears: something to hold and comfort and talk to – consolation in fantasy. On the other hand, Pickard (1961), discussing horror comics, argues that they are dangerous because they activate powerful unconscious terrors without helping to resolve them. Fairy tales, on the other hand, tend to help resolve them.

Jung (1959) suggests the reason children seem so hungry for stories:

> In myths and fairytales, as in dreams, the psyche tells its own story.

> (Jung, 1959, p. 217)

The story the psyche tells is that of its own growth towards wholeness. And it is the value of fairytales in promoting this growth that Bettelheim celebrates in *The Uses of Enchantment* (1978):

> Myths and fairy stories both answer the eternal questions:
> What is the world really like? How am I to live my life in it?
> How can I truly be myself?

> (Bettelheim, 1978, p. 45)

Fairy stories answer these questions in a symbolic way that peculiarly suits children's minds. However, the questions Bettelheim puts here are the questions that all literature explores.

What is the world really like?

During the junior years children are beginning to develop their interest in the wider world beyond home and school. Among other things, they seek stories about the exotic and distant, and about ways of life different from their own. They tend to learn more about geography and history from stories than from more formal expository writing.

At the same time, they remain interested in the local and the familiar, but their interest is now at a deeper level. They are concerned with right and wrong behaviour, with issues and with character, feelings and motives. They are exploring what the human world is really like.

How am I to live my life in it?

Stories provide the opportunity to contemplate possibilities of experience beyond those the child has experienced for herself. But because the child participates in the construction of this world and becomes emotionally engaged in it as a spectator, it provides both a picture of experience to which she can apply her perceptions and evaluations, and a mirror in which she can reflect upon herself, her feelings and characteristics, in relation to the situations and people depicted in the story. She enjoys vicarious experience in relation to which she can construct and define her own values and perceptions.

In various ways, stories raise moral issues, for example, about right and wrong behaviour, conflicts of loyalties, etc. Even fairy tales, which sometimes seem amoral (what right has Jack to steal the Giant's gold?), exhibit deep psycho-moral concerns. As Cook (1969) argues, in connection with *The Frog Prince* and *Beauty and the Beast*, etc.:

> it may not be accidental that the theme of breaking of a spell that has turned fair into foul is nearly always linked with the theme of the keeping of promises.

The keeping of promises is as much about keeping faith with oneself as about keeping faith with others. It is about maintaining one's wholeness and integrity.

While realistic stories don't necessarily flaunt psychological symbolism as overtly as myths and fairytales, they perhaps more obviously deal with questions of developing moral and emotional integrity.

How can I truly be myself?

'Know thyself' was the great, initiating injunction of Greek philosophy, and it is in the mirror of story that children can most easily reflect upon who they are, what they want and who they want to become. Two of the great stories of growing up, *Pride and Prejudice* and *Jane Eyre*, provide models of heroines becoming truly themselves, in spite of, in one case, the heroine's own vanities and prejudices; in the other, the emotional and social conditions that oppressed her. Intelligence, honesty, courage and love are the prerequisites for becoming a hero or heroine – and for becoming the hero or heroine of one's own life. This is perhaps why we need stories to do more than simply hold the mirror up to nature. We need stories in which to see reflections of ourselves as we might wish to be.

Psychodynamic symbolisation in fairytales

Fairy tales like *Cinderella* and *The Three Billy Goats Gruff* raise questions about symbolism that more everyday stories don't raise so obviously. Let me tell you a story without symbolism, but nevertheless with significance.

One day I went to collect my son from nursery and, arriving early, I looked in. My son had withdrawn from the group gathered around the teacher in the story corner, but was still listening, with a look of terrified fascination on his face. Later I asked the teacher what she had been reading, and she told me *The Three Billy Goats Gruff*. Then I understood. I used to be terrified by that story myself. But why are we scared by mere stories at all? The answer must be that the story triggers, or symbolises, a real fear that is already deep within us.

So what is it about *The Three Billy Goats Gruff* that is so scary? The troll, of course, who wants to eat up the goats. But why do we have, deep within us, a fear of being eaten up? Is it some atavistic fear from way back in evolution? Because it certainly isn't a realistic fear. We are not in much real danger of being eaten. Yet so many stories exploit this fear, from fairytales like *Hansel and Gretel, Jack and the Beanstalk* and *The Three Little Pigs* to films like *Jurassic Park, Jaws* and *Alien*. If the danger does not come from the outside world, it must come from within.

Freud's pupil, Melanie Klein, who specialised in child pychoanalysis and who invented, for analytic and therapeutic purposes, many of the play activities used in nursery education (for example, water play, clay and sand, the home corner for acting out relationships), offers a partial answer (Brown, 1964). At an early stage in our development, Freud's oral stage, we begin to develop ambivalent emotions towards our mothers, love and anger. But we feel these feelings in terms of the stage we are at: love is related to good eating and anger to bad, to frustration and biting. And we feel, in a mirror-image way, that mother feels the same towards us. In the hate-role, mother wants to bite us or give us bad things to eat. That is, she is troll-like, wicked witch-like or like the wicked step-mother who gives Snow White a poisoned apple. But hating beloved mother is too frightening an emotion to admit to or face, so it is repressed. It is, as it were, kept in cold storage until such time as we can face it and cope with it.

The story of *The Three Billy Goats Gruff* is about the triumph of good eating over bad eating. But in one respect, the story is curiously ambivalent. Are the Billygoats child, mother and father, or one Billygoat at different stages of growing up? If we take it as the former, the bearded troll is the dark mirror-image of father Billygoat, and the story, like *Jack and the Beanstalk*, is about the Oedipus complex. If the latter, the story is about successfully putting off dealing with the dangerous emotions until one is mature enough and strong enough to be able to deal with them. However, as far as my son was concerned, the emotions activated by the story were too strong to face, though they remained terrifyingly fascinating. Despite the fact that the situation was supportive, with a caring adult, the control that story, with its positive ending, symbolised was not strong enough to palliate, placate or resolve the emotions that it evoked.

One of the uses of fairy tales is to give the child a second chance to deal with potentially destructive feelings, disguising them in symbolism that is enough to activate them without being too obvious. For example, you are allowed to hate your mother in the guise of a witch or a wicked stepmother, while at the same time you love her in the guise of a fairy godmother. The same sort of dynamic applies to other ambivalent feelings, for example, about father. The argument is that all the emotions and terrors are already there within us, ticking away, and the tale is a means of defusing them. The story models or promises eventual triumph over the destructive feelings that otherwise might only find expression, but not resolution, in nightmares and destructive feelings and behaviour.

Psychodynamic motifs in stories in general

Fairytales, of course, are not the only kinds of stories that can symbolise and resolve difficult emotions. The great success of Sendak's (1970) *Where the Wild Things Are* must surely arise from its psychodynamic significance. The book begins with Max being sent to bed without any supper (wicked mother) and ends with him finding supper waiting for him (good mother). Hilary Minns (1990) found that children intuitively know that when Max is sailing away, he is sailing away from his mother, even though the book never says so. In answer to the teacher's question about why he sailed away, Gurdeep answers, "Cos he's very naughty boy'. To the same question asked again in a more elaborated form, he replies, "Cos he doesn't like her'. Children imbue the story with their own understanding of ambivalent mother–child relationships.

There are a number of books that deal with the psychological significance of fairytales. Bruno Bettelheim's *The Uses of Enchantment* (1978) is one of the most accessible and sensible. In a similar vein, Erik Erikson (1963) provides an interesting case study in which a child's observations about a favourite book give Erikson the key to his deep and debilitating fears.

Psychodynamic motifs in fantasies

Do such psychological interpretations apply in general to contemporary stories for children? We have touched on the way *Where The Wild Things Are* suggests they might. Let's consider Roald Dahl's *The BFG*. It activates the night-terrors of insecurity and the fear of being eaten, together with the fear of a father's dangerous power. But the BFG himself, a non-macho new giant (even a bit of a wimp and under-sized for a giant) provides a model of caring strength. He deals in consoling dreams. And however small the child may be, she is not morally nor intellectually his inferior. It is a tale of intelligence (so often the power of the weak in stories), moral determination and courage triumphing over brutality.

The whole story is shot through with humour, which helps to make it safe. One of the functions of humour is as a way of 'placing' fears and anxieties. In *The BFG* the humour also works in another way, for example, in the way it deals with 'whizzpopping'. Dahl, as usual, conspires with children against the proprieties and prohibitions of the adult world. Part of the courage that the child responds to is the courage of transgression, enjoying the naughtiness of being able to read about 'whizzpopping'. After all, learning controlled transgression is an essential part of growing up (What did God really want of Adam and Eve? To remain ignorant forever?).

Psychodynamic angles on everyday stories

Not every emotional problem has its roots in infancy. All the stages of life present their own challenges or problems, and there are stories to address each one. Many stories are written with a view to their being therapeutic in some way: for example, nearly every reading scheme includes a book that is designed to help children with sibling rivalry on the arrival of a new baby in the family. Typically, the baby is first feared and disliked, but then wins its way into the older brother or sister's heart.

Other stories, written purely as literature, have similar effects, symbolising causes of emotional conflicts within them – I think instantly of *Not now, Bernard* and *The Shrinking of Treehorn*. The story of *Treehorn* is itself, in terms of growing emotional independence, THE BIG GAME FOR CHILDREN TO GROW ON. In more elaborated stories or novels, the symbolisations may be less obviously evident, or may not be directed back to early childhood so much as to present situations. For example, *The Turbulent Term of Tyke Tiler*, by Gene Kemp (1979), deals with courage, loyalty, transgression and maintaining personal integrity in an everyday setting – and the question of identity is raised in a particularly challenging way!

CASE STUDY

Listening to Helen

While symbolisation within stories can be a deep source of emotional significance for children, it generally works unconsciously, and becoming aware of this significance is no part of the kind of comprehension we expect from children. It is enough that the child responds to it. Donald Fry (1985) reports discussions he had with children about their reading, and cites 8-year-old Helen as having read *The Shrinking of Treehorn* 'nine times in bed and once at school'. It is clearly a book to which she responds! As Fry says, 'Indirectly the story speaks to her about herself.'

Re-reading the story is a way of possessing it, and possessing her own experience. She refers to THE BIG GAME as 'the game of life' and says 'the game cured him'. She was struck by the way everybody fussed about Treehorn, but 'he weren't really bothered'; and by the way Treehorn's mother 'doesn't really bother about him. She's just bothered about the cake looking at it.'

According to Fry, 'it is the relationship between Treehorn and his mother that particularly puzzles and bothers her, and helps to explain why she returns to the story many times'. During the discussion, Helen compares her own mother's behaviour favourably with Treehorn's mother's. Nevertheless, according to Fry, 'she wants to avoid being fussed over and nagged at, and to feel herself in control of situations; but at the same time she wants the adults in her life to care for her and take command, especially when she is in distress'. For her, *The Shrinking of Treehorn* plays out the dilemma of the game of life as she knows it 'as many times as she cares to view it'.

In contrast, Fry cites Helen's friend, Rachel, who found *The Shrinking of Treehorn* a bit boring because she wanted him to go on shrinking and not to get big again. She had dreams of shrinking so she could go back to playgroup and was sad to wake up her normal size: 'she wanted to use the story to contemplate the possibility of growing down rather than growing up'. He suggests there might have been particular reasons in her life at that time why she might have wanted to revert to an earlier stage of security – and in the event, the story did not provide the consolation she was seeking.

Discussion points

How can you engage a child in discussing the significance of a story to her without, (a), unconsciously imposing your own ideas and agenda on the child; (b) being intrusive into what is properly private?

Hopefully, the teacher can perhaps direct a particular child towards a book that she thinks might speak to his or her condition. A teacher may feel, for example, that a child who is not yet quite old enough for *Jane Eyre* might get something of the same psychological support from reading *Black Beauty*. After all, the two stories have the same emotional hook: 'I am sentient and sensitive but powerless and speechless, misunderstood and mistreated, but I have a right to life and I will survive.' And they both come to a happy ending.

The psycho-moral dimension

Tolkien (1964) argues that fairy tales provide consolation through 'eucatastophe', or the happy ending (which is, he argues from his Christian perspective, more realistic than tragedy). The way stories mean, he argues, is not through allegory (where a suitable key to translation will provide the meaning) but through application. You can apply the story in a variety of ways to your own condition.

Similarly, C.S. Lewis (1969) argues that *The Lion, the Witch and Wardrobe* is not an allegory – though you might have fooled me! The sacrifice of Aslan on the altar to save Edmund is a very straight-forward allegory of Christ's death, although the implicit substitution theory of the atonement is theologically very medieval (not surpris-ingly, with Lewis!). What he wants his stories to do, Lewis goes on to argue, is to enable children, when they come across the Christian message, to have a feeling of familiarity, of being at home and comfortable with it, as if they have always known it in some kind of way. He argues that the moral meaning of a story is not a message or moral maxim (for example, 'Do-as-you-would-be-done-by'), but is implicit in the whole quality of the author's mind. The moral significance of a story lies in how it affects the reader's perceptions and sympathies. Response, then, operates at a deeper level within the personality than what we commonly mean by 'comprehension' or 'morals', which operate at an explicit and intellectual level.

Reader response

In some ways, the theories about significance and moral meaning in stories that emphasise how the reader responds are the most useful and productive. There is a whole industry of 'reader response theory' (see Huw Thomas, 1998, for its application to junior reading). However, there is little value in getting hung up on theory and only using stories to illustrate the theories.

Rather, we should use theory only to illuminate our experience of stories. The crucial issue to be clear about is that different readers take different meanings from a story and that the same person takes some-what different meanings from the story each time he or she reads it.

All readings are partial readings – in both senses of the word 'partial'. But this does not mean that all readings are equally valid. What 'partial' implies is that we should be duly humble about our readings. We should engage in discussion and argument because we can learn from it – both to gain new perceptions and to clarify and refine our own perceptions and expression. With children, we are concerned with the usefulness of their responses to their moral and emotional growth, though they are inevitably 'partial' and may be idiosyncratic.

The spectator role

We have already touched on response in the previous chapter, discussing what D.W. Harding (1962) calls 'the spectator role':

> True or fictional, all ... forms of narrative invite us to be
> on-lookers, joining in the evaluation of some possibility of
> experience.

Harding argues that we don't just 'identify' with the main characters, we feel *with* them and *for* them and *about* them. We review our understanding of the world in the light of the picture given in the story, and review ourselves in the light of our reflections on the story. However, although response of some kind is there from the beginning, the more reflective processes do not come about all at once.

Protherough (1983) suggests that children respond in a number of different ways to fiction. The key factor distinguishing between these ways is the relative 'distance' between the reader and the people or events in the story. Protherough's categorisation tends towards suggesting a developmental order of emergence, though being able to read at a more sophisticated level does not preclude being able also to read at a less sophisticated level, for example, with holiday reading. An adult's 'good read' may be the grown-up equivalent of children reading Enid Blyton, with her emphasis on food and 'lashings of ginger beer' (after all, food is to children's stories what sex is to adults'!). The following paragraphs follow Protherough's categories.

Projection into characters

Projection or identification is often the emotional hook for the reader, child or adult. Protherough cites some 11-year-old children's responses to a story: 'I imagined it was me whose eyes were bursting and filling up with blood, a horrible feeling'; 'I felt the skin on my back being ripped and stinging with the salt water'. Vivid and immediate as such experiences are, they preclude distance, the ability to evaluate, the recognition of irony, etc. Boys have even been known to refuse to accept or register, at the end of *The Turbulent Term of Tyke Tiler*, that Tyke was actually a girl all the time! That is how strong identification can be!

Projection into the situation

The reader is an invisible spectator alongside the characters who become friends, looking on and seeing everything that happens. As with the previous mode, the reader becomes lost in the story.

Associating between book and reader

The reader in this mode seeks links between the story and her own experience. She pictures the story in terms of her own world and her own experiences, and she wonders what she would feel, say or do if she were in the characters' situations. The child wonders, 'Am I like that?' and tests herself imaginatively against the situation – 'Would I feel that/be able to do that?'

The distanced viewer

The reader is, as it were, above the characters, responding to them with sympathy, pity, admiration, anger, contempt and so on. The reader doesn't so much feel *with* the characters as feel *about* them. Perhaps 'distance' isn't quite the word for my reactions when first reading *Mansfield Park* – I was so angry with Mrs Norris for her treatment of Fanny that I had to put the book down a number of times to cool off!

Detached evaluation

This is certainly a mode that only develops with growing maturity and doesn't really apply to primary age children except in special circumstances, probably under teacher tutelage. The reader now understands the characters as people and appreciates them as creations within the story. In later readings of *Mansfield Park*, I could enjoy Mrs Norris for being what she was, and for her role and her eventual come-uppance. With overview and hindsight, the story takes on the figure of a dance in which everyone and everything plays its part.

Different modes of response may operate during reading and in reflection after reading. Certainly there are differences between a first and subsequent readings. At first, you read for the story, not knowing what is going to happen. On a re-reading, you read to recapture something of that initial experience, but you also know what is going to happen, so you have more time to appreciate how the story is told, because you can now see the significance of details along the way for the final outcome. Harding (1962) talks about 'savouring' the story.

The effect of re-reading with younger children, however, is not necessarily like this, since even with re-reading they are unlikely to operate in the 'detached evaluation' mode, or even as 'distanced viewers'. As we saw with 8-year-old Helen, she seemed to operate primarily in the 'associating between book and reader' mode, making comparisons between her own experience and Treehorn's. Clayton (Fry, 1985), another 8-year-old, is even more deeply attached to one particular story, *Watership Down*.

CASE STUDY

What is manliness?

Initially, Clayton's sense of his own identity appeared to be wrapped up in his interest in farming, his father's occupation. He read stories, but without any special interest or passion. Then, by way of the picture-book version, he came to the full story of *Watership Down* which he read, and shared the experience of, with his father over a period of six months. His teacher was Hilary Minns, of *Read It To Me Now!* (1990) fame, and she encouraged his devotion to the story, even to the extent of involving the whole class in drama activities based on it. What with the film, the picture-book, the novel, drama and his own retellings of the story, Clayton was deeply versed in it. He not only could answer questions on it, but liked to quiz other people, including adults, about it.

His interest seemed to centre on the question of leadership, contesting the claims of Hazel and Bigwig, the fighter. Finally he wrote to Richard Adams himself about it: 'Why do you call Hazel the Captain . . . Why don't you call Bigwig the captain.' Adams replied, 'I can't answer your question in words but one day when you see for yourself why . . . you'll understand a lot including the real point of the story.'

Clayton's parents and teachers had experienced both his aggression and his sensitivity, and his teachers felt that his questioning was a process of examining aspects of his own behaviour and personality. Fry believes that when Clayton came to say of Hazel that you could 'trust him', this showed that he had already 'seen for himself why Hazel was Chief Rabbit'. In terms of the characters, the trustworthy Hazel or the fighter, Bigwig, Clayton was working out who he wants to be.

Discussion points

1 Do you have prejudices that blind you to the possible significance of an interest in aggression and warfare, whether in reading or writing, for boys' emotional development?

2 Can you help children relate their feelings about characters with their feeling their way into the development of their own characters?

Response and evaluation

However children may be responding inwardly, they cannot easily express their feelings and responses in words. Frank Whitehead (1977) observes, 'The young reader seldom finds it possible to be articulate in any specific way about what he has liked or valued in his reading'. And this applies also to what they dislike. Getting children beyond 'It was brilliant!' or 'It was boring' is difficult. What, then, can we hope to achieve by teaching? We want, like Fry, to bring out something that touches the trembling child-alive, not something precociously sophisticated like a dog in a waistcoat walking on its hind legs.

Let's consider, then, what we might do with certain passages, say, to address the objective for Year 6, Term 2:

> ... analyse how individual paragraphs are structured in writing; e.g. comments sequenced to follow the shifting thoughts of a character ...

Any passages we use for shared Literacy Hour reading, should come from a book that the children have a current familiarity with. They need a context to help them with their understanding. So let's assume that we are reading *The Secret Garden* by Frances Hodgson-Burnett (1951) aloud as a class story. To take what looks like a relatively simple descriptive passage, consider Mary Lennox's first view of the secret garden:

> It was the sweetest, most mysterious-looking place anyone could imagine. The high walls which shut it in were covered with the leafless stems of climbing roses, which were so thick they were matted together. Mary Lennox knew they were roses because she had seen a great many roses in India.
> All the ground was covered with grass of a wintry brown, and out of it grew clumps of bushes which were surely rose-bushes if they were alive. There were numbers of standard roses which had so spread their branches that they were like little trees. There were other trees in the garden, and one of the things that made the place look strangest and loveliest was that climbing roses had run all over them and swung down in long tendrils which made light swaying curtains, and here and there they had caught at each other or at a far-reaching branch and had crept from one tree to another and made lovely bridges of themselves ...

> (Burnett, 1951, p. 69)

The items that are named and located in the garden, step by step, build up a coherent picture. The coherence is not simply that the items might reasonably go together in a garden and that they build up a picture but, further, this picture is mediated to us through the eyes and feelings of Mary Lennox who is seeing it for the first time.

First, we are given an emotive pointer to how Mary sees, and how we are to imagine, the garden – 'sweetest, most mysterious . . .' and this is later reinforced by 'strangest and loveliest'. The information we are given is seen through Mary's (dare we say it?) rose-tinted spectacles and seems to follow Mary's gaze as she looks around her – high walls shutting it in, the matted rose stems, the grass and bushes . . . The information content of the sentences comes thick and fast, helping to create the sense of how overgrown and dense the vegetation is. Just as the narration follows her gaze, it follows her thoughts and feelings. Her uncertainties (not the author's, because the author certainly knows!) are represented in 'surely . . . if they were alive'. Her heightened feelings are indicated in her metaphor-making with 'curtains' and 'bridges'.

However, the meaning of the paragraph goes beyond simply following her thoughts. It operates at another, more symbolic level: the garden is roses, roses, all the way – but dead-looking, leafless roses. It is a wintry landscape. But again, roses with the hint of untamed vigour about them, thick and matted, climbing and catching at each other. Even the metaphors of 'curtains' and 'bridges', with their connotations of concealment and making connections, are covertly significant. All that roses represent in terms of love, loveliness, passion and ephemerality resonates with potentiality here. And this loveliness is all in abeyance, awaiting spring and a reawakening. What the description represents symbolically is something thematic to the whole book.

There is a lot for comprehension processes to get hold of here! However, when the reader is reading normally, and not in an analytic way, all that is likely to come over is a picture and a feeling about the scene. Response can operate – usually does operate – at a **pre-conscious** level. Indeed, the symbolic suggestiveness of roses works, if it works at all, because it operates at a pre-conscious level.

pre-conscious area of normally unconscious activity that is accessible to conscious introspection if we try

Referential (literal) meaning, then, in fiction at any rate, is inevitably bound up with emotive meaning. But only because of what we bring with us culturally to the reading – for example, about a red, red rose, about a rose that is sick, about the roses that should be brought back to Mary Lennox's pale cheek.

If, for the child reader, such symbolic resonances don't yet exist, it is through literary experiences such as this that the child begins unconsciously to imbibe cultural and symbolic meanings. It is no small part of the richness of response to have a feeling that there are meanings as yet beyond one's reach – just as poetry can communicate before it is fully understood.

The teaching challenge

So what might we ask children about this passage that will help them with the story, that will be non-deadening, that will help them develop more explicit responses? We could take a hint from the *Framework for Teaching* objectives, Year 6, Term 1: '. . . take account of viewpoints . . . explaining how this influences the reader's view of events . . . [and] how events might look from a different point of view.' While these issues could be tackled at degree level, we can also tackle them at a level appropriate to children. We might ask, as a DARTs (Directed Activities Related to Texts – see Lunzer and Gardner, 1984) discussion exercise:

- Who is thinking the garden is sweet and mysterious, strange and lovely? Why do you think so? What tells us?
- Why does everything look dead? Do you think it is really dead? Why do you think so?
- Why does Mary think it so lovely and strange? Choose a bit of the description that shows us why Mary feels as she does. How does it do so?
- Try rewriting a bit of the description, using the same facts, to make the garden seem dead and horrible. What have you had to do to make it seem like that?

Inferring feelings and motives; recognising moral issues

I have argued that some of the most important comprehension skills for children to develop are the ability to infer feelings and motives in characters and to recognise moral issues and to interrogate the text in relation to them. The *Framework for Teaching* implies these skills in the obectives for Year 3, Term 3:

> to discuss (i) character's feelings; (ii) behaviour, e.g. fair or unreasonable, brave or foolish; (iii) relationships, referring to the text and making judgements

and for Year 4, Term 3:

> to identify social, moral or cultural issues in stories, e.g.
> the dilemmas faced by characters or the moral of the story,
> and to discuss how the characters deal with them . . .

(badly written, but there it is!).

Any worthwhile discussion of a story will involve these elements. Looking at short passages in the Literacy Hour gives the opportunity to look closely at how texts tell us about feelings and motives, alert us to moral issues and prompt us into interrogation – the search for answers to questions the text itself has suggested. As the *Framework for Teaching* says in one of its better moments (Year 5, Term 1), we should:

> ...develop an active attitude towards reading: seeking answers, anticipating events, empathising with characters and imagining events that are described.

So let us look at a passage, and see how we might prompt children into an appropriate examination of it.

A possible exercise

This passage from *The Diddakoi*, by Rumer Godden (1975), comes after Kizzy, the gipsy girl who's been bullied at school, has been taken into a wealthy home. Imagine that this is about as far as we have got in reading the story.

> 'I want to see Kizzy Lovell', said Prue.
>
> 'But does she want to see you?' Peters' barrel shape filled the back door.
>
> 'But I have come to see her.' Prudence was surprised.
>
> 'We don't have to see everyone who comes. You wait there, young lady, while I go and ask.' But it was not easy to keep Prudence Cuthbert out, as Miss Brooke or Mrs Blount could have told him. Prue slipped into the kitchen after Peters and came face to face with Kizzy.
>
> Kizzy had stood rooted by the kitchen table as soon as she heard Prue's voice. Prue stopped too when she saw her and they looked at one another, 'like two kittens with their fur on end', Peters told the Admiral afterwards.
>
> Then, 'Go away,' said Kizzy.
>
> 'That's nice,' said Prue. 'When I've come all this way to see you.' Kizzy knew that was not true. Prudence had come to see Amberhurst House. 'So she could tell about it at school,' said Kizzy afterwards.
>
> (Godden, 1975, p. 57)

One way to approach this passage is to dramatise it. The children might work out that they need at least two scenes, one around the back door and kitchen, and a later scene, perhaps, when Peters and Kizzy are telling the Admiral about what happened. A child, simply reading this, might not immediately work out the two time-frames, 'now' and 'afterwards', that are needed to understand it.

Dramatising it, finding the right tone of voice, might establish what lies behind Prudence's demanding 'I want . . .' and her surprise. It doesn't occur to her that anything else counts beyond what she wants. She is a girl who is used to having her own way (as her slipping in behind Peters further demonstrates). And dramatising it will establish the tone of her voice when saying 'That's nice' – sarcastic!

A further way to explore Prue's character would be to add a third scene, where she reports back to her friends what happened when she called at Kizzy's house, or to hot-seat a child in role as Prue about what happened.

Meanwhile, what does Kizzy feel? Hearing Prue's voice caused her to stand 'rooted by the kitchen table'. The image of the kittens suggests the edgy hostility of the meeting (while also reminding us of the protective cordon of adults now around Kizzy). Her brief 'Go away' confirms the interpretation. She is nervous, possibly frightened, and doesn't want to see Prue. And this interpretation is also supported by the way Peters, blocking the doorway, is apparently trying to protect Kizzy.

As a piece of guided groupwork, you could ask the children:

- Rewrite this passage as a dramatic script. How many scenes will you need?
- Are there any speeches you will need to invent that are not written as speech in the story?
- What tone of voice is each speech said in?

Such a task fulfils more than one aspect of the objectives – it touches on objectives to do with dramatic scripts. The questions are leading questions, suggesting what the children might need to do. For example, the question about 'how many scenes' suggests they might need more than one. The question about inventing speeches might lead them to wonder how they might get across the point that Kizzy knows what Prue is saying isn't true.

Further sorts of questions might include writing a brief character sketch of Prue and of Peters from the evidence here and predicting what might happen in the future. For example, the hostility between Prue and Kizzy means, surely, there is a show-down to look forward to! And we might even expect a reversal – Kizzy no longer scared of Prue. We read on in anticipation that the unhappy situation depicted here will be resolved in some way. We read on, interrogating the text for clues and answers. What will happen next, now that Prue is in the house? Will they fight? Etc.

Beyond this, there is the question of the theme of the story – discrimination and bullying against a 'diddikoi', and the moral issues about fairness, good-neighbourliness and friendship.

These are bigger issues than the snippet we are looking at can open up, but using the snippet as a reminder of the story up until this point, we could ask:

- What is the challenge or problem that Kizzy has to face?
- Who are her opponents?
- Who are her helpers?
- What would be a good outcome to the story?
- What questions do you want (a) the next page; (b) the story to answer?

STORY IN THE CLASSROOM

The National Curriculum and National Literacy Strategy

In 1979, Chris Woodhead, now HMCI, said about teaching literature, 'We are not yet clear about what counts as an appropriate educational objective in this area'. Despite the plethora of objectives subsequently formulated in the *Framework for Teaching*, some uncertainty in this area remains, and remains healthy. After all, as D.H. Lawrence (1925) says, 'If you try to nail anything down in the novel, either it kills the novel, or the novel gets up and walks away with the nail.'

For practical purposes, then, we need to consider the legal requirements upon us and how to interpret and implement them in a way that doesn't kill novels or cause children to walk away from them. For Lawrence, 'the novel is the one bright book of life' that 'can make the whole man alive tremble.' We have seen something of 'the whole child alive' trembling in the experiences of Helen and Clayton, discussed above. Whatever else we do, we must 'trust the tale' and allow for the possibility that reading stories can have more profound effects in people's lives than any programme of educational objectives is likely to bring about.

One thing is certain. The sort of literary criticism that we learned at secondary school and at college is *not* appropriate for children. Junior children do not operate in the mode of 'detached evaluation'. Protherough (1983) remarks, 'By presenting stories as 'work' rather than a source of enjoyment, we may hamper rather than assist [children's] development'. In foregrounding the importance of 'response' in the primary years, Martin and Leather (1994) argue 'for more status to be given to the very personal way in which readers are affected by what they read'. So, no mini-lit. crit., please!

This does not mean that we can't ask any kind of analysis or evaluation from children. What is important is what kind, and how we ask them to do it. Understanding and feeling work together in response and personal development. With junior children we operate within the personal and subjective areas of response, we don't aim for the impersonal and objective analysis. Nevertheless, much of the personal and subjective should be made explicit and become subject to socialised scrutiny – which is why we ask children to put things into words and to discuss and compare their responses, or to work collaboratively on re-creative activities like dramatising episodes, designing bookjackets, etc.

All the same, as we find in relation to other genres as well, much of the best comprehension is what is implicit in imitation – when children try to write in ways suggested by their reading. And part of comprehension should also be the children's comprehending things about themselves as a readers, reflecting on their developing skills, needs and responses.

The National Curriculum

The National Curriculum says that, among other things, at Key Stage 2 children should be:

* encouraged to develop as enthusiastic, independent and reflective readers ... and have opportunities to read extensively for their own interest and pleasure ...
* encouraged to respond imaginatively to the plot, characters, ideas, vocabulary and organisation of language in literature ...
* taught to evaluate the texts they read and to refer to relevant passages or episodes to support their opinions.

This concern with enthusiasm, pleasure and imaginative response is important to hold on to. Though imaginative response means different things in relation to each of the items in the subsequent list, the main emphasis here falls on the subjective in children's reading experience. Finally, 'evaluation' is equated with opinions, personal preferences – but opinions supported by reference to relevant instances. The subjective is to be made more subject to scrutiny by the beginnings of reasoned literary argument – 'the common pursuit of true judgement' (Eliot, 1933).

The National Literacy Strategy

How are these concerns to be put into effect? The objectives in the National Literacy Strategy's *Framework* will give us a clue as to what is expected. For example, in Year 3 children should be taught:

* to compare a range of story settings and to select words and phrases that describe scenes

- how dialogue is presented . . .
- to be aware of the different voices in stories . . . showing differences between the narrator and different characters . . .
- to investigate the styles and voices of traditional story language . . .
- to identify typical story themes . . .
- to identify main and recurring characters, evaluate their behaviour and justify views
- to re-tell the main points of a story in sequence; to compare different stories; to evaluate stories and justify their preferences
- to refer to significant aspect of the text, for example, opening, build-up, atmosphere . . .
- to distinguish between 1st and 3rd person accounts
- to consider credibility of events . . .
- to discuss (i) character's feelings; (ii) behaviour . . .; (iii) relationships . . ., referring to the text and making judgements.

All this in Year 3, along with everything else! Daunting, isn't it? However, what makes it so daunting in prospect is, perhaps, our thinking about these requirements in too abstract and literary critical a way. When we look at the very brief suggestions about how these requirements might be implemented, we find things like using puppets to present stories, looking at story openings and endings and using them in their own writing, and talking about the use of adjectives in descriptions. Even the most abstract-sounding objectives can be satisfied in straightforward ways. For example, credibility can be discussed in terms of whether certain stories or events could *really* happen, and the question about themes could be tackled by asking, 'Who can tell me what the story is about? Tell me in just one sentence!', and then writing down the answers for further discussion. These activities aren't too daunting!

So the question about the *Framework for Teaching* objectives is really about how to interpret them in terms that are appropriate to the children's interests and capabilities, and which are not inimical to their enthusiasm, independence and imaginative responsiveness. The objectives represent the kinds of issues you would want to talk with children about in any case. Presented formally as it is, the 'Framework' could suggest a programme where the objectives and the theory are the tail that wags the dog. But if you hold on to the dog firmly enough, it is the tail that wags!

The objectives do not determine your particular choice of stories. They can provide approaches to discussing elements in any stories that you choose and a vocabulary and bank of ideas for thinking with. Approached with self-confidence and an eye on what is important, the *Framework for Teaching* objectives are not really a problem.

The framework of the Framework for Teaching

The *Framework for Teaching*, while spending most of its energies on spelling out the organisation and objectives of the Literacy Hour, confirms what the National Curriculum says about independent reading. Children should 'be interested in books, read with enjoyment' and 'develop their powers of imagination, inventiveness and critical awareness'. Independent reading and listening to stories take place outside and additionally to the Literacy Hour.

The function of the Literacy Hour is to provide explicit teaching and instruction through shared text, word and sentence level work and guided group and independent work at all three levels. And this work is designed to feed the literacy skills that children are developing and exploiting in independent reading and in other areas of the curriculum.

Independent reading

Motivation and opportunity

Motivation and opportunity are essential. I remember being motivated, during the days of post-war austerity and sweet rationing, to read my first children's novel, an imperialistic and racist Puffin called *David Goes to Zululand*, by being bribed by my parents with the promise of my own tray of home-made fudge. I sat in my father's study while he wrote maths textbooks. This anecdote raises a number of issues:

- Not all motivation is necessarily intrinsic, though one hopes that the intrinsic motivation of interest and enjoyment will take over before too long!
- Boys can be particularly reluctant to read independently, so teachers may have to resort to seeking out or providing materials that wouldn't necessarily be chosen for their literary and social desirability. Since interest and enjoyment are motives as well as goals, it is vital to provide material that children enjoy. My first novel started with an air-gun and ended with an express rifle and rolling in elephant dung to conceal the human scent – a boys' book!

Fry found that the first 'story-book' that Clayton spontaneously told him about was the programme for the Smithfield Show which he had attended with his father!

- Parental example, involvement and support are extremely desirable – as the tale of Clayton also suggests.

Motivation

Forms of extrinsic motivation include:

- reading records in which the child can tick off books read and see the list grow (NB publicly visible charts can be dispiriting to the slower readers)
- for younger children, readers' badges children can wear any day they have finished a book
- after reading to teacher, reassuring discussions about skills they are developing and books and materials they might enjoy
- having steps of improvement and indications of interest rewarded by growing privileges, for example, being able to take one of teacher's own books home.

Intrinsic motivation can be encouraged by:

- reading good quality literature to children daily
- providing non-fiction as well as fiction materials on subjects of interest to the children – not necessarily reading books. After all, Clayton came to *Watership Down* through a book of stills from the film and, prior to that, Raymond Briggs' *The Snowman*
- promoting a 'reading culture' within the classroom, where children talk about and recommend books, lend and borrow books, keep a reading diary and list any book they want to recommend publicly so that other children can consult them about it – maybe, even do a poster to recommend it (I remember Enid Blyton stories circulating in the classroom without reference to the teacher)
- discussing books with the teacher, and the teacher discussing the (children's) books she has enjoyed or found interesting on a particular topic – shared experience and enthusiasm is a great motivator
- becoming expert – *the* expert – in some particular area, as Clayton became on farming and *Watership Down*. I remember how a topic on birds and flight grabbed one academically very average boy, Darren, who subsequently became a keen bird-watcher. He even returned from his secondary school to borrow a quite high-powered adult book to help with a project he was doing on how birds are biologically adapted for flight – a book that I've regretted losing ever since!

The general idea is to get the children to see themselves as readers, to gain in self-esteem through their reading and to discover that books can enrich their lives and open up new worlds for them.

Opportunity

Opportunity involves both providing time and suitable reading materials. Dedicated reading periods, daily or two or three times a week, whatever you choose to call them (USSR – Uninterrupted Sustained Silent Reading, DEAR – Drop Everything And Read, ERIC – Everyone Reading In Class, or whatever), are highly desirable. They give reading a high profile, they provide quiet so that children can get lost in the story and they give children the chance to see an adult reading. Children need sustained periods of at least 20 minutes to half an hour to get into a story and to gain the benefit of sustained reading for developing their reading skills. Children become measurably quicker and more accurate over a period of sustained reading, up until the time fatigue sets in.

The advent of the Literacy Hour must not be used as an excuse to curtail dedicated private reading time. To do so would be to go against the National Literacy Strategy, all that we know about best practice and the purposes of reading. We do not help children to read in order to do the Literacy Hour. We do the Literacy Hour in order to help children read.

Children tend to borrow books more readily from a class than a school library, and from a school rather than a public library. Nevertheless, visits to a library for choosing books are an 'occasion', and a good children's librarian is an invaluable resource, both to the teacher for advice and to the children to talk about the books that are available. Don't just borrow boxes of books from the Schools' Library Service, but persuade a librarian to come in and talk about them. The more enthusiastic adults 'selling' reading, the better!

Parental support

Engaging parental interest is important. It should be encouraged to go beyond simply signing a form to say the child has done some reading. In these days of expecting primary children to do homework, it is not unreasonable to ask for 15 minutes or half an hour a night taken away from television or the computer, or for some other regular period to be devoted to reading at home.

In the early years, this will be reading with an adult, but in Key Stage 2 it may be more independent. However, engaging parental interest in what the child is reading and making sure the child feels that interest remain very important. The parent can not only listen to reading but can read the story for him/herself also and discuss it with the child. Think of the story of Clayton (I promise, I won't mention him any more, after this!). It is invaluable to establish that reading is something grown-ups do too, and are interested in.

Classroom activities supporting independent reading

One of the great motivating activities in relation to private reading is public discussion, sharing experiences. One sort of discussion is that which goes on with the teacher. This may take the form of talking about the story while the child is reading it – maybe listening to the reader and then discussing what has happened, modelling the skills of empathy and interrogation. Another activity is the 'reading conference', maybe at the point at which the child is choosing a new book, when the agenda consists of discussing with the child her feelings about her developing reading skills and her thoughts about the ending (how was it right for the story?), judgements about the book just finished and preferences about what to read next.

Reading diaries
The child can also keep a 'reading diary' on a regular basis, recording the times she has spent reading at home or at school, what she has been reading, and any things she has noticed about reading and herself as a reader, for example, what she has enjoyed, new words, how she worked a difficult word out, what she felt about what she was reading, what interested her especially, whether it made her think of any experiences she has had herself.

A regular time should be given each day for keeping the diary up-to-date. Certainly entries should be made after finishing a book and about her reasons for choosing and her anticipations about the next book. It is both a help to the teacher to be able to refer to it, and a help to the child to get into the habit of reflecting both on what she has read, on herself as a developing reader and on her interests.

Sharing experiences of books: group reading
Where there are multiple copies of a book, as is the case with some schemes and resources providing trade books, for example, The Scholastic Literacy Centre (1993), group reading is possible. Groups should be carefully selected, with four an optimum number, and certainly no more than six. The children may read around the group, or they may read silently up to a predetermined stopping place, and then address the issues and questions supplied. These questions may relate to the relevant *Framework for Teaching* objectives, but should always tend to develop children's picturing, attentiveness to language, reflectiveness and anticipation, their empathy and judgements, and their responses and evaluations.

Sharing experiences of books: critical recommendations
Whether spoken or written, formulating critical recommendations of books for peers can focus and clarify children's comprehension and response. We think new things as we put our thoughts and feelings into words. Some sort of proforma can help to structure

such recommendations – as simple or complex as you think useful. For example, you could select ideas from the following:

Information about the book

- Name of book and author
- What sort of a book is it? (funny, sad, frightening, exciting; adventure, school story, historical, fantasy, etc.)
- What is it about? (One sentence, please)
- What is the setting? Where does it happen? When did the events take place? What sort or group of people are involved?
- Who are the main characters in the story and what are they like?
- What happens to start things off? What are the problems the main characters have to face?

Response and opinion

- Describe an episode you particularly enjoyed to give a taste of what the book is like.
- Is there any description or use of language you particularly liked?
- How did the book make you feel?
- What sort of people will enjoy it, and why?
- Give it a star rating: * ** *** **** *****

Group presentations

Individuals or small groups can work together on a story to produce a display for the rest of the class. Such displays might include a poster to sell the aspects of the story that the children decide are most important, a selection of quotations around a portrait of a character, chosen to illustrate his/her personality or a picture of some episode with speech and thought bubbles attached to characters to represent the sub-text of feelings and motives.

In some stories the sequence of time may be important, so that, for example, the events of *Tom's Midnight Garden* (Philippa Pearce) may be easier to grasp using two parallel time lines, one for Tom and one for Hatty, with the children working out how to relate them. In other stories, ones that involve journeys, for example, *The Silver Sword* (Ian Serraillier), *Children on the Oregon Trail* (A. Rutgers van der Loeff), *The Hobbit* (J.R.R. Tolkien), maps of the real world or imagined country may be helpful, with the track of the geographical journey itself becoming a time line of episodes.

Some stories are based firmly within particular historical events, and while the story supplies much of the necessary information, further explorations growing out of, and feeding into the story can be helpful. For example, *The Silver Sword* (Ian Serrallier), *Carrie's War* (Nina Bawden), *Friend or Foe* (Michael Morpurgo), *The Machinegunners* and *Blitz* (Robert Westall) and even, stretching a point, *When Hitler Stole Pink Rabbit* (Judith Kerr), all have a Second World War background. Some framework of historical knowledge will help to contextualise the stories and this could be presented as a display. And the War as a historical topic is enriched and deepened by the reading of relevant novels.

Displays or big books of children's written work relating to a story can be produced. For example, children can write about episodes from the point of view of a different character from the one focalised in the text, they can write the diary of a character, or, in the case of school-based stories, they can write the children's reports. A group with a tape-recorder can script and record a discussion about a book, dramatise an episode as a radio play or conduct interviews with characters from the story.

The aim of all such activities is to get the children discussing the story, seeing different angles on it, working out the presentation and exploring the wider historical and geographical contexts. Part of what they will be doing is what the National Curriculum asks in relation to information skills, the 're-presentation' of information in different forms in such a way that it is thoroughly understood.

Reading aloud to the class

This remains a valuable activity even after children have become readers for themselves. It provides practice in attentive listening and focuses on comprehension, without any distraction from problems with decoding. It can provide experience of more complex literary texts and language, mediated by the teacher's intonation both in reading narrative and descriptive passages and in animating dialogue, so that it is easier to comprehend. It can provide an opportunity to introduce authors and stories, for example, classics, that children might not tend to choose for themselves. It can provide experience of extended attention and recall with longer stories read as a serial. It provides a common, unifying experience for the whole class, even while the spread of reading skills among the children is getting wider. And it can provide a context for the text, sentence and word level work you do in the Literacy Hour.

Traditionally, such reading aloud tends to take place at the end of the day, when children are tired and prepared to sit (if they are not fractious!), in order to draw children in together. But other times are possible. Graham and Kelly (1998) cite the dramatic effect that reading an enormously popular novel from 9.00 *a.m.* each morning had upon punctuality!

Whenever the reading takes place, the book should be selected with care, the way it is introduced should be considered – how do you raise interest and expectation in what is to come? Do you remind the children about the previous episode, or get them to remind you?

You should practise your reading to ensure that it is fluent and dramatic, and suitable stopping places should be determined upon in advance. Further, the teacher should consider whether it is appropriate to stop and question children at any point during the reading or after the reading. What kind of questions do you ask? **Closed questions** about the facts of the situation? **Open questions** about how they think characters might feel or how they feel themselves, about what they think of the characters' behaviour, etc.? The advantages of such focused questioning have to be balanced against the disadvantages of interrupting the flow of the narrative – and making it seem like work!

closed questions
questions with a definite right answer, asked to test children's knowledge

open questions
questions without a 'right' answer, and to which single-word answers are not appropriate, asked to stimulate thought and imagination or elicit personal experiences and responses

Story work in the Literacy Hour

The *Framework for teaching* spells out a lot of activities and an array of contexts, from whole class to group and individual activities, under immediate teacher guidance or without. The activities need not be confined to the Literacy Hour, but are appropriate within it. What I shall aim to do here is suggest some sorts of activities that fit the requirements and help expand the children's enjoyment and understanding of a particular story, using *The BFG* by Roald Dahl (1984) as the example.

Let us assume that the story is being or has been read aloud to a Year 4 class and the children have enjoyed it. After all, it is funny, it is a bit rude and activates fears that then come under the control of humour; and in the relationship between Sophie and the BFG children can sense some parallel with their relationships with powerful adults and be reassured that intelligence is a way of dealing with situations.

Whole-class shared text work

Consider the objectives for Year 4, Term 1:

> to investigate how settings and characters are built up from small details

and:

to identify the main characteristics of the key characters, drawing on the text to justify views and using the information to predict actions.

These issues are picked up again later in the year, for example:

to understand how the use of expressive and descriptive language can, e.g. create moods, arouse expectations, etc.

We could choose the opening chapter to discuss settings, descriptive language, mood and expectations. But let us for the moment consider how characters are built up. How is the BFG himself introduced and established?

Character is usually built up on the basis of appearance, behaviour, speech and the motives and feelings that the reader is either told about explicitly or that the reader infers. We will want to guide children's attention to these issues.

In the night-time setting, the BFG is 'something very tall and very black and very thin' doing mysterious things after peering in at windows. The rather grotesque initial description of his face is topped off with the eyes, about which there is something 'fierce and devilish'. No wonder Sophie is convinced he is going to eat her!

Back in the cave, however, when he takes his black cloak off, Sophie sees that his dirty waistcoat has no buttons, his trousers are far too short and he is wearing 'a pair of ridiculous sandals'. The term 'ridiculous' begins to attach to his whole appearance. Then he speaks: 'Ha! What has us got here?' Even his grammar is ridiculous.

So much for context. As a passage of text for shared study, let's look at the first half page of the chapter, 'The BFG'. You read it to the children, with them following the enlarged text.

The Giant picked up the trembling Sophie with one hand and carried her across the cave and put her on the table.

Now he really is going to eat me, Sophie thought.

The Giant sat down and stared hard at Sophie. He had truly enormous ears. Each one was as big as the wheel of a truck and he seemed to be able to move them inwards and outwards from his head as he wished.

'I is hungry!' the Giant boomed. He grinned, showing massive square teeth. The teeth were very white and very square and they sat in his mouth like huge slices of white bread.

'P...please don't eat me,' Sophie stammered.

> The Giant let out a bellow of laughter. 'Just because I is a giant, you think I is a man-gobbling cannybull!'

> (Dahl, 1984, p. 25)

Because you want interactive participation from the children, you can't determine exactly how the discussion will go. But you will have prepared questions and have an aim. You could start off by asking about how Sophie feels (and how they know), and then about how the children feel – do they share Sophie's fears? If not, why not?

Now is the time to start looking at the detail of the description and at the giant's language. If the children have laughed at the two similes, about the truck wheels and the slices of bread, they are hardly likely to feel too scared for Sophie. You could ask them what was funny – presumably it is something to do with their picturing. You could ask whether the children think they are good similes, and what they make us feel. There would be scope for suggesting further similes, for example, about his eyes, his laugh, his sandals (cf. 'herring boxes without topses. . .').

Then there is the question of the Giant's language. How far is it a kind of baby-talk? If you can probe the children to come to some such kind of description ('Who do you know who talks a bit like "I is hungry!"?'), then you can ask about how this makes you feel about the speaker. Is he really scary? And touching on the issue of prediction, is he likely to eat Sophie up?

A harder question for children to answer, because they are not yet very good at such inferences, is to ask, 'What was the Giant thinking when he sat down and stared hard at Sophie?' Even if a child replies, 'He was thinking of eating her', hopefully another child will disagree, and a useful discussion could ensue.

A yet harder question might be, 'What was Sophie doing while the Giant stared at her?' You might prompt the children by further asking, 'Who thought his ears were enormous? Who thought they were as big as the wheel of a truck? Did the Giant think it?' In doing this, you would be starting to touch on questions of viewpoint, anticipating objectives in later years. Such questions presuppose a grounding in empathic inference.

Whole-class sentence level work
Sentence level work could look at the Giant's language, focusing on his grammar. You could ask children to correct 'What has us got here?' and 'I is hungry' and, as much more fun, to try composing sentences in the Giant's style, for example, 'Give we the book', 'Please don't eat I'. Such activities can easily be followed up in group

and individual guided work, for example, scanning the whole book for further examples and rewriting some part of the story from the BFG's point of view in his own words! BFG-talk is an excellent entry into looking at grammar and agreements.

Grammar is not the only thing to look at at sentence level. We can also look at stylistic devices, for example, as we noted above, in our passage similes are important. Not only should children be considering the structure of similes, but also their range of effects, for humour, exaggeration, vivid picturing and so on. Similarly, they can look at the sentence construction of comparisons for example, 'Your head is emptier than a bundongle' whatever a 'bundongle' may be!

Once more, children are going to learn much more about similes and comparisons by making up their own, based on examples, than by simply studying them. *The BFG* provides a good model for children to start from, inventing their own gross and grotesque descriptions. And if this produces inventive insults, rejoice in the creativity of language! A wall display entitled 'Inventive Invective' would, no doubt, go down a treat.

Whole-class word level work

The BFG is a great gobblefunker with words. Consider the sentence, 'Greeks is full of uckyslush'. Children will work out that 'uckyslush' seems to be composed of 'yucky' and 'slush', and because it relates to Greece, it will mean 'sloppy grease'. But a 'bundongle' is more of a problem. Yet from the context children should be able to determine some of its characteristics. They could provide their own invented definitions and etymologies, following the conventions of a dictionary.

BFG-talk is a good way into talking about phonological chunks (how do you read the invented words, letter-by-letter, or finding pronounceable chunks?), spellings and pronunciations (for example, 'human beans', all the puns about 'Turkey' and 'turkey', 'Greece' and 'greasy', etc., 'MY BREKFUST IS REDDY'), and the morphological composition of words like 'hippodumplings'.

What is the link between the words 'scrumplet', 'scrumdiddlyumptious' and 'delumptious'? 'Scrumptious', of course: a word which is early nineteenth-century colloquial American, of unknown origin. Only one of my various Oxford dictionaries offers 'delicious' as a meaning, though I would have thought that this was its primary meaning nowadays (and only by extension applicable to small children, whom we sometimes say 'look good enough to eat'!). And presumably Dahl thought so too, since eating (and drinking) is what *The BFG* is all about!

What other words or word-parts contribute to these portmanteau words? How do we know that 'scrumplet' is a noun and 'delumptious' is an adjective? What other words end with '-let' and what does '-let' mean? What other words end with '-ious'? Where does the expression 'portmanteau words' come from, and why? All these questions, and questions like them, can prompt a range of shared and guided explorations.

Summary

Through myths and legends and stories, peoples transmit their sense of cultural identity and values from generation to generation. Stories also contribute to individual identity as we explore and develop our own perceptions, individuality and values through the stories we tell and the stories we hear and read. Children have a natural hunger for stories 'to grow on'.

But to conduct an intellectual or literary critical examination of stories is not the aim of primary education. Our aim is to help children explore stories in their own terms, in such a way that they develop individually and culturally through them. We must learn to trust the story. If, through the emotional empathy generated by *Tom's Midnight Garden* (Philippa Pearce), the child senses something of the haunting sadness of friends growing away from each other, and is reduced to tears by the final rediscovery (and maybe becomes inquisitive about her own Nana's childhood), is this not more important than literary analysis?

There are, however, things in relation to stories that we can usefully explore and examine with children – responses and evaluations, historical and cultural backgrounds, use of language and structure in stories. But the ways these things are best examined and explored with juniors are not abstractly, not objectively, but with the subjectivity of felt experience, in discussing reactions and interpretations, and responding expressively through writing and presentation. It could be that the most important part of the child's experience of literature is hidden from the teacher, in the child's quiet reading and re-reading of things that speak to her condition. If this is the case, the teacher has done her job, having helped the child become autonomous, at least in this respect.

- Stories are one of the primary ways in which we represent our experience to ourselves in order to make sense of it.

- Response to stories can operate at psychological depths that do not lend themselves readily to classroom examination, but these may be the most important responses.

- Children can grow personally, intellectually and morally through their response to story.

- Reading stories both widens children's experience vicariously and deepens it by the way they engage with them: for example, by identifying with characters and experiences and evaluating them; by comparing themselves and their own experiences with the characters and situations in the story.

- The primary classroom examination of stories, while it may look at technical and structural elements, is not primarily concerned with academic issues and objectivity, but with exploring personal and subjective responses by sharing, discussing and representing them.

Further reading

Benton, M. and Fox, G. (1985) *Teaching Literature: Nine to Fourteen*, Oxford
A book that every teacher of this age-group should take into account, it is virtually a standard text about ways of promoting imaginative reading.

Martin, T. and Leather, B. (1994) *Readers and Texts in the Primary Years*, Open University
This book explores the concept of response at length, emphasising the ways in which response at the primary stage is more personal and idiosyncratic than intellectual and academic.

Thomas, Huw (1998) *Reading and Responding to Fiction: Classroom Strategies for Developing Literacy*, Scholastic
In a unique book, Thomas provides a well-written, accessible application of structuralist and post-modernist critical ideas to children's literature, and shows how they may be valuably exploited in the classroom.

Tucker, Nicholas (1981) *The Child and the Book*, Cambridge
A very readable modern classic about the psychological significance of children's books and children's reading, this is a book that enriches our understanding of the personal meanings of stories.

5 Reading poetry

Objectives

When you have read this chapter, you should be able to:

- reflect on the power of poetry both to entertain and to vitalise a sense of the potentialities of language, life and experience

- recognise some of the technical ways poetry works to achieve its emotive effects

- interpret the statutory requirements and the *National Literacy Strategy Framework for Teaching* in a way that is faithful to poetry and to children

- plan purposeful approaches to the reading of poetry, both through appropriate provision of materials and through more direct and directed teaching activities.

Introduction

While poetry can appeal to readers in a wide variety of ways, one of its most important potentialities is to speak very directly to, and for, our inwardness of experience – that part of us from which our passions and our sympathies flow. From this arises poetry's power to express our deepest feelings for us, to console us in the most extreme experiences of life and to open up for us new worlds of experience or new ways of experiencing the world around us.

Children, unless or until socialised otherwise, respond readily to the power of language expressed in rhythm and imagery, so it behoves us as teachers in the primary years to ground children in an appreciation of good poetry that will survive adolescence and prove talismanic for the rest of their lives.

THE POWER OF POETRY

Though poetry is still a thing that scares many adults, including teachers, it doesn't frighten children. Adults have been through secondary school and have been made to feel inadequate and insecure because poetry is full of 'hidden meanings' couched in difficult language and is subject to arcane technical analyses, symbolised for many by the daunting expression 'iambic pentameter'. Primary children haven't been through secondary school and happily remain innocent and uncorrupted by academic teaching.

The poetry they tend to have encountered consists largely of nursery rhymes and humorous or nonsense poetry written by people like Roger McGough, Brian Patten, Roald Dahl and – oh, so many contemporary names! – Allan Ahlberg, Michael Rosen, Kit Wright, Ian McMillan, etc. For primary children, their experience of poetry has been fun.

No wonder, then, that poetry has overtaken stories as many children's preferred reading. The poems they read give immediate rewards – they tend to be funny, undemanding and short. Often, they are rather anarchic in the way they play with language and in the meanings and images they create. They provide the pay-off and the rewarding sense of having completed something more quickly than a story does. And they can easily be shared with a friend.

We have to have doubts, however, about the long-term effects of allowing primary children *only* to encounter contemporary comic poetry. It neither opens up the world of wonder and awe that poetry, perhaps uniquely, can unfold, nor does it open up the great tradition of English poetry. It is a shame that few children today have the experience of some of the great hymns of the language – the imagery of 'And did those feet in ancient times' and the mystery of 'Immortal, invisible, God only wise'. It is every child's birthright to feel the transporting wonder of Coleridge's 'Kubla Khan' and know Blake's 'Tyger, Tyger' off by heart.

I can remember when, aged 8, I was gob-smacked by a poem that a boy I knew recited to me on our way home from school. He had had to learn it off by heart, and I didn't let him go before I'd learned it off by heart myself! It was G.K. Chesterton's 'The Donkey':

The Donkey

When fishes flew and forests walked
   And figs grew upon thorn,
Some moment when the moon was blood
   Then surely I was born.

With monstrous head and sickening cry
   And ears like errant wings,
The devil's walking parody
   On all four-footed things.

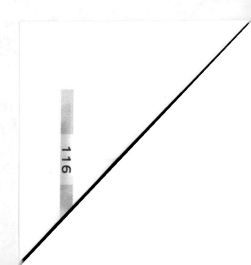

> The tattered outlaw of the earth,
>   Of ancient crooked will;
> Starve, scourge, deride me: I am dumb,
>   I keep my secret still.
>
> Fools! For I also had my hour;
>   One far fierce hour and sweet:
> There was a shout about my ears,
>   And palms before my feet.

> *G.K. Chesterton*

Here was a richness of mystery and emotion that grabbed me and I wanted to make it my own, to possess it. The immediate hook was those opening images, so simply expressed yet so evocatively vivid, and the feeling of being an outsider expressed in the second and third stanzas. I did not understand all the language, but I did feel the emotion. Not that I could put it into words. It is only now, as an adult looking back, that I can see something of what the poem symbolised for me.

As the donkey is dumb, so the child is dumb before the adult – and yet knows the angry frustration of being dumb. The poem is a celebration, in a world that seems to want to crush it, of the stoic strength of developing individual consciousness. Knowing the poem gave me a heart-warming sense of validation and inner triumph – it's all right being *me*, however much my ears stick out! I went home with a glory in my head.

Poetry can be a consolation, a stay and a touchstone throughout one's life – and a large part of the reason for offering a full range of poetry to children is to give them the opportunity to encounter its sustaining power. But doing so raises interesting problems for teachers. Not just, how do you do it, what poems do you choose? But, what sort of comprehension are we talking about? When the poetry is being at its most successful for the child, when it is expressing the unknown, the inexpressible, the otherwise unformulated and unformulatable, what are we going to ask the child about it? If the poetry is working, anything we can ask about it is going to be a trivial irrelevance. And, at worst, we have the power to kill the poem stone-dead for the child.

THE FRAMEWORK FOR TEACHING OBJECTIVES

In the light, then, of what poetry can mean in a child's (and an adult's) life, what should our teaching objectives be? The National

Curriculum (1995) is thin on poetry, mentioning it only under 'Range': it talks about 'figurative language', 'good quality modern poetry' and 'some classic poetry'. There is nothing specific mentioned among the Key Skills, although responding 'imaginatively to the ... organisation of language' does have application to poetry. The *Framework for Teaching* (DfEE, 1998) objectives, however, include many references to poetry. Under the heading 'Range', emphasis falls on poetic forms and themes – but mostly on forms.

Why this emphasis on forms? Is it because they are teachable in a way that can be tested? Is it an aspect of the incipient Gradgrindery in the *Framework for Teaching*? Let's consider the case of 'cinquains', an especially privileged form, receiving more than one mention. Has a serious poet ever written a serious poem in this form? No. Who had ever heard of cinquains before Sandy Brownjohn popularised the notion in *Does It Have To Rhyme?* (1980)? No one. You feel that the lists of forms were probably taken straight from Sandy Brownjohn's headings without further thought.

Sandy Brownjohn's concern is primarily with developing children's appreciation of poetry by getting children to write, sparked off by introducing them to poems and to forms which are within their capacity to imitate. *Writing* using forms like the cinquain has its place because some of the simple forms are manageable by children, while the forms of the poetry they should be *reading* may not be so manageable. Strangely, the *Framework for Teaching*, then, would appear to have its eye, when discussing range, more on children's creative writing than on their reading.

The objectives that apply to poetry fall into certain general categories:

- reading aloud and performance
- study of layout and form, together with experience of a range of genres
- explorations of figurative language, language play and rhymes
- selecting poems, expression of preferences and responses
- familiarity with some poetry from previous ages and other cultures
- familiarity with some significant poets and their styles
- writing poems, based on models and on personal feelings.

The objectives are couched in very academic language, and many could appropriately be tackled at secondary or first degree level! For example, academic-sounding expressions include 'compare and contrast ...', 'understand the terms ... ballad, sonnet, rap, elegy ...', 'understand the use of figurative language ...' Quite a strong emphasis in relation to poetry, as elsewhere in the objectives, falls on learning technical terms: rhyme, alliteration, simile, archaic, couplets, style, half-rhymes, rhythm, assonance, connotation, ambiguity, implied or multi-layered meanings, the names of poetic forms, etc. Enough to frighten teachers without a literary background – and with!

The danger with all this is that it so terrifies teachers that they approach their teaching with an academic straitjacket on. Yet the objectives are not bad in their spirit. It is the letter of them that can be deadening. Neither their expression nor the rather haphazard scattering of them over the years and terms is very helpful. So let's now consider what is good about them.

The emphasis on hearing, speaking and performing poems

This is good because poems are, by their nature, about the sound of language, and about expression. Working on a reading or performance is an oblique way of exploring the construction and meaning of a poem, and it makes the child really familar with the text. Naming sound effects like assonance makes more sense in a context of trying to bring out the sound patterns in a poem. The requirement for reciting poems means learning them off by heart, and this is a way for children to come to possess them for life.

Selecting poems, expressing preferences and responses

This requirement extends along a continuum from choosing poems to discussing their impact. Expressing preferences can extend from saying, 'It's great!' or 'It's boring' to discursive analysis. Even simple questions like 'What bits do you like specially? What bits do you like saying and getting your tongue round?' lead children towards considered thinking. One way of reinforcing preferences is finding ways, like personal anthologies, for children to record and publicise their favourite poems. Kaye Webb's *I Like This Poem* (1979) is a delightful anthology of children's choices, with each child saying something about why he or she likes the particular poem. A home-made anthology like this edges children towards expressing their responses and discussing them with others, thus reformulating and refining them.

The requirement to explore poets and poems from earlier times and other cultures

This precludes the danger of only giving children experience of contemporary comic poets. It opens up a sense of history and continuity, provides a wider range of experiences and introduces children to the great tradition of English poetry in both its historical depth and in the way that it has spread around the world, gaining as it does so from other cultures and historical experiences, as with the great tradition of Caribbean poetry. The specification of Shakespeare is invaluable. Children can, if taught properly, come to love Shakespeare before the dry academic approaches of exam courses kill off any potential enthusiasm. Leon Garfield's *Shakespeare's Stories* with Charles Keeping's glorious illustrations, is a real turn-on for junior children as a way of approaching Shakespeare and coming to his language.

The study of significant poets

The notion that poets are real people can be vastly enhanced by having poets in school. But how many of these count as 'significant', I wouldn't like to say! But the study of a major poet and his poems in his context can create datum points for children's developing experience. There is, for example, an excellent teaching pack for primary schools, *Introducing Wordsworth* (Martin, 1998), produced by the Wordsworth Trust, that would support a study that goes beyond those blessed daffodils and places Wordsworth in his landscape and timescape. Other poets, like Shakespeare (of course), Blake, Coleridge, Tennyson and John Clare, lend themselves to similar treatment.

The exploration of, and play with, the expressive potentialities of language

Playing with language comes naturally to children – it is part of the learning process. While the 'Objectives' place a disproportionate emphasis on rhyme in the junior years, the total contribution of sound effects in poetry cannot be stressed too much. The naming of parts is not as important as the response, but it can focus attention and fix experiences. Accuracy when naming parts is important, however. *Educating Rita* got assonance wrong – and, as far as I know, I'm the only person ever to have commented on it!

Again, similes and other figures of speech, such as metaphor, alliteration, onomatopoeia and so on, are important for children to experience and experiment with, though less important for them to be able to name. Few of us can name many of the figures of speech that traditional rhetoric elaborated endlessly. But we tend to use them and respond to them without even realising. For example, the expressions 'sweet and sour', 'ice-burn', 'a white lie', 'bittersweet', 'parting is such sweet sorrow', 'a living death', 'love-hate relationship' and 'a snail's fury' are oxymorons – but to be ignorant of the name doesn't preclude one's responding to them as striking expressions of some of the paradoxes in our experience.

The emphasis on writing poetry, using poems that have been read as models

Like performance, writing is an oblique way of exploring how another poem works. For the Elizabethans, imitation was a noble aim, to naturalise a foreign influence and make it our own. The Kingman Report (1988), one of the publications leading towards the National Curriculum, quoted Octavio Paz with approval: 'every creative act begins as imitation and ends as invention'. Of course, a child can read with enjoyment poems she cannot hope to emulate. What you might ask a child to imitate is one aspect of a poem – its theme, its use of alliteration, a phrase to develop or whatever. The influence of a poem may only emerge in a child's writing after a period of incubation.

The thing that children are perhaps least good at imitating is metre, the rhythmic underpinning of a poem. Unless they can get it into their heads, as is possible with a limerick, they cannot manage it. It is better to try to give them another form to follow that they can cope with, because children quickly learn that poems, to be proper poems, have to have some sort of ritual form. So, for example, if you are interested in alliteration, don't ask the children to imitate iambic pentameters, but given them another form, for example, asking then to alliterate two or three words in each line and repeat the last word of each line as the first word of the next.

Here, in the chaining and the alliteration, is a formal structure within children's capabilities, and which creates a sense of poetic ritual which corresponds well with this Year 5 boy's emotional reaction to caving for the first time:

Speliogenesis

A silhouetted cave stands in the murky mist of the moonlight,
Moonlight formations move across a pool of crystal,
Crystal clear stalagmites dance across the cave in the candlelight
Light shafts swoop across the cavern,
Cavern echoes ring out . . .

Imitation is not the only form of priming in the writery school, but providing models is likely to be part of any approach you take to creative poetry writing. So the writing may as well be meshed in with the reading.

These, then, are the soundly based approaches that the 'Objectives' promote. But beyond this, before we move to discussing the practical things we can do as teachers, we need to consider the dimensions of poetry, its height, its breadth, its depth, and to consider how poetry works, including those aspects that get scant attention in the *Framework for Teaching*.

THE DIMENSIONS OF POETRY

Lines, and how the poem sounds

Reading a poem is different from reading a story or anything else in prose for one major reason: a poem highlights how it sounds. If you don't hear it in your mind's ear, then you'd better read it aloud! The play of rhythm, intonation and sound-texture are vital to its nature. The language is not intended to be transparent, but to make you feel its weight, its warp and woof.

The reason a poem looks different from prose on the page is because it is spatially divided up into lines, and these lines demarcate auditory rhythmic units. A line ending, even if there's no punctuation marking it, constitutes a rhetorical articulation, a minimal pause. Reading a poem well is, in the first instance, very largely a matter of finding the right balance between reading it according to the lineation and reading it according to the flow of the words in the sentences. C.S. Lewis (1954) talks about 'double audition', the way the reader needs to be alert to the demands of both metre and meaning in establishing the overall rhythms.

Metre and free verse

Sometimes the lines have regular, repeated rhythmic patterns (and the line endings may be further highlighted by rhymes). Poems like this are said to be written in metre. Other poems are written in 'free verse' without any clear metrical patterning. Nevertheless, the lineation marks some kind of rhythm, often the natural rhythms of the speaking voice. Free verse is often designed to imitate spontaneous speech or thought, as if we are listening to somebody speaking or even as if we are sharing the streamy flow of the poet's thoughts and perceptions – in some cases, hardly structured by syntax.

Metrical verse can achieve similar effects, as Shakespearean soliloquies and Wordsworth's blank verse show. But it can do many other things as well. It can, most obviously, highlight its own artificiality. Poetry is a verbal art, and arts are, by their nature, artificial. It is just that, with some genres, like film and the novel, we are so enculturated into the artificiality of the medium that we tend to think of it as natural. Free verse often aims to achieve a similar naturalisation. But metrical verse insists on its artifice. Nobody ever spoke in rhyme or ballad metre. But one thing that metre and rhyme do is make the poetry memorable. Indeed, this was, in the days of oral culture, the prime purpose of rhythm and rhyme – to aid memory. My bet is that you can remember, or part-remember, some metrical poetry, but you can't remember any free verse!

Metrical verse is more (or seems more) deliberated and permanent than free verse. The syntax of metrical verse tends to be more structured and organised. Free verse aims to give the impression of transience, of improvisation and being caught on the wing. Consider, for example, those free-verse anecdotes of Michael Rosen's about life in his family with his brother. It's difficult to call them poetry at all, they are so natural-seeming, and the artifice is so down-played, with the lineation simply reinforcing the spoken phrasing. The artifice is in seeming so natural. Read them aloud, and you read them well. The punch-lines work: it's the way he tells them – or rather, the way he lineates them.

Rhythm and stress

English speech is naturally rhythmic and the rhythms result from the interaction of a number of features relating to syllables, stress and meaning. A syllable is centred on a vowel sound, the pulse of vocal energy. This pulse may be relatively stressed or unstressed in relation to the adjacent syllables.

Words of more than one syllable exhibit patterns of stress, with some syllables stressed in pronunciation at the expense of others. For example, consider the word 'patterns': the stress falls on the first syllable, and the second syllable is relatively unstressed: The '-terns' part is not pronounced like 'terns' or 'turns', but more like 'tuns'. If you were to stress the second syllable at the expense of the first, /puhTURNS/, nobody would know what you were talking about. Note further that, with a word like 'present', if you say /PREZunt/, it is a noun or adjective, but if you say /pruhZENT/, it is a verb:

Let me present you with this present.

This grammatical stress distinction applies in many words, for example, refuse, reject, conscript; but not all, for example, process, express.

On top of the stress patterns of polysyllabic words, sentences tend to have stress patterns depending on both their syntactic structure and the information content. For example, function words tend not to be stressed except where required for pragmatic purposes – 'You say you saw *a* cat, but was it *the* cat?'

And above the syntactic and semantic/pragmatic functions of stress, there are two further related tendencies in English that have a strong influence in poetry: the tendencies to stress alternate syllables and to have stresses occur at regular time intervals (the tendency to 'isochrony'). So if you pack in more syllables between two stressed syllables, you have to say them more quickly. Compare a line from Coleridge with an alternative version:

> With a leap and a bound the swift anapaests throng

> With leaps and bounds swift bison throng

Which line feels faster, more bouncy and energetic?

Metre

Metre in English poetry exploits stress rhythms. On top of all the influences on stress patterns mentioned so far, metre in poetry imposes its own expectations about regular, repeated stress patterns. These metrical patterns may coincide with or run counter to the 'natural' stress patterns, and the great rhythmic subtlety of English metrical verse is dependent on the interplay, 'double audition' or 'counterpoint' (to use Gerard Manley Hopkins' term) between the implicit metre and natural speech rhythms, creating the potential for the subtlest modulation or the most emphatic and dominating beat. For example, consider Wordsworth description of climbing while birds-nesting when a boy:

> . . .Oh! when I have hung
> Above the raven's nest, by knots of grass
> And half-inch fissures in the slippery rock
> But ill-sustained, and almost (so it seemed)
> Suspended by the blast that blew amain
> Shouldering the naked crag, oh, at that time
> While on the perilous ridge I hung alone,
> With what strange utterance did the loud dry wind
> Blow through my ear! the sky seemed not a sky
> Of earth – and with what motion moved the clouds!

> (from Wordsworth, *The Prelude*, Book 1, line 330*ff*)

Here the impetus of the sentence grammar allows no stopping at line-endings but pushes on with breathless exaltation. The iambic pentameters are almost, but not quite, imperceptible. Contrast this with the totally different, but equally dramatic, emphatic rhythm of Byron's:

> The Assyrian came down like the wolf on the fold
> And his cohorts were gleaming in purple and gold;
> And the sheen of their spears was like stars on the sea
> When the blue wave rolls nightly on deep Galilee...

(from Byron, 'The Destruction of Sennacherib')

The metre here determines the rhythm. It is anapaestic, like the line from Coleridge quoted above. Each line consists of four anapaests or metrical 'feet' of three syllables each, with the last syllable stressed. This is particularly clearly seen in the third line where every third syllable is a content word, and all the other unstressed words are function words.

Iambic metres and their variations

The commonest metres in traditional English poetry are iambic. That is, the metre is built up from units called 'iambic feet', each of two syllables, with the second one stressed. If you've got five of these 'feet' in a line you have an iambic pentameter. Shakespeare, sonnets, blank verse and a good deal else are written in this diDUM diDUM diDUM diDUM diDUM metre. What you will notice is that it exploits the tendency to alternating unstressed and stressed syllables.

The iambic pentameter has so strong an effect that, if it is foregrounded, it can be wearisome. However, it can be varied in various ways. The commonest ways are:

- foregrounding the rhythm of the sentence and letting the sentences spill over line endings on to the next line (these are called 'run on' lines)
- starting the line with a stressed syllable
- adding or taking away unstressed syllables, so either slowing down or speeding up the movement
- having some sort of a rhythmic break or caesura in the middle of the line.

The Wordsworth passage above illustrates all these variations. Generally, the effect of the iambic pentameter is so potent, you can play fast and loose with it and still experience it as the background metre. The crucial element is the five beats per line. For a further example of the fluid variations discussed above, look at the example of Tennyson's blank verse on page 125.

English metres are stress-syllable metres, not syllabics

If I have spent too long on this subject, it is because there is so much ignorance about it, and this ignorance even shows itself in the *Framework for Teaching* objectives. Among the Year 4, Term 3 objectives, one is concerned, among other things, with children understanding the term 'rhythm' and identifying rhythms in poems, and this is followed by the objective, 'to clap out and count the number of syllables in each line of regular poetry'. This suggests that the writers of the *Framework for Teaching* are so ignorant of the nature of English metres that they think that the number of syllables is the critical thing. They need to be informed: English poetry is not syllabic like French and Japanese. In English, stress is the critical factor. English is a stress-timed language and English metres are stress-syllable metres.

Rhythm and rhyme
Rhythm is more fundamental to poetry than rhyme. Again, it shows the hopelessness of the *Framework for Teaching* in the face of poetry that it devotes numerous objectives to looking at rhyme and rhyme schemes, and never says anything sensible about rhythm at all. Yet you can easily teach your children to clap to the stress patterns of poetry rather than to the number of syllables. In choral work, it is hard to get them *not* to over-emphasise the stress patterns and chant the poem!

The texture of language, the texture of life
The focus on sound in poetry shows itself in a variety of ways. Rhythm, metre and rhyme we have already discussed in relation to their effects on the patterning of sound. And we could add to the pattern-making potentialities of language alliteration, assonance and consonance (the 'rhyming' or chiming of vowel sounds and consonant sounds respectively). The sound patterns of language in poetry contribute markedly to its effects, meaning and memorability.

Imitation
There are further uses of the sound elements in language that also contribute to poeticality. These may be grouped under the general heading of 'mimesis' or imitation. The obvious example is onomatopoeia, where the sounds of the words in some way imitate what they describe. Here is an example from Tennyson:

> Dry clash'd his harness in the icy caves
> And barren chasms, and all to left and right
> The bare, black cliffs clang'd round him, as he based
> His feet on juts of slippery crag than rang
> Sharp-smitten by the dint of armed heels –
> And on a sudden, lo! the level lake
> And the long glories of the winter moon.

> (from Tennyson, 'Morte d'Arthur')

In this passage, the first five lines are full of hard, harsh sounds – clotted consonants and constricted vowels. Even the echoing of sounds clanging from the cliffs is imitated in the alliteration and the assonances (dry-icy-right; barren-chasms-black-clang'd-crag-rang; sharp-armed; smitten-dint). Then the last two lines come as a total contrast, with their liquid consonants and long vowel sounds.

Ted Hughes, in *Poetry in the Making* (1967), talks about 'words that live' – words that appeal directly to the senses: words

> we hear, like 'click' or 'chuckle', or which we see, like 'freckled' or 'veined', or which we taste, like 'vinegar' or 'sugar', or which we touch, like 'prickle' or 'oily', or smell, like 'tar' or 'onion'. . .

While it might be going too far to call such words 'onomatopoeic', they give a sense of the texture of the world they describe. Consider Hopkins'

> Glory be to God for dappled things –
> For skies of couple-colour as a brinded cow
> For rose-moles all in stipple upon trout that swim . . .

This provides many examples of the ways 'words that live' can work, making a sound-pattern that is itself a part of the meaning. Fred Sedgwick (1997) cites a wonderful discussion of this poem with a class of 5-year-olds, starting from the question, 'What do you think *couple-colour* means?' Once the children work out that it means two colours, the discussion flows:

> 'couple like two is like two colours on a cow's back . . . like on a fish, when you've caught it, the different colours . . . I like the f's and the s's in the second verse . . . but look, there's lots of f's in the first verse . . .'

Hughes himself, describing an otter, contrasts its movements in the water and out:

> Underwater eyes, an eel's
> Oil of water body. . .
> . . .Walloping up roads with the milk wagon.

> (from Hughes, 'An Otter' in *Lupercal*)

These are words you can feel as you say them, moving with the texture of life.

Rhythmic imitation

Rhythm can also be used for imitation. We have already discussed how it can be used to imitate the speaking voice or the mind thinking. Thom Gunn exploits it in that rare thing in English, a syllabic poem, 'Considering the snail':

> . . .I cannot tell
> what power is at work, drenched there
> with purpose, knowing nothing.
> What is a snail's fury? All
> I think is that if later . . .

> (from Gunn, 'Considering the snail' in *My Sad Captains*)

The rhythms seem hesitant, tentative, broken by the line endings. Here part of the meaning is what Ogden and Richards (1923), called signs of difficulty of reference. The rhythms imitate the expression of questioning wonder, someone searching for the right words.

The simplest form of rhythmic imitation is imitating some rhythm that exists in the real world. There are, for example, two famous poems that imitate the rhythms of a steam train, Auden's 'The Night Mail', beginning:

> Here is the Night Mail crossing the Border
> Bringing the cheque and the postal order . . .

> (from Auden, 'The Night Mail')

and Robert Louis Stevenson's 'From the Window of a Railway Carriage', which begins:

> Faster than witches, faster than fairies,
> Bridges and houses, hedges and ditches . . .

> (from Stevenson, 'From the Window of a Railway Carriage')

Both poems use metrical feet that start with a stressed syllable, and create urgency by varying the number of unstressed syllables between the stresses.

A poem that builds up speed with the steam engine is Stephen Spender's 'The Express'. And so does the reverse menu I learned at my mother's knee:

> Coffee, coffee, coffee,
> Cheese and biscuits, cheese and biscuits, cheese and biscuits,

> Prunes and custard, prunes and custard, prunes and custard,
> Beef and carrots, beef and carrots, beef and carrots,
> Fish and chips, fish and chips, fish and chips,
>   Soooooooooooup!

Rhythm can not only imitate things, but also emotions. 'Skimble-shanks: the Railway Cat', by T.S. Eliot, has a very exciting rhythm:

> There's a whisper down the line at 11.39
> When the Night Mail's ready to depart,
> Saying 'Skimble where is Skimble has he gone to hunt the thimble?
> We must find him or the train can't start.'

> (from Eliot, 'Skimbleshanks: the Railway Cat')

The rhythm here does not imitate anything specific, but it has a gusto and urgency that carries the story along.

So, if you are going to ask children to clap or tap in time with anything about a poem, clap in time to the rhythm, i.e. to the stress pattern, not to the syllables. More important, make sure that the rhythm comes across in performance, in individual reading and recitation or in choral work. But remember, the rhythm is not the same thing as the metre. Rhythm takes the meaning and the flow of the sentences into account, along with the metre.

THE TICKLE FACTOR AND THE TINGLE FACTOR

We began this chapter by remarking on the prevalence of contemporary comic poetry in primary schools and said, 'Fine, as long as it's not the whole diet'. Now I want to consider a balanced diet. While there are many dimensions to balance, the main one I want to dwell on is the balance between poems that tickle the chuckle-button and poems that prickle the back of your neck.

There is a great tradition of comic poetry in English, from 'John Gilpin' onwards, including many of the great nineteenth-century writers like Lewis Carroll and early twentieth-century writers like A.A. Milne, T.S Eliot and Hilaire Belloc. So don't get stuck on Spike Milligan, Brian Patten and 'jelly-belly' rhymes, good fun though they are. There are more kinds of comic and of nonsense than one.

If children are to grow in their appreciation of poetry and to go on reading it beyond primary school, they must encounter (to borrow Treehorn's phrase) poetry to grow on. There's drama and awe in Tennyson's 'The Eagle':

The Eagle

He clasps the crag with crooked hands;
Close to the sun in lonely land,
Ring'd with the azure world, he stands.

The wrinkled sea beneath him crawls;
He watches from his mountain walls,
And like a thunderbolt he falls.

Alfred, Lord Tennyson

It's also short enough to learn easily – as I remember doing. I also remember the emotions it roused in me – and the inspired painting I did! There is a good deal you could discuss – after all, the 'Objectives' do require you to discuss figurative language, personi-fication and so on. And you could go on to reading Emily Dickinson's 'A narrow fellow in the grass', Lawrence's 'Snake' and some of Ted Hughes' poems. Here are poems about a response to nature that recognises both the majesty and the terror of it.

While there is not space or occasion here for spelling out the whole range of poetry that might provide 'tingle' experiences, it will perhaps be valuable to mention narrative poetry, because this is a genre that hardly exists in contemporary poetry. You have to look back to an earlier age for the great poems like the ballads of Robin Hood, parts of 'The Rime of the Ancient Mariner', 'Young Lochinvar', 'Hiawatha', 'Morte d'Arthur', 'The Lady of Shallot', 'The Charge of the Light Brigade', 'The Ballad of "The Revenge"', 'The Highwayman', and so on. Not many of these poems were orig-inally written for children, but they are well suited to children approaching puberty and beginning to rehearse aspects of their adult roles: romance, courage, duty, tragedy and death.

IMPLICATIONS FOR PRACTICE

Children's readiness to read poems, even their preference for reading poems, given the choice, must depend on how poetry is introduced to them. An enthusiastic teacher who reads well-chosen poetry aloud with pleasure, expression and conviction will find chil-dren enquiring about poems they enjoyed listening to, and wanting to read them for themselves. And the nature of poetry books is that readers then continue to browse through the book. Any new poems they find they enjoy, they will want to share with friends and a chain reaction ensues. But all this presupposes a good selec-tion and display of poetry books and the initial lighting of the blue touch-paper!

Listening to poems can extend and expand children's range of experience and depth of enjoyment of poetry. Where a child may find a poem difficult or too long to venture into on her own, she may be happy to listen to it and tackle it with the focus and support of a class or group activity.

Here I shall try to summarise the kind of approaches to teaching poetry found in, for example, Benton and Fox (1985) and Carter (1998), that constitute 'good practice' and that will fulfil the requirements of *Framework for Teaching*. These approaches are designed to help children to capture their first reactions and to develop and refine their responses and their knowledge.

- *First encounters* Listening to poems; reading them; jotting down first impressions in an unself-critical, headlong fashion; asking children to make pictures in their heads, based on phrases in the poem
- *Exploring a poem to increase comprehension* Children in pairs sharing their first impression jottings; in groups, reading the poem aloud so as to express its form and meaning best; exchanging written impressions prior to discussion; small group exploratory discussion about meaning, without teacher; choosing a title (if this has been withheld), speculating about the story or character behind the poem; re-writing the content in another form to see what is lost; conferencing with teacher
- *Exploring a poem in terms of form and historical background* Discussing technicalities with teacher; learning about context of poem and poet from teacher or written materials; discussing technical effects in groups with a view to best reading or performance
- *Asking questions* The children formulating questions for themselves – what they want to know; for each other, factual and open-ended; and in groups framing their own questions about the poem for subsequent discussion with teacher
- *Becoming familiar with a poem* Learning by heart; expressively engaging with the poem, for example, in dance, art, making poem-posters; developing performance, etc.
- *Composing, writing own poems in response* In imitation of theme, form, figurative language
- *Collecting poems* Collecting and writing out personal favourites; critical selection for class anthologies; choosing for a poetic 'Desert Island Discs'; searching for poems on a theme or in a form
- *Performing, exhibiting and publishing* Recitation, choral speaking, dance, for example, for assembly; exhibition of art work, for example, illuminated texts, illustrations; word-processed books of class poems, etc.

These activities deal largely with imaginative response and are reasonably congruent with the *Framework for Teaching* objectives. My following observations largely follow the general pattern outlined above but pick up particularly on certain elements.

Listening

While children should be able to listen to tapes and to other people reading poems, the teacher has a prime responsibility to teach herself to read well and to practise the poems she reads to the class. If the poems are well chosen and worthwhile, and the reading is professional, the children will soon learn to attend to them. You can even discuss with the children the skills of listening: picturing the person and situation which the poem implies, picturing the scene described, feeling into the feelings, going with the flow of the language, observing its patterning, thinking of any questions it raises and trying to answer them, comparing it with other poems or experiences.

In some schools, assembly is a time for listening to poems – a poem a day throughout the year will provide the children with a wide experience. And making copies available for anyone who especially likes a particular poem will help children to feel a special relationship with the poems they have picked out.

Some teachers start the classroom day with a poem – attention, but no comment called for. The same poem, listened to in silence, is repeated each weekday until Friday, when it is discussed. By this time the children should be thoroughly familiar with it, they may even know it virtually off by heart. And they may have discussed it amongst themselves. But the silent listening is an occasion for working out one's own response and evaluations over time, without the need for instant and unreflective reactions – without even the need, initially, of trying to put it into words. Too many of our reactions, for example, to paintings, are instant, and strategies for holding back from the rush to judgement can lead to more reflectivity. A snap judgement like, 'It's rubbish!', is hard to go back on.

Reading, speaking and performing poems

Working on a public reading of a poem is a way of getting to know it extremely well. If the teacher explains how she practises reading poems for reading to the class, the children will accept its importance. We are not dealing here with elocution, but expression – reading for meaning. This can involve individuals or small groups working (perhaps with a tape-recorder) on a poem. Anne Harvey's *He Said, She said, They said* (1993) is an anthology of poems with conversations in them, ideally suited for small group performance, but other kinds of poems can also lend themselves to being divided into parts.

Alternatively, poems can be spoken chorally, with the group of children working out how they should speak it – in parts or in unison, quietly and softly or strongly and forcefully, with or without percussion to reinforce the beat. For example, Byron's 'The Destruction of Sennacherib' might go well with the percussive sounds of rattling spears and clashing armour getting gradually louder. Such small group speaking could be an appropriate Literacy Hour activity, since working out how to speak a poem is learning about what the poem means and how it means it.

Memorising poems

Benton and Fox (1985) remark, 'Memorizing "Ozymandias" at the age of ten can damage your health'! But they follow this remark with a 'But . . .' The desire to know a poem by heart can arise naturally out of genuine enthusiasm. It can be 'a potentially sustaining investment for later life', especially as people tend naturally to turn to poetry to express feelings at emotional junctures in their lives.

So should children only learn poems they desperate want to, or should they be made to learn 'teacher's-choice' poems off by heart? Both are possible, with suitable encouragement. With 'teacher's-choice', you can 'sell' the poem and inveigle children into learning, as discussed below. Group situations can support individuals, as with the learning and singing of nursery rhymes in Key Stage 1. In general, one should try to make it a matter of 'learning by heart' rather than 'learning by rote'.

In fact, Sandy Brownjohn (1982) found that children, already well into poetry, were enthusiastic about learning poems off by heart, particularly when given a free choice. There was no compulsion, but two-thirds of the children chose to do so, and their choices were varied and interesting, and included 'adult' poems that the children probably didn't fully understand, but which they responded to the music of. Children's ability to choose poems for themselves depends – obviously! – upon their acquaintance with, and access to, a range of poems. Brownjohn herself, as the teacher, learned one off by heart which she recited to the class, an achievement she found surprisingly rewarding and exhilarating!

Repetition is essential in learning off by heart – but the repetition can be made fairly painless. For class learning, you can put the poem up prominently somewhere, and the children read it aloud (*sotto voce*!) in passing each time they go by. You get them to re-read the poem a number of times, getting them to notice a new 'hook' each time: patterns of words (thematically linked words, repeated phrases, etc.), alliterative patterns, rhymes and half-rhymes, assonances, etc. And these hooks can be coded in colour on the class copy.

You read a strongly rhythmical poem, and ask them to work on a performance reading, doing justice to the rhythm and to emotional expressiveness. Reciting in unison helps support the slower learners. All these are purposeful excuses for repetition and attending to the memory-supportive sound patterns of the poem. For learning individual poems, children can apply the same sort of techniques.

Memory depends upon sight as well as sound (differently for different people), so writing out the poem and illustrating it can help, especially if the illustration has a narrative element to it. Learning the poem can help understanding just as work on understanding can help the learning.

Learning and reciting funny poems can be its own reward and may be a useful way to get reluctant boys into poetry. It is particularly important in this situation to insist on a good public performance. Children collapsing into giggles to cover up their failings is even worse in class than it is with so-called carol singers! This is a situation where some private lunch-time tuition might save the day.

Expressive engagement

Just as the National Curriculum specifies 're-presentation' as the culminating element in information skills, so translating the meaning, feelings or impact of a poem into another medium, dance, drama, art or music, may be the rewarding way for children to explore a poem and make it their own. Indeed, it could be that it is the best way with some poems (remember Tennyson's 'The Eagle'?). Painting a mural (following Rousseau, possibly) might allow children to explore the majesty and terror of Blake's 'Tyger' more satisfyingly than discussion. Sedgwick (1997) cites an instance where children's imaginative painting of the Lake Isle of Innisfree was a useful precursor to their discussion.

Children writing their own poems

What we are concerned with here is not so much the whole area of creative writing and poetry writing, but the kind of way that imitation is a means of coming to grips with a poem and learning more about it. One very natural response to a poem or a picture one enjoys is to want to do something like it. Imitation is somewhat like 're-presentation' and is a mode of comprehension – possibly one of the subtlest indices of comprehension, if only in terms of what is attempted, not what is achieved.

The work that the *Framework for Teaching* suggests on lay-out and form in poetry, together with learning the technical terms, becomes a much more vital activity if related to children's own writing. Sedgwick (1997) quotes John Mole:

> the way of encouraging the writing of poetry which I find most rewarding is *formal*, in the best sense of the word ... the classroom seems more relaxed and humming with invention when there are rules ...

This is in accord with Sandy Brownjohn's approach (1989) that begins with language games before moving on to the introduction of specific techniques and forms. Only when children have some grounding in these matters does she concentrate more on themes and ideas for writing about. Latterly she has dealt more in using poems for imitation (for example, Brownjohn, 1993a, 1993b).

Models, techniques and constraints are, in the right context, creatively liberating. Even so simple a strategy as writing, not in your own voice, but in the voice of another character, can free the flow of language, and such simple techniques as using repetition can give form and structure and a sense of deliberation to a poem. It is an everyday form of magic.

Performing, exhibiting and publishing

A sense of audience provides both a goal and a discipline for work. Whether the performance or exhibit is related to a 'proper' poem or the children's own poems, the aim of doing justice to oneself and the poem and a feeling of responsibility towards the audience, provide a sense of purpose. Similarly, written end-products need to be 'written in best' or word-processed, illustrated or illuminated. Brownjohn (1989) remarks, 'I have found that typing out the children's work and putting it into a large class poetry book does almost more than anything else to encourage children and give them confidence.'

Carter (1998) cites another, and potentially the most educative, kind of publication: children discussing their work with teachers and others. In some ways, the teacher giving attention and being interested in what the child has to say about the process of producing the work and what his or her aims and intentions were, is the most rewarding form of publication for the child. Brownjohn, likewise, is ready to give help and advice on technique (for example, where line-endings might come) and takes children's work home to read at leisure, when she can give it her full attention. She tells the children this, and thinks they appreciate it. It provides not only feed-back but the flattery of being taken seriously.

Exploratory discussion and conferencing

Exploratory talk is crucial – the tentative expression, the testing and developing of personal responses in discussion with other, non-threatening people. I have left this way of working with a poem till last, because there is so much to say about it, and the discussion of the rest of the chapter will grow out of it.

Is it not enough that children should laugh at comic poems or be thrilled or stunned by deeper poems? In certain cases, perhaps, yes. But more common is the situation of feeling something of the magic of a poem, but needing to talk yourself into a deeper understanding or experience of it. Even if a teacher-dominated discussion might do damage to children's feelings about a poem, children's discussions (even if nerve-rackingly for the teacher not under her immediate control) can be valuable, and can become more valuable, the more experience of such discussion the children have.

Whole-class discussions and small-group discussions have limitations as well as uses. In the whole-class discussion, the limitations include the dominance of the teacher's agenda and children's deferral to the teacher for angles, ideas and judgements; and the fact that relatively few children take an active part. Small-group discussion, on the other hand, may lack focus or lose its way in fruitless literalism.

Carter (1998) advocates the conferencing strategy developed by the National Literacy Project: small groups, with a scribe, who have to report back ultimately to a whole-class plenary, with the teacher finally making a summary and adding her own two-pen'orth. However, we all know as adults how unsatisfactory plenaries are. The danger for children is that the teacher's comments may come to seem the authoritative and only valid part, whereas it is the small-group work that has most potential for helping children to develop.

Carter talks about the children in small groups taking 'themselves on a sort of mental walk through the poem'. How might this go? Douglas Barnes explored the dynamics of such discussions in *From Communication to Curriculum* (1976). He called the children's groping towards a meaning in their discussions 'exploratory talk'.

CASE STUDY

Talking amongst themselves

Here is a transcript of such a discussion between four 11-year-old girls. They have simply been asked to discuss a poem called 'The Bully Asleep' by J.H. Walsh. Bill,

continued...

the bully, falls asleep in the classroom, and other children draw the teacher's attention to the situation. She says to let him be. Jimmy and Roger discuss how they can take revenge on him while he's asleep, but Jane feels sorry for him.

1 Well, the teacher's bound to notice.
2 Yes, really . . . because I mean . . . I mean if . . .
3 Or she could have gone out because someone had asked her for, or something . . . she probably felt really sorry for him so she just left him . . . The teachers do . . .
4 What really sorry for him . . . so she'd just left him so they could stick pins in him.
5 Oh no, she probably . . . with the 'whispered' . . . said 'whispered' . . .
6 Yes.
7 Yes, but here it says . . . um . . . oh 'Stand away from him, children. Miss Andrews stooped to see.'
8 Mm.
9 So you'd think she would do more really.
10 Yes, . . . you'd think she'd um . . . probably wake . . . if she would really felt sorry for . . . sorry for him she'd . . .
11 She'd wake him.
10 (cont.) . . . wake him.
12 Oh no! . . . No, she wouldn't send him home alone . . . because . . . nobody's . . .
13 His mother's bad.
14 Yes.
15 His mother would probably go out to work.
16 Yes he'd get no sleep if his mum was there.
17 Might have to . . . might have to turn out and work.
18 It might be . . . his mother's fault that really he's like this.
19 Oh it will be . . . It always is.
20 Look here it says um . . . 'His eyes are . . .' Where is it? 'His dark eyes cruel and somehow sad.'
21 I think that puts it doesn't it?
22 Yes.
23 There's always something like that.
(Pause)
24 He's unhappy. (Whispered)

(Barnes, 1976, pp. 26–7)

The first thing that strikes one, reading this transcript, is how disjointed it seems. But this is the nature of informal conversation, especially when people are thinking aloud. They seem to understand each other, be sharing a common mind.

Without any teacherly direction, they tackle the poem as it takes them. They treat it as a real-life episode to discuss, and are particularly taken with trying to interpret the teacher's role. It almost seems, at one point, they think the teacher overhears the plans for revenge and does nothing about it. They bring their knowledge and experience to bear in trying to make sense of the situation.

continued...

But how they do this is significant. Barnes observes that the language of their collaborative thinking aloud is marked by hypothetical expressions, 'she could have gone', 'she probably felt', 'You'd think . . .', 'Might have to . . .' This expresses a kind of tentativity that keeps possibilities open: every statement is open to correction or amendment, just as it implicitly appeals for agreement or confirmation. Interpretations are not foreclosed.

If children are to take an active part in their learning, exploratory talk, full of hesitations, false starts and so on, is one way in which they can bring what they are learning into relation with their existing world knowledge and views. There has to be a place for such vulnerable expression, and it may need the absence of the teacher to flourish.

Such small group discussion depends on the children 'expecting to find the text meaningful and therefore being willing to stay with it long enough to construct a meaning for themselves'. In this example, the approach is open and the children stick closely to the text, even if their remarks are not always what an adult might consider relevant and appropriate, and even if there is a tendency to accept uncritically whatever the other children say. Nevertheless, the girls' discussion compares favourably with that of one group of boys, in a similar situation, who treated their poem as if each line of it had a fixed 'right meaning', which closed approach precluded exploratory talk and the kind of discussion which might have helped them to make something of the poem.

Discussion points

1 How would you judge if a discussion had been worthwhile or a failed opportunity?
2 Can a teacher give pointers for discussion without setting the agenda?

CASE STUDY

Children on the Lake Isle

Discussions like the one given above are not solely the preserve of Year 6 children. Fred Sedgwick (1997) quotes a discussion by 7-year-olds about Yeats' 'The Lake Isle of Innisfree'. The discussion is just as focused, being concerned with decoding and meaning ('live' [adjective] you said, it's really 'live' [verb]'), with one child drawing another back from raising extraneous issues with the reproof, 'We're looking at this poem here'. The children quote from the text and try to determine its meaning, generally by paraphrasing and naturalising the language:

'"for peace comes dropping slow". Slowly peace comes . . .
There's tons of bees buzzing round in the glade and a glade is a kind of space in a wood.'

continued...

Sometimes they worry away at a phrase, never coming to a conclusion, but going round and round it again and again:

> '"Nine bean rows", that's a kind of mystery ... [then a good deal later] This poem's upside down ... nine bean rows, nine rows of beans ... that's upside down ...'

In context, it could be (but it is not clear) that he is questioning the grammatical inversion, 'Nine bean rows I will have there'. Certainly, at a later point, the grammar causes one or two confusions: 'What's "wattles made"?' 'I don't know.'

At one point they discuss the place-name itself, perhaps naively, but nonetheless relevantly:

B	It's inside a free, inside you're free everywhere
E	You're free everywhere and you can go anywhere on the island
T	But what about this first bit, what does Innis mean?
E	Inside this island, it's free on this island and if you go anywhere else you are stuck and if you go on this island you are free ...
J	It's really noisy in the city and it's really quiet on the island
E	Yeah and you're really free on the island ...

(Sedgwick, 1997, p. 170)

However misdirected and literal their way of trying to interpret the connotations of the name, they are getting at something true about the poem. They stick with the poem, correct some of their own misreadings, naturalise the poem to something they can understand and respond very positively and directly to the mood of the poem. It is hard to think that a teacher-led discussion would have led to more real learning.

Discussion points

1 Which is better, the teacher setting questions for the children or the children setting questions for the teacher?
2 After reviewing the tape of a discussion, what sorts of issues (if any) might the teacher usefully return to with the children?

The role of the teacher

If such discussions are part of Literacy Hour activities, the teacher will be available for guidance, even if not for the whole discussion. The guidance might take the form of setting initial questions or foci for discussion or asking the children to record any questions that their discussion alerts them to. The teacher might be listening in to, and possibly joining in, the discussion once it is under way. She may then nudge it in desirable directions or comment favourably on it before moving on. What might limit the usefulness of her joining in would be if she takes over the discussion or imposes her own agenda or judgements. The teacher must learn to trust the poem *and* the children.

Getting a small group to report back to her at the end of their discussion, or getting the children to tape-record their discussion, can be useful for focusing the children on the task, and for giving the teacher an idea of how profitable the discussion is being. After listening to the tape, the teacher may feel the need, for another occasion, to give guidelines for future discussions: for example, asking people to speak in turn, so that everybody can, and has to, contribute; to start every contribution with 'Perhaps ...'; or whatever rules she feels will help a particular group of children towards collaborative exploration.

Being open to the poem

Reading a poem is not like working out a problem – though that may be an element in reading. It is not about finding the right answer, or even understanding a concept. It is a different ball-game altogether. It is about being open to and affected by the poem.

What reading poetry certainly should *not* be, for primary school children, is an exercise in mini-literary criticism. Despite the way that the 'Framework for learning' objectives are written, all those protocols and prohibitions about practical criticism that some of us learned for A-level, do not apply at primary level. At primary level it is entirely appropriate that children should discuss and use their own experience in discussing a poem. They should seek parallel, illustrative and contrasting experiences in order to throw light on the poem. It is about being open to the poem and open to one's personal observations and experiences. And in a discussion situation, it is about being open to other people's responses, insights and experiences and bouncing ideas off each other.

Keeping close to the text

In addition to openness, we would want to find a sense of relevance and appropriateness, based in reference to the text. This might show itself in a willingness to question or take further other people's comments. For example:

B   What's core?
E   Our heart is the core
T   The middle of our heart is the core
J   like the middle of the island

(Sedgwick, 1997, p. 170)

The value of discussion

Discussion is a skill in itself, and is in some ways a model of the individual comprehension process. As Vygotsky (1962) suggested, verbal thinking is internalised dialogue, developed from the social experience of talking together. Some of this talking together is with peers, some with teachers. For us, as teachers, part of the challenge of teaching poetry comprehension is to allow the children to experience exploratory dialogue in order to be able to internalise its processes.

The approaches we have discussed have dealt, on the one hand, with indirect, oblique approaches of two kinds, through learning by heart, art and writing, and through learning about the techniques and forms of poetry. On the other, we have considered more direct approaches, through discussion. Now, perhaps we should consider how these things can all work together, within the model of the *Framework for Teaching*.

LITERACY HOUR WORK ON A POEM

Here I discuss how we might approach a particular poem. A big text version will be needed for the whole-class work. The discussion is designed to include as many aspects mentioned in the *Framework for Teaching* as possible. In real life, one would be more selective. The text is Shakespeare's song from *The Tempest*:

> Full fathom five thy father lies;
>> Of his bones are coral made;
> Those are pearls that were his eyes;
>> Nothing of him that doth fade,
> But doth suffer a sea change
> Into something rich and stange:
> Sea nymphs hourly ring his knell.
>>> Ding-dong!
>> Hark! now I hear them,
>>> Ding-dong bell!

Tackling a Shakespeare poem satisfies the criteria about using poetry from other ages and from significant poets. Since the poem needs both some introduction to contextualise it and because some of the grammar is strange, you might tell them something of the story – a kindly spirit called Ariel is singing a mysterious song of consolation to a young man who believes his father has drowned in a shipwreck. If you are tackling *The Tempest* more extensively, a fuller telling of the story would be appropriate (for example, using Garfield, 1988). And if you can get a recording of the song being sung, so much the better. This could be used to raise the question of genre, a song within a play. How important are the words in songs? How does singing make it different from saying it?

In any event, you will want to read it to the class, both with the children simply listening to it, and then subsequently, with them following the text. It would be worth getting an initial, private response to the feeling of the poem/song before looking at the text, perhaps by asking children to write down individually any descriptive words they feel appropriate.

Some questions about vocabulary will arise, and the simplest thing would be to explain about fathoms, sea nymphs and knells. It will also be useful to point out that coral was rare in Shakespeare's time, and was treated as a semi-precious stone; and that, in the 'language of jewels', pearls are associated with pain and grief.

But any questions about the curious inversions of grammar, let the children raise and puzzle over for themselves. In the whole-class session you might want to concentrate on more objective elements, like the rhymes, the refrain, the rhythm. These require more in the way of informed input, whereas the puzzles are best left for exploratory talk among the children in their groups.

The technical elements of rhyme and so on are best tackled first in relation to reading aloud, to choral reading and performance. If the first reactions have thrown up any descriptions of the mood the poem gives rise to – weird, sad, scary, dream-like or whatever – then you should seek children's suggestions about how you could read it as a class. Does it lend itself to parts? Would a background of strange sounds work well? Any other sound effects? Would girls' or boys' voices be better for different parts? Could a reading slightly out of phase, like an echo, be effective?

How should the structural characteristics of the poem affect the reading? For example, what do the layout on the page, the indentations, the rhymes and rhythm suggest? What other patterns of sound would one like to bring out? What are the key ideas or images that need to be foregrounded? Using different coloured highlighting pens on the enlarged text can help you in discussing these patterns. Working out a performance could be a whole-class or a small group activity. And by the time you have done all this, the children will pretty well know the poem off by heart. You could encourage them to do so for their performances.

Another aspect of the poem you could explore is the language and imagery. This is perhaps best done in small groups, but you might like to suggest a focus for discussion, but what sort of focus? Ideally, you want the children to make discoveries for themselves, even if they are not what you had in mind. Your aim is that children should be learning about how to read poems by opening up their responses to the poem. It doesn't matter if they get some things wrong (as you see it) or miss some things. Shakespeare can take it. So you could ask, 'When you hear the words, what do you see in your mind's eye? How does it make you feel? What do you think is happening? How would it make Ferdinand feel, seeing that he believes his father has drowned? Are there any puzzling bits? How does the puzzle make you feel?'

Fred Sedgwick (1997) quotes and comments on two discussions between some 8–11-year-olds on this poem. Here I select some bits from the transcripts:

> I thought it was about a statue ... There's been a shipwreck, you can tell because there are fish and there are bones, and there's pearls ... What is this sea-change? ... That's the tides ... Or it could be that he has died, and he has turned into a swarm of fish ... the sea-change is the weather changed and he got shipwrecked ... Rich and strange, that's the pearls that were his eyes ...
>
> He's changed into a fish – No, he's changed into a skeleton ... his bones turned into coral – and his eyes, his eyes, his eyes ... under the water all the colour came out of his eyes, and they went grey like pearls ...

> (Sedgwick, 1997, pp. 167–8)

The children talk themselves through the poem and into an understanding. They are focused and uninhibited, without wondering if they've got the right answer to satisfy the teacher. Some of the things they say are very mundane and literal, but perhaps these remarks constitute necessary clarifications and points of departure for their further thinking. Other comments which we might feel are off-beam, still add to the rich soup of suggested meanings ... Other perceptions are vivid and arresting. I doubt if I, as a teacher, could have given them an interpretation that would satisfy them better!

Any individual work that might be done on the poem had probably best be creative in some way – illustrating it, writing poems of their own (for example, Ferdinand's elegy for his father), writing an undersea description (maybe Tennyson's 'Kraken' could contribute here, along with the Cheltenham and Gloucester television commercial!), or writing about grief and consolation in relation, say, to a pet that has died. Discursive writing is unlikely to be profitable, even though discursive talk is.

Summary

Poetry, hopefully, has a new lease of life today, in the adult world, among children and in education. However, in encouraging its enjoyment, as teachers, we must not provide a diet solely of comic and performance verse nor dry up the sap of living response in children by concentrating on analysis and technique. Children should be encouraged to listen to poetry with attention and to learn poems off by heart. They should read widely, and this means the provision of poetry books as part of the normal reading materials in the classroom.

Poetry activities in the Literacy Hour should both introduce children to challenging poetry and to technicalities, but not at the expense of imaginative response. Critical to the development of response and analysis are exploratory discussions in small groups and the creative work, including poetry writing, that individuals develop in response to poems they have read and enjoyed.

- Children should encounter not only comic but also more serious kinds of poetry, to experience not only the 'tickle' but also the 'tingle' factor.

- This means poetry needs to be made available to children, by having it read to them well, and by having it available to read.

- Poetry can speak to our inwardness, to a sense of awe and wonder and potentiality that is not otherwise often experienced.

- With Key Stage 2 children, the kinds of response to poetry we are seeking to develop are not primarily analytic but personal, indicated by enthusiasm.

- It is unlikely children will be able to explain why they like what they do, so teaching approaches need to be oblique.

- Activities related to poetry are various, from listening to, speaking, and reading it, to learning it by heart, making selections and collections, imitating it in writing, devising presentations, art-works or performances, and exploring its structure and language in teacher-led sessions, or exploring its meaning in small-group discussions with other children.

Further reading

Carter, Dennis (1998) *Teaching Poetry in the Primary School*, David Fulton
Written in the light (or shadow, as he sometimes sees it) of the NC and the NLS, this book provides good advice and suggestions about 'modes of encounter between children and poetry', based on the Clwyd Poetry Project.

Sedgwick, Fred (1997) *Read My Mind*, Routledge
A stimulating and readable book based on the author's deep personal commitment and wide experience of teaching poetry in schools with children of all ages.

Wilson, Anthony with Hughes, Sian (eds) (1998) *The Poetry Book for Primary Schools*, The Poetry Society
An exciting compilation of inspirational pieces by well-known contemporary poets, many with considerable experience of working in schools.

Information and study skills 6

When you have read this chapter you should:

- be able to discuss the various skills involved in understanding information texts

- have available a repertoire of strategies for challenging and prompting children into understanding information texts

- be able to plan, prepare and implement a progression of activities that develop information skills

- be able to assess children's information skills and devise remedial strategies as required.

Introduction

In our present-day world, a child who does not grow up able to cope with written information and instructions is socially, intellectually and economically disadvantaged. While you can live a decent (if dull) life without novels and poetry, you can't live happily or make a decent living without swimming confidently in the sea of information in which we sometimes feel we are drowning! We need to be able to read the news and new information in our own specialist fields, we need to be able to cope with bureaucracies and business, and we need to be able to access and assess information relevant to the ways we spend our leisure and our money. And we also need to learn to decide what is relevant to us and to ignore the rest.

This means that children must learn not to be outfaced by written information and documents, to be prepared to learn from them and to learn to take a critical or sceptical slant on what they read. Children need to learn the skills and confidence to use written texts and to discard what is not of use or interest to them. And they need so to understand what they read that they can use the information for their own purposes.

We tend to take, and teach, an almost religious reverence for the written word and books. Maybe we feel we must read every word – for a sense of completeness or because we are afraid of having missed something. But not every book or text is 'the life-blood of a master spirit'! Milton's freedom to publish has to be matched by our freedom not to have to read every word that's printed! It may be true one should read every word of a novel, but not necessarily of an information text. There are new reading skills to be learned – skills of location and selection as well as of attention and assimilation.

Part of learning to read is learning how not to have to bother to read certain things – you may never need to read a whole book again! You certainly would not want to read a whole bus timetable. I'd be surprised if you read all of this book, or read it in the same order as it is presented! But I do hope you find some ideas to exploit in it – and that you have the skills to find them and to make them part of your thinking! After all, comprehension means relating what you read with what you already know, thus expanding and modifying your knowledge and understanding. And this act of relating things involves making judgements about meaning, relevance and reliability.

I will begin this chapter, then, with a discussion of the requirements of the National Curriculum and the National Literacy Strategy *Framework for Teaching* and discuss them in relation to various accounts of what constitutes information or study skills. In some ways I prefer the term 'study skills' because it has wider implications than 'information retrieval skills', which is what 'information skills' is sometimes taken to mean (see Horner, 1998). The statutory requirements certainly imply the wider view.

THE REQUIREMENTS OF THE NATIONAL CURRICULUM AND THE NATIONAL LITERACY STRATEGY

Some background

The HMI report *The Teaching and Learning of Reading in Primary Schools* (1990) found that:

> in Key Stage 2 (7 to 11 year olds) reading received less
> systematic attention as the children grew older and other
> demands arose from the widening curriculum. By Year 6. . .
> the majority were not being challenged to develop advanced
> reading skills. . .

Certainly there is some tendency, after initial reading skills have been established, to let reading look after itself. Once children are 'reading widely on their own', what more is there to do? Reading is so much part and parcel of every activity in the KS2 classroom, everything the children do is surely, *inter alia*, reading practice? And if they are reading information books for project work, etc., surely they are developing and practising information skills?

Yes and no. Certainly any reading activity is going to help reinforce word identification skills, but I think that even as adults most of us feel our study skills aren't everything we would like them to be. We would all like to be able to gather the gist of what we are reading more quickly and efficiently. We would like to be able to skim effectively, and to feel sure we haven't missed out on anything important. We would like to be able to find resources and find our way round these resources more capably than we do. We would all like to be able to take notes efficiently and effectively. All these things are advanced reading skills. And like all skills, they can be learned more or less well, sooner or later. As teachers, we will want our children to learn them sooner and learn them well.

HMI (1990) noted that classes achieving high standards were characterised by the wide variety of reading materials, in addition to scheme materials, that were provided, and this provision was not left to chance. The teachers planned it so that children read a good variety of fiction and poetry and information from both books and non-book sources. The non-books materials included instructions, signs, maps, lists, indexes, directories, newspapers, magazines and advertisements.

In May 1994, the SCAA *English Draft Proposals*, spelled out some of the advanced reading skills with which HMI had been concerned:

- the confidence to choose and read more challenging texts
- an increasing sensitivity to meanings beyond the literal
- a growing ability to distinguish between more and less significant aspects of a text
- asking and answering questions about a text
- an ability to summarise the main points of a text and relate their summary to the full text
- the use of appropriate reading strategies when seeking information
- a growing ability to use reference skills to find specific information
- the increasingly confident use of information retrieval systems and libraries . . .

The need both to provide information materials for reading and to develop a specific set of skills appropriate to reading information was clearly on the agenda.

The National Curriculum

In 1995, the National Curriculum specified that children at Key Stage 2:

> should read and use a wide range of sources of information, including those not specifically designed for children

and that they:

> should be taught how to find information in books and computer-based sources by using organisational devices to help them decide which parts of the material to read closely . . .

Information or study skills were required to be an explicit, not just an implicit, part of the curriculum.

Children should be given the opportunity to read information texts for different purposes, for example, for general interest or for study purposes, and should be helped to adopt appropriate strategies for the different purposes. In relation to study purposes, for example, working on a topic or project, they should be taught to:

- pose pertinent questions about a topic they are investigating
- identify the precise information that they wish to know
- distinguish fact from opinion
- consider an argument critically
- make succinct notes
- use dictionaries, glossaries and thesauruses to explain unfamiliar vocabulary
- note the meaning and use of newly encountered words
- re-present information in different forms
- use library classification systems, catalogues and indexes.

These specifications are so succinct but suggestive that they leave much of the interpretation and elaboration to the teacher ('Use your loaf!', as Sir Ron Dearing put it). For example, do children need to identify 'the precise information' *before* or *after* they find it? That is, do they have to be totally clear about what facts they are searching for before they begin, or is it that they need to be able to recognise unexpected but relevant facts when they come across them? It would be a pity to limit children's enquiry to 'information retrieval', although this is a term used by Horner (1998), writing on behalf of SCAA. One's reading should open one up to new perceptions, not simply be a resource for supporting one's old ideas.

The National Literacy Strategy

The National Literacy Strategy, on the other hand, aims to be more precise and prescriptive.

In 1998, the National Literacy Strategy listed Non-fiction Reading Comprehension amongst its objectives from the beginning of Year 1. This is followed by Writing Composition, the specific objectives of which include what the National Curriculum means by 're-presentation', the recording or reporting of the information acquired from reading by either 'putting it in your own words' or translating it into some other format or medium.

The point about 're-presentation' is that the information is not just to be copied out, but is to be exploited, interpreted or transformed in some way that requires the child to have processed it mentally before reproducing it in some transmuted form. These are sophisticated skills which, like effective note-taking, are taught as Study Skills with higher education students. But now they also find a place in primary education – though presumably not at the same level of sophistication! There is a recognition that reading for information demands its own array of advanced reading skills, and that children should be encouraged to develop them from the beginning.

THE CATEGORISATION OF INFORMATION SKILLS

One of the more influential categorisations of information skills was propounded by Winkworth (1977) and has been discussed by Wray (1985, 1994), among many others. The categorisation is presented as a series of steps in undertaking a task:

1 Define subject and purpose: having a need for or interest in acquiring some information.
2 Locate information: you have to know where and how to find the sort of information you want.
3 Select information: some information will be relevant to your purposes, while some not.
4 Organise information: different bits of information may need to be related to each other for your purposes.
5 Evaluate information: you need to decide whether you have sufficient information and whether it is reliable.
6 Communicate results: this assumes the purpose is communication, not use.

This categorisation is fine for thinking about a research exercise or using a timetable. It appears to have been devised in relation to topic or project work. But it doesn't in any way deal with reading information for interest's sake. It will not describe the activities of a boy reading up about his favourite football team, for whom *any* information may be grist to the mill. It does not apply in all details to reading for more organised information, as with a boy reading a book about how aeroplanes fly – he wants to know it all, and he has no previous information in terms of which to evaluate what he reads. He wants to *know*, and maybe he wants to *use* the information in designing a glider, but he has no (immediate) interest in communication (but maybe a home-made glider should count as 're-presentation'?).

Similarly, the communication criterion does not apply to reading instructions or recipes: you don't read a recipe to communicate the information, but to use it in making a cake or whatever. Nevertheless, any information search will involve some of these steps, even if we have to stretch our definitions a bit. After all, 'If I'd known you were coming I'd have baked a cake', does suggest a cake *can* be some kind of communication!

A categorisation of skills does not, in itself, suggest a programme of instruction in skills over the primary years. It deals with the use and co-ordination of different skills in a coherent procedure. This procedure can be carried out at different levels of sophistication. What this procedural model offers, then, so far as programme planning is concerned, is a goal. It doesn't specify how you get to that goal. That is a subject we will return to in due course, later in the chapter.

Search, comprehend, exploit

We can perhaps group Winkworth's six procedural skills under three more general imperatives: search, comprehend, exploit. And we can do the same with the National Curriculum and Literacy Strategy requirements.

In relation to information texts, we can summarise the requirements of the National Curriculum and the Literacy Strategy, discussed above, under the three general headings:

- search skills, including alphabetic skills
- comprehension skills, including critical skills
- and exploitation skills, including note-taking and re-presentation skills, using information for new purposes.

For example, if we look at the objectives for Year 3, Term 1, we can see that '18 to locate information . . .' belongs under the 'search skills, including alphabetic skills' category; 16, 17, 19 and 20, concerned with distinguishing genres and grasping the gist of passages, belong in the critical comprehension category; and 21 and 22, concerned with recording and writing, using the information acquired by reading, belong in the 'exploitation' category.

Alphabetic and search skills

Alphabetic and search skills are concerned with finding suitable information sources. First you need to decide *what* information you are seeking, then you have to decide *where* you might look for it and then you need to know specifically *how* to locate it.

Alphabetic skills: looking up words

First, you need to know or decide what you are searching for. Imagine you have come across the word 'artefact' in your reading and want to find out what the word means. Where will you look? Presumably, in a dictionary. How will you find the word? You use alphabetical order. But how do you use alphabetical order? First, you open the dictionary near the beginning, because you know that the first letter, 'a', comes at the beginning of the alphabet. Then you look at the top of the page to see the header word and compare its spelling with your target word to see whether the first letter is 'a', or comes before or after it; and if it is 'a', to see whether the second letter comes before or after, or is, 'r', and so on. Thus you decide which direction through the dictionary to turn the pages ... Then you may need to scan the page, looking at the head-words ... I could go on spelling out the programmed stages of looking up a word, but you would learn more from doing it yourself and noting the complex of programmed procedures you employ!

It is good to be reminded what a complex procedure it is – even when you know the alphabet perfectly well. How much more diffi- cult it must be if you have to repeat the alphabet *sotto voce* to yourself in order to work it out! Simple practice at saying the alphabet, starting at different points; working forwards and backwards, saying which letter comes next; saying if a letter comes before or after a given letter; trying to open a dictionary at roughly the right place in the alphabet and putting letter cards or words into alphabetical order, all help with establishing that flexible, over-learned knowl- edge of the alphabet that is invaluable for looking things up effortlessly.

Looking up spellings

You might now like to think out what the procedure is for using the dictionary for looking up a spelling, rather than a meaning. For example, how do you spell /artefact/? Try noting down the proce- dural programme a child needs to apply. This is a much more complicated task than looking up a word when the spelling is known. When a spelling is not known, the child has to hypothe- sise about possible spellings, using phonic skills and knowledge of plausible spelling sequences, and then check them out. And if she uses the *Oxford Primary School Dictionary*, she may misleadingly be led to believe that 'artifact' is not an acceptable spelling!

In practising this skill, children need to dare to guess about possible spellings. They should be encouraged to try writing out a spelling, sounding the word in chunks as they go, and looking to see if it looks right. Then they can look it up in the dictionary. If the hypothesised spelling is proved wrong, they need to consider alternative ways of spelling the word. Of course, children will find really anomalous spellings like 'psychic' or 'wraithe' or 'gnome' impossible, unless they have some partial visual memory of the word. The teacher can drop hints if the word is really obtuse – for example, the teacher could inform the children that the word /sign/ is related to /signal/, or that /knowledge/ is related to /know/. But what the teacher will primarily aim to do is remind the children of spelling patterns they know and which might apply. The teacher tries to encourage children to explore and deploy the knowledge they already possess.

In general, alertness to spelling patterns and hypothesising about possible spellings can be encouraged by playing 'alternative spelling' games. A rhyming dictionary could be helpful. How many ways of spelling /peak/ are there? 'Peak', 'peek', 'peke' and 'pique' are all legitimate. But adding incorrect spellings are also instructive – 'ball', 'bawl', 'baul', 'borl' and 'boarl'. The game is to find incorrect spellings that can be justified by analogy with other words, for example, Paul, or, board. Such games feed into spelling alertness and the development of orthographic reading skills. And you can use the rime-onset domino cards we referred to in Chapter 2 to help.

Choosing a research target

So much, then, for alphabetical skills. Now we need to look at the broader picture, which starts with deciding what kind of information you are looking for. Choosing the research target depends upon intended outcomes. Imagine a child is interested in the topic of volcanoes. He may simply want a book about volcanoes; or he may have more specific questions in mind – What is a volcano? What kinds are there? Can you tell when a volcano is about to erupt? Why aren't there any in Yorkshire? If the boy is simply interested in the subject and is choosing a book to read, then the target is simply a suitable book or two.

If, however, the intended outcome is related to a topic on volcanoes and the activity has a particular goal, for example, a written project or an explanatory table-top model, then determining research targets may be more complicated but also more specific. There may be stages to go through in this:

1 Review what you know about volcanoes.
2 Decide what sort of things you would like to know about, for example, What's it like inside a volcano? What happens to people when there's an eruption?
3 Decide what sort of re-presentations might be best to show what you've found out, for example, building an exploded model of a volcano or writing a booklet about famous eruptions in history.
4 Consider what sort of information you might be looking for, for example, an annotated diagram or picture of a volcano.
5 Write out questions you would like answers to, for example, What makes a volcano erupt? What happens when it does? Where are the nearest volcanoes? When did they last erupt? Were any people hurt?
6 Put questions into a coherent order, so that any answers will flow one into the next.

This last requirement is perhaps the most difficult. For example, the child has to understand that to consider the question why there are no volcanoes in Yorkshire, requires him first to know what conditions create volcanoes in general and whether these conditions apply to Yorkshire. Teacher help is likely to be required in thinking this sequence through.

Finding the literature
Then there are the skills of knowing where you might go to look, who you might write to, where to find addresses, how to find your way round a library, etc. In the first instance, children will probably have to look either through a pre-selected topic box of books or in a class or school library. In the topic box, children may simply look at covers and titles to choose a suitable book to start looking at.

With a library, there is the organisation to negotiate. Children will need to be taught about how the library is organised and how to find books on specific topics. Different libraries are organised in different ways, but children's attention should be drawn to signs, shelf-labels, catalogues, subject indexes and so on. If children are using a public library, they should also be ready to seek assistance from librarians who are generally eager to help and use their expertise when presented with a specific challenge (librarians actually *like* people, especially children!).

There are also IT information sources: for example, the school may have CD-ROMs of encyclopedias, etc., and even an Internet search engine. However, accessibility and time constraints are likely to limit the usefulness of IT except for special purpose and occasions. But children can be encouraged to use home resources if available.

Certainly, colour printouts of useful illustrations and diagrams can add a great deal to the presentation of topic work.

Finding your way round a book

An important comprehension skill is knowing how to find your way round a book: using the title, contents and blurb (the description of the book on the back cover) to evaluate its usefulness; and then the contents page, index, chapter and sub-heading to find your way round the information. You can play information search games with a list of questions and a pile of books. For example:

1 Select two children and let them decide who is to be the instructor and who the hunter.
2 You ask the question, for example, Is a Fly Agaric poisonous?
3 The instructor then has to decide what the question tells her about the subject, talking it through, for example, 'I don't know what a Fly Agaric is, but if it is a fly and could be poisonous, it might be a stinging or biting insect. Or it could be a snake. Or it might be poisonous to eat. Let's see if we've got a book about insects or snakes or a book about things to eat.'
4 The instructor has to tell the hunter what to do, for example, 'Read me the names of the books on the table. Is any of them about poisons or snakes or insects or things you could eat? Right, look at the mushroom book because that's the only one about things that you can eat. Look at the contents page. Is there a chapter about poison? Right, look up page 40, then. Can you see anything about Fly Agaric? Nothing on that page? Are there any sub-headings? No. Right, look at the first sentence of each paragraph. No mention of Fly Agaric? How long is the chapter? That's too long. So let's try the index at the back. Look up Fly Agaric. Is it there? What page does it say? Look up page 114. Is it about Fly Agaric? Can you see anything about poison? Read me what it says. Right, Fly Agaric is a poisonous mushroom, but not as poisonous as Death Cap.'

This method of getting the child to talk through the procedure allows you, and the rest of the children, to monitor what is going on, and by making the procedure explicit, it confirms the skills involved and helps the children to internalise them. As all the children will want a turn, it is best, perhaps to do it with one or two children in a whole-class shared-text session and then to let small groups practise it as a guided activity.

Skimming and scanning

The example given above involved the use not only of the large-scale organisational features of a book, title and cover, contents page, and index, but also more local features like sub-headings and paragraphs. It also involved skills like skimming and scanning. These are skills that can be practised separately.

Skimming is the process of flipping through the pages fairly fast, trying to locate the sort of places where you might find what you are looking for. You might be noting page headings, sub-headings and illustrations, seeking something relevant to your purposes. At a slightly more sophisticated level, you might look at the first sentences of paragraphs, because in non-fiction texts, the first sentences of paragraphs are often the 'topic sentence' that tells us the main idea or subject of the paragraph. If you are lucky, the book may provide a summary at the end of each chapter, so you can readily use the summaries to find out whether you need to read the chapter more thoroughly.

When you are not really looking, sometimes a word that is of special significance to you, like your name, or a word connected with a particular interest of yours, will seem to leap out of the page at you. 'Scanning' is the term for exploiting this potentiality in skilled reading. Your brain is seeking words that are meaningful to you faster than you can consciously pay attention. The knack of scanning is to let your pre-conscious brain work on your behalf by asking it to look for particular key words. So, in the example given above, it was not necessary for the hunter to read every word, but to let his eyes wander down page 114, looking out for the key words 'Fly Agaric', 'poison' or 'poisonous'. Hopefully, the words will leap out of the page at her.

Children can be given practice in skimming by getting them to try to find the relevant part of a book without using the contents or index pages, simply by flipping through the book, taking in the minimal amount of information from headings, pictures, captions and so on. It is not a fool-proof method of finding what is wanted, but it can save time.

Similarly, you can get children to practise scanning. For example, when we are using a dictionary, we may well skim the page headers to locate the right page, but it is probably quicker, then, to scan the page, letting your eye seek your target word, rather than methodically working out where it is according to alphabetical order. Head words in dictionaries are printed in **bold** to facilitate successful scanning.

Scanning can be practised on photocopied pages. You can give the children a question to answer from the text and let them choose a key word from the question to scan the page for, to help them find the answer. Hopefully, the children will be able to answer the question more quickly by scanning than by reading the whole page. After all, the skills of skimming and scanning are part of the process of not spending unnecessary time and effort in seeking information, of not having to read whole textbooks ever again!

Critical comprehension skills

Comprehension depends upon intensive reading of the text, not skimming or scanning. We have said that comprehension is a matter of actively making sense of a text by interpreting the new information in the light of what we already know, and reorganising what we already know in the light of the new. How much we comprehend depends to a large degree on how much we know about the subject beforehand, because understanding builds upon what we already know and bring to the text. Activating what we already know is a skill in itself, and this is why we ask children to remind themselves of what they already know about a topic before they begin. Then comprehension depends upon how effectively we read the text, being alert to the links, connections and structure of the information.

It certainly help with comprehension if we have some idea, a kind of preview, of what we are going to read before we begin. Titles can be very important for providing such contextualising pre-organisers, and some texts provide brief summaries at the beginning of each chapter. Similarly, summaries at the ends of chapter, designed as useful reminders of what the chapter has dealt with, can provide a useful succinct structural framework in case, while reading, we can't see the wood for the trees. The sophisticated reader may well read the summary at the end of the chapter both to decide whether the chapter is worth reading and to act as a pre-organiser before reading the chapter.

A good model for writers of information texts is to follow the bishop's advice about sermons to the new curate: First, tell them what you're going to tell them. Then tell them. Then tell them what you've told them. Not a bad model for lessons, either – though some psychologists think people need to review information *five* times, not merely three, before it becomes lodged in long-term memory! We all know the experience of having to read and then re-read a text, sometimes more than once, to make sense of it. The strategy of re-reading, after a break, is something we may need to help children with.

The value of prior knowledge

One of the problems for children is that they don't necessarily have much information to bring with them to an information text, nor a framework of ideas that permits them to determine relevance and the relative importance of different pieces of information. To return to our example of the boy who wanted to find out about how aeroplanes fly: without some established concepts or without a framework of questions to guide his approach to the text, it is questionable how much coherent sense he will take from it. Without sufficient background in physics, he may, mistakenly, interpret the diagram of the 'angle of incidence' in terms of the wing sliding up a ramp of air and interpret the arrow representing 'lift' as the air dynamically pulling upwards on the wing.

Because of these problems, texts for children are specially adapted in their kinds of explanations. As we saw in Chapter 3, texts tend to be written with a certain kind of reader in mind, and offer hand-holds for that reader to grasp. Readers are expected to fill in certain gaps in the text and make 'bridging inferences' which depend upon the knowledge the reader brings to the text. Writers for children try to make these gaps as small (and the inferences as easy) as they can. Some try to make their writing as narrative-like as possible.

Even so, there is a tendency for writers to over-estimate how much children already know and bring with them. Those hand-holds, relating to prior knowledge and experience, often aren't effectively there for the children. The teacher's role often is, when a child has problems with understanding an information text, to help the child find her own relevant prior experience and apply it to the context.

The registers of information texts
Further, the styles of writing (registers) of information books can create obstacles for young readers in addition to any difficulties they may have with the content. For children who are used to chronological narrative following the actions of individuals, non-chronological writing and impersonal and generalised expression can be difficult to grasp. And such writing also tends to use unfamiliar grammatical constructions like passives. Argument and explanation often require, at the text level, abstract patterns of organisation and, at the sentence level, complex grammar, with subordinate clauses, logical connectives and condensed information content (consider this sentence, for example!).

Sub-headings, etc.
Children need to be specially introduced to the use of chapter headings, sub-headings and other structural devices to help them see the overall pattern of what they are reading. One good way of getting them to understand this is, as a DART (Directed Activity Related to Text) activity, to get them to put sub-headings into a passage of text, in order to make its structure clearer.

The organisation of information

We can discuss some important criteria in relation to structure and expression in comparing two books about dinosaurs, one a reference book, the other a reading-scheme book. The Piccolo *Dictionary of Dinosaurs* (Bastable, 1977) begins with a section, 'How to use this book', guiding the reader through, not only the organisation of the book, but also through the information in a very helpful way – if the child has the patience to follow its advice.

The Collins Pathways *The Age of the Dinosaurs* (1996) is organised differently, since it is not an out-and-out reference book but is something of a hybrid. It tries to avoid too much solid writing and technical language. For example, it avoids the terms 'ornithischian' and 'saurischian', and explains the distinction between 'bird-hipped' and 'lizard-hipped' body forms with a helpful diagram that distinguishes clearly between the upright stance, high-held body and straight legs of bird-hipped dinosaurs, and the low-slung bodies and exaggerated cabriole legs of the lizard-hipped dinosaurs. As a more modern book, it uses colour and graphic presentations more than the older book, which depends much more on words.

The Pathways book has an index and a bibliography but no contents page. The timeline along the bottom of the pages has inadequate explanation. While, with the help of the index, specific information can be identified, the book is designed more to fascinate by facts than as a text-book or research tool.

The styles of exposition are different. The Piccolo book, for example, tells us the weight of Apatosaurus (or Brontosaurus) and graphically explains this as 'the same as about six elephants!' The Pathways book provides a picture and a size-indicating icon showing two buses '× 2' – which might mean, but probably doesn't, that it was as big as four buses! The Piccolo book tells us that Archaeopterix was 'pigeon-sized', but the icon in the Pathways book shows a bit of a bus '× 1/10', which is not very helpful! The Piccolo book wins on imaginability.

But its linguistic expression is sometimes a bit more complex. Compare these two passages:

> . . .if it [Archaeopterix] had not been discovered with fossil feather impressions it surely would have been classed as just another small, land-bound dinosaur.

(from the Piccolo Dictionary of Dinosaurs, *p. 16)*

> Archaeopterix looks like a small dinosaur from its fossil skeleton. But a close look at the fossil shows the outline of feathers surrounding the bones.

(from The Age of the Dinosaurs, Collins Pathways, *p. 11)*

For a child, the hypothetical 'if it had not . . . (then) it surely would . . .' construction is potentially very confusing. Because, in fact, it had been and it wasn't – if you see what I mean! By hypothetical indirections pointing directions out is too sophisticated for most child readers.

In many ways, while the dictionary gives more information more authoritatively, and its style of writing is quite bright, the grammar and solid masses of print might be off-putting. By contrast, the layout, pictures and presentation of the Pathways book will make it much more attractive to children.

What I want this comparison to do is not to recommend one of these books in preference to the other (after all, the Piccolo book is probably no longer in print), but to indicate some of the kinds of criteria which you might apply in selecting information books for children, like authoritativeness, accessibility and user-friendliness in language and presentation.

Critical reading

Critical reading extends the notion of comprehension beyond simply understanding what has been presented by linking it into your existing corpus of knowledge. It involves evaluating what has been comprehended. You don't passively absorb what the writer tells you, but you decide whether it is fact or opinion, whether it is relevant to your purposes, whether it answers all the questions you have, whether it fits in with what you already know and, if not, whether it is reliable, etc.

Self-monitoring comprehension

Self-monitoring comprehension is perhaps the first and most important critical skill: to be alert to whether you have understood what you have read or not, and whether you need to re-read it or seek some further information elsewhere. This issue was discussed at some length in Chapter 3.

The easiest situation for a child is to recognise when she doesn't know the meaning of a particular word. It is harder to recognise when you haven't understood a sentence, and even harder to recognise when you haven't understood the relationship between information in different sentences.

Part of the problem is that children don't necessarily expect to understand everything they read – after all, a lot of what goes on in the world must necessarily pass them by, whether it doesn't relate to their interests in life or whether they don't have the background information to relate it to. But children do have a natural curiosity, and it is our job to enlist this curiosity in the search for meaning. We want children to feel annoyed if they don't understand something and to insist on explanation.

One way of promoting such attentiveness is to tell them you are going to try to trick them with some nonsense that doesn't fit into a passage. For example, the activity below for upper juniors asks the children to cross out any nonsense or irrelevancies that have been introduced into the passage. (This activity to be carried out initially in pairs to promote discussion and explicitness.)

Cross out any bits in the following passage that don't belong and stop it making sense:

The word 'dinosaur' means 'terrible lizard'. Dinosaurs lived on earth for over 150 million years and died out 64 million years ago. Man has only lived on earth for a little over 2 million years, so men were very frightened of dinosaurs and lived in caves to hide from them. Dinosaurs were reptiles, and had cold blood. They all laid eggs. They sat on their eggs to keep them warm.

With younger children, you may need to provide more immediate and gross contradictions, for example, 'Rabbits only eat grass and lettuce and things like that. They specially like sardines.'

Making notes

Making notes actively organises understanding and assists memory. It is not only a useful skill for many practical purposes, but it is also a useful activity for teaching and checking on children's critical comprehension.

The purpose of note-making is not just to help memory but also to help the note-maker organise her new knowledge. Organised knowledge is more memorable than unorganised knowledge; and the process of organising it makes it yet more memorable!

Making notes involves and develops various critical skills. Good notes both select the important information and record its hierarchical structure, using sub-headings, indentations, numberings, etc., to organise the information. Critical reading, then, involves selection and attention to the hierarchical structure of the information, for example, what is the key information, what is secondary or simply illustration.

Children have to be taught how to take notes to focus their reading. They won't be able to do this without guidance and practice. You can introduce some of these skills through listening comprehension:

- You tell the children you are going to read them a passage and they each have to think of a suitable title for it. After they have done this, they discuss their titles in small groups (four is optimal) and choose what they think is the best title. You read the passage again, for them to check they are happy with their title. Then you can have a plenary discussion, with people explaining why they think their titles are best.

- You provide the children with some questions relating to a passage you are going to read to them. You tell them they mustn't write anything down till you have finished reading. This ensures that they will have had to remember the information but will probably not remember the exact wording, so they will have to find their own words. Then, in small groups the children can discuss their answers and agree on a version. You read the passage again for them to check and confirm an answer they want to stand, which, as before, they can justify in a plenary discussion.

- You tell the children the subject that you are going to read a passage about, and in small groups they write a set of questions they would like the passage to give them answers to. Then you read them the passage, and they record the answers they found, and also make notes on what interesting information they learned that they hadn't been looking out for. They should also note the questions they did not get answers to and try to think why not (were they the wrong questions? was the passage inadequate?) and where they might look to try to find the answers. Groups can share their experiences.

Similar activities can be carried out using written passages, but the great danger with this is that children are inclined to write out, word for word, what is in the text, because they feel this is the certain way to get answers right. Much 'topic work' tends, sadly, to consist of such basic copying.

We want the information to go through the children's understanding and to stay in the children's heads, and simple copying doesn't promote this. A better arrangement is to get children to read up the information, make notes on it, and then write up their topic from the notes, rather than straight from the textbook. In this way, the children will have had to process the information. Part of this processing is the note-making because making notes demands the crucial skills of selection and distillation, and actively organises understanding.

The following devices variously help children to select the most important information, to escape from dependence on the wording of the text and to clarify the information structure. The texts initially should be photocopied passages that the children can write on:

- *Underlining key words or ideas* with a limited number of underlinings allowed, enforcing selection (this is an activity initially best carried out in pairs to promote explicit discussion). As a development from this, the children may then write out phrases, using the key words, to make the ideas clear. Then they can organise the phrases as a list, possibly changing the order, if this will make things clearer, numbering the items.
- *Constructing checklists*, for example, of materials or procedures needed for a recipe or a construction or looking after gerbils.
- *Graphic (in the first instance, wordless) representations* (for example, how to make a cake; how the pyramids were built; a categorisation of dinosaurs; drawings from descriptions). The children can use diagrams, maps, flow-charts, strip cartoons, etc., as appropriate.
- *Making up a matrix to record information* (initially, the matrix may need to be given; then making up a suitable matrix in relation to information being sought is one task, and filling it in is another) A matrix might look like Figure 6.1.

Figure 6.1

Animals in the Mezozoic Era

	Type	Walked on	Food
Dinosaurs	bird-hipped	2 legs and 4	vegetarians
	lizard-hipped	2 legs	carnivores
		4 legs	vegetarians
Other animals: icthyosaurs, rhynchosaurs, placodonts, etc.			

- *Making up a word explosion or web from a central concept* While the matrix requires decisions about some initial categories, a web can tend to grow more organically, even if a point comes when it needs to be revised and redrawn. See Figure 6.2.

Figure 6.2

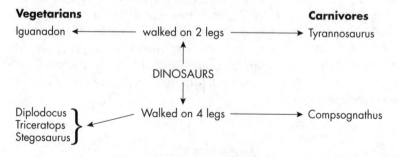

Vegetarians   **Carnivores**

Iguanadon ←——— walked on 2 legs ———→ Tyrannosaurus

↑

DINOSAURS

↓

Diplodocus
Triceratops } ←——— Walked on 4 legs ———→ Compsognathus
Stegosaurus

- *Using a proforma for recording* (a), what you already know; (b), what you want to find out; (c), what you have found out, including anything you hadn't anticipated; (d), what you now think/feel about the subject. This sort of proforma can be used subsequently as a 'writing frame' (see David Wray, *Teaching Writing at Key Stage 2*, in this series) for subsequent extensive writing.

Writing summaries of passages is a very sophisticated activity, too hard for many students (never mind children!), who still copy out key sentences! But writing summaries or numbered notes can readily develop from some of the activities given above, particularly the first one. Here is an example of how this might work in a sequence of lessons.

Example: an integrated comprehension teaching activity (Year 6)
Provide the children with copies of the chosen passage and then read it to them aloud. Ask them if there are any words they don't understand and try to explain them. Explain to the children that they might not understand all the ideas, but this doesn't matter, because as they read and re-read the passage, some of the ideas will get clearer and, in any case, what you want them to do is to choose the five most important ideas that make sense to them. Once they have chosen them, they can underline them. Let them discuss their choices in small groups, but let each child make up his or her own mind about what to mark up.

Consider the following passage as an example:

> Ekranoplans were first invented in Russia in the 1960s. They were kept secret, but photographs from the world's first spy satellite, used by the USA, revealed the existence of the so-called 'Caspian Sea Monster', a craft that was much bigger than any aeroplane that has ever flown. The ekranoplan is a strange cross between a ship and an aeroplane. It flies in the air, but very close to the ground or sea, because it depends upon 'ground effect'. 'Ground effect' occurs when wings are flying close to the ground and flying becomes much easier. Many sea-birds use this effect when flying long distances over the sea. 'Ground effect' has two useful consequences. First, because of the air that is 'trapped' between the wings and the ground, heavier weights can be carried by smaller wings. Secondly, less power is needed to keep the craft flying. Heavy loads can be carried very fast for long distances. Such craft could have both military and commercial uses: for example, invasion forces could use the speed and radar invisibility of low-flying ekranoplans to achieve surprise landings; and fresh food could be carried cheaply for long distances around the world. We will surely see more of these once-secret 'sea monsters' in the future!

Imagine you are one of the children. What are the five most important facts you would underline? Remember, only five underlinings, only one main idea per underlining!

Imagine you had underlined the following ideas:

1 Ekranoplans were first invented in Russia
2 a cross between a ship and an aeroplane
3 it depends upon "ground effect"
4 Heavy loads can be carried very fast for long distances
5 Such craft could have both military and commercial uses

When you come to write up these points as notes, you might decide that the last point is really a development or extension of the fourth point, not a totally new point, so the numbering and layout should show it belongs to point number 4. You might rewrite and number these facts thus:

1 Ekranoplans were invented in Russia
2 They are a cross between ships and aeroplanes
3 They use 'ground effect' to help them fly
4 (a) They can carry heavy loads very fast over long distances.
  (b) They can be used for both military and commercial purposes.

The second lesson in the sequence follows next day. It is a good idea to provide a bit of mental distance by waiting overnight before you ask the children to write from their notes. This assists the re-presentation (as required by the National Curriculum) of the ideas in the child's own words. Putting things into their own words, or into their own medium for presentation, ensures the information has gone through the brain, and not just from eye to hand as in copying!

By the time 24 hours has elapsed, the children will have forgotten the wording of the original text, but hopefully, with the aid of the notes, they will not have forgotten everything! The hope is that anything they write will tend to be in their own words rather than slavishly following the original. Though, of course, some crucial phrases will tend to come through in the notes.

You can use the children's notes in two different ways:

• ask the children to use them to write a summary
• ask them to use the notes, and what else they can remember, as the basis for writing on the subject.

If the children set out to write a summary, you could ask them to try to link the ideas within sentences, allowing them only two or three sentences. They might come up with something like this:

Ekranoplans, which were invented in Russia, are a kind of cross between ships and aeroplanes. Using 'ground effect', they can carry heavy loads very fast over long distances and so could be useful for either military or commercial purposes.

If the children were now to look at their versions along with somebody else's version, and they were to look again at the original, they could compare their results and interpretations about what were the most important ideas in the passage and decide whose was the best summary.

With the extended writing task, you will ask children to write using their notes and what else they can remember. Perforce, because they cannot remember the wording of the original, they will be putting the ideas into their own words, reconstructing the meaning in the process and making it their own. If you set the task of writing an article, it may be a good idea to specify a target audience, for example, the audience for a school newspaper. If you give them a title like 'Future transport is here today!', and you have discussed the way newpaper articles have to grab the reader's attention from the first line, you might get:

Is it a ship? Is it a plane? No, it's an ekranoplan! Russia's secret invention may make the world a smaller place . . .

IMPLICATIONS FOR PRACTICE: AN INFORMATION SKILLS PROGRAMME

The *Framework for Teaching*, with its objectives, proposes something very much like a programme for teaching, but it is characterised by suggestiveness and gaps, rather than being a coherent and comprehensive syllabus. The objectives are characterised by some amazingly high-falutin' language, for example, Year 3.2: 'discuss the merits and limitations of particular instructional texts . . . and compare these with others . . . to give an overall evaluation'!

Such expression seems designed to scare teachers, let alone children! Sadly, in writing brief specifications it is hard to avoid such language. But in practice, what does this objective mean for 7–8-year-olds? It will mean things like: Does it have coloured/ good diagrams or illustrations? Is it attractive and interesting? Can you read it easily? Does it tell you what you want to know? Has it got a clear contents page and index? The important point is that from the beginning, children are being asked to evaluate and have opinions, not merely to be passive consumers of texts.

Part of the teacher's task is to translate such specifications into the appropriate and the manageable. Not all the objectives translate into such appropriate aims and activities. Some remain over-sophisticated, for example, 'distinguishing between implicit and explicit points of view'! Others seem to be repeated with variations from year to year – for example, the objectives seem very concerned about 'persuasive writing', presumably in the hope of innoculating children against commercial and political exploitation. It is the teacher's job to grade the work appropriately for the children at different ages.

What I propose here is a programme that more than fulfils the *Framework for Teaching* and statutory requirements. I don't claim it is perfect – it is for developing and expropriating as teachers think fit. After all, it was itself developed from some ideas in Wray (1985)! The very process of kicking it around is a positive and creative process – like the 7-year-old's evaluating 'the merits and limitations' of texts!

A POSSIBLE PROGRAMME FOR TEACHING INFORMATION SKILLS IN KS2

It is assumed that children have basic reading skills and a knowledge of the alphabet from Key Stage 1. The programme in every year, including Year 3, should contain a revision element. This is because the skills are cumulative, not sequential, hopefully building up a wide range of study skills.

Year 3

Alphabet and language skills
- Put words in alphabetical order using first letter.
- Understand purpose and format of dictionary, encyclopaedia and information books.
- Use first letter to find word in dictionary or encyclopaedia.
- Use simple dictionary to find word meaning.
- Add newly-met words to class word book, giving meaning and an example of use in the context of a sentence.
- Hypothesise possible spelling of word and check in dictionary; if unsuccessful, hypothesise another possible spelling, and check.

Search skills
- Choose topic to investigate.
- Think up and write down questions to investigate.
- Find book on particular topic by looking on shelves, using simple classification scheme.

- Use book title, cover, blurb to determine subject.
- Use contents page and index and page numbers to find specific subject.
- Identify and use organisational features in texts, for example, headings and sub-headings, captions to pictures.
- Scan chapter for relevant illustrations, sub-headings, etc.
- Scan text to find relevant key words.
- Read sentence and paragraph to check relevance of information.
- Find information from computer sources.

Comprehension skills
- Understand difference between fiction and non-fiction, for example, by sorting books, passages of text.
- Recognise difference between different sorts of non-fiction texts, for example, in sorting reference books, timetables, directories, information books, how-to-do-it books, etc.
- Cope with more formal, impersonal information texts.
- Read passage and give it a title and summarise what it is about in one sentence.
- Answer simple closed questions on passage.
- Make simple bridging inferences.
- Identify a number of key points in a text, for example, the important points about looking after a gerbil.
- Look at functional and personal tenor of, for example, letters, to decide what their purpose is (for example, to share news, seek information, complain, etc.) and how formal or informal the writing is.
- Choose appropriate pictures as illustrations.
- Relate new information to what is already known, for example, recognise nonsense, irrelevances, similarities, etc.
- Report on relevance and usefulness of book.
- Follow procedural texts effectively, relating instructions, lists of materials and diagrams.

Note-taking and re-presentation skills
- Underline important information in paragraph.
- Use/record information as appropriate.
- Put in own words information derived from pictures.
- Use other formats to record information, for example, checklists under headings, matrices, flow charts, quiz writing.
- Write down in own words answers to own questions.
- Use different formats to present own information, for example, writing, pictures, charts.
- Use information orally – talks, 'hot-seating', quizzes.

Year 4

Alphabet and language skills
- Use second and third letters to put words into alphabetical order.
- Find words in dictionary and encyclopaedia using second and third letters.
- Use volume titles of encyclopaedias to find correct volume.
- Use page header words in dictionary to locate target word.
- Open dictionary in roughly right place.

Search skills
- Distinguish text types by reference to layout, organisation and language, for example, between recipe books, information texts, instructiona texts, drama, poetry, etc.
- Brainstorm questions on a subject and re-order them into logical sequence.
- Use shelf titles and simple classification systems.
- Assess usefulness and ease of use of book by glancing through it and checking on organisational features, for example, sub-headings, bullet points, etc.
- Use contents page, chapter heading, sub-heading, index and scanning for key words to find specific facts.
- Skim first sentences (often topic sentences) of paragraphs to find location of relevant information.

Comprehension skills
- Read continuous text and remember main points.
- Identify topic sentences in paragraphs.
- Recognise when you don't understand something and use appropriate strategies, for example, re-reading, looking up word, using context cues, asking.
- Use glossary to understand difficult words.
- Use search and comprehension skills to answer specific questions.
- Check information found in one book against another.
- Relate new information with already known.
- Relate information from different sources and check for fit.
- Supply own related/relevant examples.
- Distinguish between facts and opinions, for example, in advertisements.
- Discuss persuasive writing, for example, in advertisements, how it works.
- Look at arguments, for example, in letters to the local paper – how do people use evidence, try to change attitudes?
- Look at relation between headlines and story in newspapers.
- Identify, for example, by underlining, most important information in a sentence or passage.

Note-taking and re-presentation skills
- Select key words/phrases from text to act as memory notes.
- Make notes in graphic form of word-web around central concept.
- Rewrite information in own words using notes alone.
- Using information gained for writing imaginative story.
- Re-present information using charts, diagrams and pictures as appropriate.
- Write own booklet on subject researched.
- Compile book-list of books used.

Year 5

Alphabet and language skills
- Use a thesaurus to find words of similar meaning.
- Use dictionary to explore complex words, affixes, roots, etc.

Search skills
- Use cross-references in an encyclopaedia.
- Use more complex classification and cataloguing system in library.
- Find and compare different sources.

Comprehension skills
- Evaluate usefulness of books and other sources of information, for example, CD-ROMs.
- Summarise useful information gained.
- Distinguish fact and opinion, for example, in journalism.
- Identify/imitate linguistic devices of persuasive language.
- Interpret diagrams, graphs, tables, etc.
- Identify and compare characteristics of different kinds of writing, for example, chronological writing like diaries and reports, instructional texts like how-to books, explanatory texts, letters and persuasive arguments by considering their use of language, for example, tenses and voice of verbs, connective phrases and structure in sentences.

Note-making and re-presentation skills
- Make notes by jotting down main ideas of paragraphs.
- Consult two or more books on subject before beginning to present information gained.
- Making notes for different purposes, for example, to talk to, in story-telling, for working up into writing.
- Re-present information in a variety of ways, for example, booklets, models, posters, tape-recordings, flow-diagrams, etc.

Year 6

Alphabet and language skills
- Understand guide to pronunciation in dictionary.
- Understand significance of abbreviated information about words in dictionary.
- Begin to use adult dictionary with more complex information.

Search skills
- Review information about information books, for example, date of publication, bibliography, other works by author.
- Use full range of library skills to find and review relevant materials.

Comprehension skills
- Cope with some texts written for adults – newspapers, journals, cookery books, dictionaries, etc.
- Identify characteristics of different genres of writing, for example, by comparing texts.
- Finding main ideas by scanning for organisation of text, skimming for key words/phrases, seeking topic sentences.
- Reconstruct main ideas, perceiving links and connections
- Check information against own experience, for example, supplying own examples, checking for counter examples.
- Evaluate information – 'How does he know?' How well is it presented?
- Evaluate persuasive writing – 'How's he trying to get at me? What's in it for him?' How is it done?
- Reflect on implications and consequences of information.

Note-taking and re-presentation skills
- Identify and write out topic sentences in sustained passage
- Rewrite as a summary
- Organise notes taken on a text into headings and sub-heading
- Collate information from a variety of sources under headings and notes for writing from.
- Re-present information in coherent, organised continuous writing, with paragraphs, sub-heading as appropriate.
- Re-present information through inter-related text, diagrams, tables, etc.
- Adapt re-presentation for different media, audiences, etc., for example, present as information booklet/package for Year 2/3.

Summary

Reading information texts involves learning a new set of skills on the part of the child reader. Some are search and research skills, like using alphabetical order, finding one's way around the organisation of a book, using the classification system in a library and framing a research topic. Some are to do more directly with reading itself and comprehension. These skills include learning to reading more formal, impersonal and grammatically complex texts that are not organised in a narrative or chronological way, and learning when *not* to read the whole text if it is not relevant to particular research purposes. Some are to do with remembering and using the information from the texts, and these skills include identifying and evaluating key ideas, note-making and the child presenting information in her own words for her own purposes.

These skills cannot be learned effectively without deliberate and explicit teaching. Simply giving project or topic work that requires the use of these skills does not ensure that the child invents them for herself. A cumulative programme of teaching over the Key Stage 2 years, designed to mesh in with, and support topic work so that its usefulness is evident, is the most effective way to ensure these long-term life skills have a secure foundation.

- Information or study skills need to be taught explicitly.

- These skills fall into four general categories: alphabet and language skills, search skills, comprehension skills, and note-taking and re-presentation skills.

- Alphabet and language skills involve learning to use alphabetical order to find references, interpret information about words and their use.

- Search skills involve both determining the focus of a research topic and finding relevant material. Finding relevant materials involves library skills and skills in negotiating the organisation of texts.

- Comprehension skills involve both coping with the non-chronological organisation of material and impersonal and complex language, and recalling relevant pre-existing knowledge and integrating new information with it.

● Note-taking and re-presentation skills involve recording for future reference the structure of the key ideas of a text and the ability to express those ideas in other words or modes of communication (for example, diagrams, models), and to use those ideas within a wider autonomic purpose.

Further reading

Littlefair, Alison (1991) *Reading All Types Of Writing*, Open University
A useful book covering the differing challenges for children of reading texts written in different genres and registers.

Mallett, Margaret (1992) *Making Facts Matter: Reading Non-fiction 5–11*, Chapman
Theoretically based, yet very practical with many classroom examples and an emphasis on *enjoying* information.

Neate, Bobbie (1992) *Finding Out About Finding Out*, Hodder and Stoughton
Like the previous book, Neate discusses register, and goes on to provide practical advice about teaching children to get the most out of information books without resorting to copying verbatim. Very helpful.

Reid, Dee and Bentley, Diana (1996) *Reading On! Developing Reading at Key Stage 2*, Scholastic
Though brief, each chapter, on a whole range of areas in this readable book, is pertinent and illuminating about how to encourage critical and responsive reading.

Wray, David and Leewin, Maureen (1997) *Extending Literacy: Children Reading and Writing Non-fiction*, Routledge
Wray, as elsewhere, provides useful, practical classroom material, especially on writing frames.

Assessment and intervention 7

When you have read this chapter, you should be able to:

- discuss the different purposes for which assessment can be undertaken and characterise the approaches taken in following up the different purposes

- implement useful classroom formative assessment practices

- apply what you have learned from formative assessments in practical classroom planning and interventions.

This chapter distinguishes between two different functions of assessment: on the one hand, for controlling the education system, for accountability and measuring levels of attainment; and on the other, for helping teachers to match their teaching to the children's abilities and needs. The emphasis then falls predominantly on the second of these two functions, discussing appropriate classroom approaches to assessing and recording children's progress in ways that can feed into better informed teaching and more rounded judgements about attainment.

THE PURPOSES OF ASSESSMENT

If education is about empowering people, assessment is sometimes seen to be the other side of the coin, in which those in authority exercise their power over those being educated. The assessors determine how the assessed shall be valued, for example, what pay or what doors shall be open to them, what level of instruction or education they shall undergo next. This is what makes Pearson *et al.* (1998) say that 'at every level of analysis, assessment is a political act'. Assessment is generally scary for those being assessed.

But not all assessment is as bad as that. Assessment can have two different purposes: on the one hand, the purpose can be to provide information about how schools and individual children measure up to standards of performance; and on the other hand, it can be to identify class or individual needs in order to facilitate purposeful teaching. Measurements of performance standards take place at the end of a period or process of instruction and are called 'summative' assessments. Assessments that take place during a process of instruction in order to help fine-tune the teaching to the needs of the children are called 'formative'.

According to Coles (1998), the first of these two purposes:

> often . . . has very little to do with helping the individual child and a lot to do with accountability within the school system.

The purpose of SATs (now National Curriculum Tasks and Tests), for example, is to do with accountability. SATs are meant to help to raise standards by measuring school performance, for example, for producing league tables, and to provide parents with information both about schools and about how their children measure up. That is, they aim to provide summative assessments of children's, and schools', attainments. The standards involved, for example the Level Descriptions, are **criterion-referenced** – that is, the yardstick for measurement involves pre-determined attainment targets constituting absolute standards. While Teacher Assessment, akin to on-going coursework or portfolio assessments, was conceived as a complementary element in National Curriculum testing, SATs came to dominate the highly political agenda of national assessment procedures.

criterion-referenced and norm-referenced testing
criterion referenced refers to fixed standards in tests, while norm-referenced refers to comparative performance – how a child performs compared with the average for her age

Reading tests, on the other hand, tend to be **norm-referenced** rather than criterion referenced. They provide a 'reading age', in order to measure a child's reading performance against a normative standard based on average child performance. Children are not measured against an absolute standard, but against each other. Such tests tend not to provide much information that is useful for teaching purposes. According to Coles (1998):

> a lot of this assessment is the practice of measuring reading rather than analysing it.

This type of assessment 'masks the complexity of the process and leaves argument about the teaching of reading up in the air' (op. cit.). The information it provides is not usable either for assessing teaching methods nor for guiding immediate teaching goals and strategies.

The classic case of a reading test that doesn't provide information that is of genuine use to the teacher is the Schonell Graded Word Reading Test. Children are asked to read a list of words ('tree little egg milk . . .' etc.). Consequently, the words are read without the support of any meaningful context. Allowing no help from semantic or syntactic cues, this is a pure test of bottom-up attainment. In its nature, then, it can tell you nothing about fluency, reading for meaning, and comprehension. It can tell you nothing about interest and motivation. It can tell you nothing about the skills and strategies that the child employs or fails to employ in a real reading situation. It probably doesn't even tell you how the child attempts to identify the words in the word list – logographic sight recognition, synthetic phonics, partial or full alphabetic reading or whatever. It doesn't tell you what skills the child has or doesn't have in her repertoire nor how she is inclined to deploy them. It probably tells you vastly less that is useful for informing your teaching than you already know. But it does provide an objective measure, a number you can write down – for whatever purposes you write down numbers.

Of course, not all reading tests are of as limited a nature as this. What is clear is that tests become more useful and meaningful, the more closely they approximate to ordinary reading situations, with meaningful continuous text. But even the most complex and sophisticated of standardised tests do not cover all aspects of reading and in any case, as Coles remarks, 'children's reading is not improved simply by being measured'.

Problems about what to assess and how to assess it

We have discussed the Schonell Grade Word Reading Test in terms of how limited a sampling of reading skills it employs. And indeed, most standardised tests are designed with only one approach to teaching in mind – in the case of Schonell, look-and-say. But the whole array of reading skills is quite hard to get at for testing purposes. Sue Horner (1998), writing on behalf of the Schools Curriculum and Assessment Authority (SCAA), describes the model of reading that National Curriculum tests seek to assess as, at the lower levels, placing emphasis on accurate and fluent reading and on reading with understanding. She goes on, 'While response to texts is included at all levels, it becomes more prominent later, as do strategies for information retrieval'.

In relation to this model, she identifies a fundamental problem of assessment as 'whether to try to get directly at the reading act or whether to rely on evidence derived from speaking or writing'. For example, if you assess a child's comprehension from written work based on retrieved information, how do you distinguish between the contributions of 'reading with understanding' and written composition skills?

About SATs, Horner comments, 'In the main, the tests for 7- and 11-year-olds contain questions which expect short, correct answers, so the opportunity for recognizing multiple readings of texts is not extensive'. Such closed comprehension questions (often multiple-choice questions) is one way to side-step the problem of assessing writing rather than reading skills. Clearly, Horner recognises the limitations of this approach – limitations which are discussed at greater length below.

Among other, related, challenges to test developers, she cites the problems of 'whether and/or how to separate decoding, understanding, responding and evaluation for assessment purposes' and 'what significance to attribute to the mode of response (written or oral), since the level descriptions are not prescriptive about this'. Designing such tests clearly is full of problems – how to sample the full range of things you would like to test, how to get at covert skills from overt behaviours.

The balance between summative and formative assessments

formative and summative assessments formative assessments are designed to help the teacher know where children are at and what to teach next, and may be qualitative in nature, while summative assessments provide quantitative data at the end of a programme, and are useful for accountability purposes

Horner distinguishes between the **summative assessments** with which national tests are concerned, and the place of **formative assessment**: 'the provision for identification of progress within a key stage, that is, formative assessment, is for teachers to decide as part of their ongoing, day-to-day teaching'.

She says this within the context of saying 'how the curriculum is taught . . . is up to teachers and schools,' and making the point that, in the system of 'best-fit' level description assessment:

> the UK model could be seen to fail to make the vital link between what is taught and what is learnt, since differentiation is made evident at the end rather than during the process of teaching the curriculum.

(Horner, 1998)

This possible failure to incorporate formative assessment in the national tests (as compared with national systems in other English-speaking countries) is (I think, and I think she thinks) a strength. It places the importance of teachers' on-going formative assessments, leading to customised and differentiated teaching, centre-stage. It relates to Sir Ron Dearing's 'Use your loaf' injunction and clearly places responsibility and initiative in the hands of the teacher. But whether this is how governments see it is a different matter!

This discussion of national testing, then, highlights certain issues as the domain for the formative assessments that we should be making in classrooms:

- the formative assessment of decoding skills

- assessing of literal comprehension through short answers
- assessing more complex kinds of comprehension through both speech and writing
- assessing response and evaluation through both speech and writing.

These are issues to which we will return.

Qualitative versus quantitative assessments

At the same time as there is a strong governmental move towards national testing in order to improve educational accountability, there is also, going in a different direction, 'a new movement to align the assessment instruments with ordinary classroom tasks ... a move from quantitative to qualitative data' (Coles, 1998).

The two different approaches to testing have different purposes and tend to operate on different time-scales. Governments, concerned with accountability, look to the year, the phases of education, the large scale, and want a summative assessment to measure what has been achieved. Like OFSTED, they want a measure of value for money. They want to know whether standards of reading have changed over time and whether their policies have made any difference. Consequently, they have a predilection for traditional, conservative, quantitative measuring procedures that have proved successful in the past and that will allow comparisons over time to be made. Hence the tendency to rate 'pencil and paper' tests more highly than teacher assessments, and the current demand from OFSTED for more reliable standardised tests.

The teacher, on the other hand, operating from teaching intervention to teaching intervention, lesson to lesson, works on a much smaller time scale and wants formative, qualitative assessments to help her provide appropriate prompts and guidance and to plan the next step for her children.

This requirement marries in with the philosophical underpinning to the 'new paradigm' approaches. These approaches are sometimes claimed to be '**post-modern**' (Harrison *et al.*, 1998) in that they question certain traditional certainties, for example, about the 'meaning' of a text. Is the meaning of a text a discrete object, waiting to be unearthed like buried treasure (for example, by Horner's 'short, correct answers'), or is the meaning something that happens in the reader as the result of the dialogue between the reader and the text? Harrison *et al.* cite Derrida's dictum that the reader's role is not to discover meaning, but to produce it; to dismantle the text and rebuild it another way.

post-modernist criticism a school of literary criticism, concerned more with how texts mean than what they mean, more with the role of the reader than the writer, and more with socio-political origins than literary-moral significances

Before we dismiss Derrida's ideas as French intellectual flummery, consider our notion that meaning depends on what the child brings to the text as well as what the child takes from the text; the notion of 're-presenting' information (i.e. dismantling it and rebuilding it in another medium or exploiting it in a different context, for another purpose), and of encouraging critical and sceptical reading (diminishing the authority of the text). While the last two points are not quite what Derrida was driving at, they are not a thousand miles away from it.

Though we do not generally ask children to 'read against the grain' of a text because reading *with* the grain is still a challenge (and usually more rewarding), and although we initially encourage children to become consumers of texts, because the ability to consume has to be well established before the ability to deconstruct texts becomes possible, we are concerned with developing skills with the potential to lead on to yet more sophisticated skills. Derrida's ideal reader approaches the text with his own agenda. The child initially has no such established agenda, and is only beginning to build up her world-view in terms of which she interprets what she reads.

The subjectivity of the supposedly 'objective'

One of the critical perceptions underlying the 'new paradigm' is that even the most 'objective' of summative measurements of reading, so beloved of national testing, are built upon a foundation of innumerable subjective decisions. These decisions can occur both in the designing and the implementation of the tests – as SATs have exemplified over the years. Vincent (1994) noted that the SEAC requirement for objective timed tests did not marry well with reading as defined by the National Curriculum – 'This is a formula for bad tests'. More recently, 'Marking choas undermines tests' (TES, 6 November 1998), reports that the marking of the 1998 SATs for Key Stages 1 and 2 has been castigated both for excessive subjectivity (English) and for marking down highly relevant and well-informed answers that do not fit the marking criteria (Science). And even Chris Woodhead, the HMCI, has recently said (TES, 18 December 1998) that SATs are unreliable because 'the tests are not the right tests ... we need standardised tests in literacy and numeracy', the tests have changed so much over the years that it is not possible to make comparisons over time, and because the teachers cheat! Across the range, SATs do not command great respect as a reliable form of summative assessment.

'Responsive assessment'

On the more positive side, post-modernist ideas have led Harrison *et al.* to propose the notion of 'responsive assessment' – a notion I interpret as not *peculiarly* post-modern but in accord with the humane tradition of English studies over the last 60 years or more, represented by Denys Thompson, D.W. Harding, David Holbrook, Harold and Connie Rosen, James Britton, John Dixon and Douglas Barnes, etc.

'Responsive assessment' is characterised by being local and small-scale, involving teacher-, self- and peer-assessment, and being open to negotiation and avoiding premature closure in deciding on criteria. Instead of working towards a single global measurement, 'responsive assessment' recognises that reading is a multi-faceted activity involving the whole person.

Harrison *et al.* quote with approval Stake's view with regard to the problem of data reduction and the reduction of the assessment of complex skills to a single score: 'Oversimplification obfuscates'. For example, multiple choice comprehension tests are seen as manufacturing reliability at the expense of penalising subjective, creative or unexpected responses – a point that Horner (above) recognises. And 'reading ages' tell you nothing about the nature of the reading processes, the skills, awarenesses and motivations of the readers.

On the other hand, performance assessment through portfolio approaches and instruments like the Primary Language Record (see below) are seen as privileging the role of the reader and the reader's responses and as means of capturing unanticipated outcomes and acknowledging the dynamic model of the reader as meaning-maker. Portfolios can incorporate a great range of different kinds of evidence, including child-initiated responses and activities related to reading, ranging from written reports to tape-interviews and discussions. Activities such as DARTs (Directed Activities Related to Texts, discussed in Beard, 1987) are seen as offering a range of practical approaches for opening up texts for dialogue and debate, and as encouraging active reflection on, or reconstruction of, texts in ways that enable readers to become co-authors of the meaning.

In these contexts, the role of the teacher may be more that of *chairing*, than *guiding* pupil-centred group discussion (Beard, 1987). Or, as we have suggested throughout the book, the role might be to set up tasks for unsupervised small group discussions which permit more democratic exploratory talk. If comprehension of text is dialogic, an interaction between reader and text, then group discussion activities, which are by nature dialogic, are an externalised exercise in processes that the child can subsequently internalise. Exploratory and problem-solving discussion provides the child with a model of taking into account and weighing differing viewpoints and perceptions, and working towards a fuller, and possibly more balanced, interpretation.

Such approaches are classroom-centred and can provide assessment information that is of direct value both to the teacher and to the child, who becomes through such assessment activities more engaged and reflective about her own reading and comprehension processes.

The dialogic nature of comprehension

The processes of discussion alert the child to the partiality of individual responses – partiality in the sense both of being biased and of being incomplete. Ideally, it alerts her to the fact that comprehension is not absolute but relative, and that comprehension can change and develop with new insights. The processes of discussion require the child to put her thoughts into words in ways that subject them to both her own and other people's scrutiny. And ideally, she in turn scrutinises other people's contributions. In fact, however, it rarely occurs that one child will criticise another's contribution, either because she doesn't taken on board what is being said, doesn't realise it conflicts with her own views – or out of delicacy! Children may need to be prompted into recognising, facing and working through disagreements or conflicting perceptions. The processes of recording responses in writing, either individual or group consensual, cause the child to organise and structure her thinking in a reflective way in the process of organising and structuring her expression.

For the teacher assessing these responses, the task is not so much to measure them against a yardstick of correctness, as to evaluate their coherence and completeness as well as the skills, sensitivities and conceptual alertnesses that are demonstrated. The teacher's job is not to bring the child to some notional right answer, but to respect the child as someone trying to make meaning and to play a facilitating role in helping the child towards further, new or more inclusive meanings.

This does not mean, of course, that any view or interpretation is as good as any other or that children should not be expected to comprehend factual information accurately. The teacher's role may require her to remind children of known information or to feed in new information, if it is relevant, to help correct or balance children's interpretations.

Dialogue with the text

The notion of dialogue with the text tends to mean different things when we consider reading information texts and reading literature. While reading literature involves the dialogic play of inference, empathy and elaboration from the beginning, the process of understanding an informational text involves some level of submission to the literal meaning of the text before the 'dialogue' between the reader's existing mental constructs and the new information comes into play in making connections and inferences, and elaborating by finding her own examples to illustrate the concepts in the text. Again, evaluation will tend to follow interpretation, whereas with literature, some kinds of evaluation (evaluation *within* the story, not *of* the story) are integral with interpretation.

Responsive assessment and responsive teaching

What 'responsive assessment' is concerned with is primarily assessment that formatively supports the teaching-and-learning interactions of the classroom. The sorts of assessment I am concerned with here, then, are not accountability-oriented tests like SATs, but formative assessment procedures that will help you obtain insights that can be used to help children learning in the ways they individually make sense of the texts they read. The argument for responsive assessment cannot be applied to national testing because it doesn't lend itself to summative and numerical results.

'Feedback' and 'feedforward'

The National Curriculum Task Group on Assessment and Testing report (TGAT, 1988) said:

> The assessment process itself should not determine what is taught and learned ... Yet it should not simply be a bolt-on addition at the end. Rather, it should be an integral part of the educational process, continually providing both 'feedback' and 'feedforward'. It therefore needs to be incorporated systematically into teaching strategies and practices at all levels.

The danger with assessment systems is that they become the tail that wags the dog. Once a test is in place, we tend to teach to the test. For example, the prevalence of multiple-choice testing in the United States has led to a real concern that children are not being taught to develop joined-up learning and thinking and expression. The problem, say Pearson *et al.* (1998), 'is not that teachers teach to the tests but that teachers need tests worth teaching to'.

However, whether it is possible to design tests worth teaching to remains an open question (see Hayward and Spencer, discussed below). Pearson *et al.*'s conclusion, after a very extensive period of developing a 'new paradigm' New Standards set of assessment instruments over a number of years and over a number of states in the US, was that it was more problematic than they had originally supposed: 'what we learned, we think, is that there is no substitute for a good curriculum and that the assessment has yet to the built that can stand as a surrogate for curriculum'.

Assessment should not determine what is taught, but what is taught next

Even if assessment should not determine the curriculum and what is taught overall, it should inform what is taught *next* and how it should be taught. Assessment is the starting point of the teaching cycle and not the end of it. It properly precedes planning because you need to know what it is appropriate to aim for in your planning; and knowing what you want to achieve depends upon your assessment of where the children are at and what the children need to learn or practise next. So we can picture the teaching cycle as in Figure 7.1.

Figure 7.1
The teaching cycle

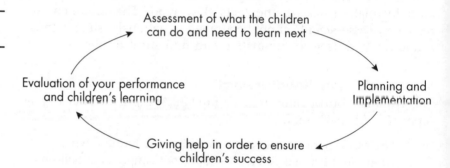

In this version of the teaching cycle, I have put planning and implementation together simply in order not to have too cluttered a picture, and they are pretty obvious elements anyway. The things I want to lay emphasis on are the elements at six, nine and twelve o'clock. Nine o'clock can be seen as 'feedback' and twelve o'clock as 'feedforward'.

Giving help in order to ensure success

This relates to Vygotsky's (1962) principle that what children can do with help today, they can do on their own tomorrow. And to the principle that nothing succeeds like success. The kinds of ways we might give help in different situations have been an element in the discussion throughout this book. But the point I want to make here is that, when we are concentrating specifically on assessment, however much we want to assess children in real contexts, not in artificial test conditions, the aims of evaluation and instruction are sometimes in conflict. If you want to see how a child manages on her own, you must forgo giving her help.

The example of miscue analysis

For example, let us consider the situation of conducting a miscue analysis (see Bielby, 1998, for a fuller discussion of conducting and interpreting miscue analyses). You have provided the child with a reasonably challenging passage to read (you aim for, maybe, 85–90 per cent accuracy because you need enough miscues to analyse). So far the situation isn't much different from normal reading (where, as Marie Clay (1991) says, you should aim for 90–95 per cent accuracy to facilitate self-tutoring). You listen as the child reads – this is normal – but you also record the reading so that afterwards you can mark up the child's version verbatim on a photocopy of the text.

But where the situation differs markedly from an ordinary listening-to-readers session is that you have warned the child that you are not going to help or say anything because you want to see how she copes on her own. You forgo giving her help or taking advantage of useful opportunities for teaching. Of course, if the child is really struggling or becoming distressed, you break the protocol. You stop the strict assessment procedure, apologise for having asked her to do something too hard for her and do something else to redeem the situation, like treating the occasion as an opportunity for shared reading, so that she doesn't feel a failure and develop an aversion to reading to the teacher.

Marie Clay's (1985) protocols for doing running reading records, while very similar to miscue analysis, differ in this respect. The teacher can do some minimal teaching or provide help, and these occasions are scored in the marking. Since running reading records were developed for use with early years children and are carried out using the child's current reading material, they are a kinder, less artificial and less off-putting procedure, as is appropriate for younger children. Running reading records are about as close as it is possible to get to avoiding the conflict between the aims of assessment and instruction.

The way running reading record procedures have been exploited and distorted for SATs purposes at Key Stage 1 demonstrates very clearly the conflict between formal assessments and teaching purposes. The SATs procedures are not primarily designed for diagnostic purposes, with the aim of helping the child. The *texts* used in the tests are standardised, not adapted to the individual child, and miscues are marked as errors in order to derive scores. The bias is towards quantitative, rather than qualitative data. But how else could Sue Horner and SCAA (see above) separate out decoding from understanding, response and evaluation?

The criteria in miscue analysis and running records

Practice in administering miscue analyses or running reading records makes the teacher alert to children's strategies and facilitates her ability to interpret children's difficulties and miscues. After doing a few miscue analyses, you will tend, ever after, to interpret what you hear diagnostically. In fact, this analytic sensitising of the teacher is one of the main spin-off benefits of doing miscue analyses!

The key elements in interpreting miscues are to determine which sources of information (semantic, syntactic and graphophonic) the child is using in her reading, and to determine measures of accuracy and self-correction. These are the same things that the teacher should be alert to in listening to readers, and should be prompting the child to develop.

The scoring in miscue analysis is not primarily designed to enable the teacher to make comparisons between children, because the children will be doing the analysis task on different texts. Of course, it is possible to make comparisons between children, but only in the most general way, for example, 'A is guessing too much and needs help with applying graphophonics. On the other hand, B is okay on the graphophonics, but needs to take the context more into account to help her make intelligent guesses when she comes across irregularly spelled words that won't submit to phonic decoding'.

But what miscue analysis is primarily designed to do is to indicate the effectiveness and the balance between bottom-up and top-down skills and the level of self-monitoring in the individual child's performance. The purpose of the analysis is to alert the teacher to the skills that the child seems to be weak in and least able to incorporate effectively into her reading strategies. This kind of assessment, then, provides qualitative, rather than quantitative information.

With a different text and texts of different levels of difficulty, the child doing a miscue analysis might well achieve a somewhat different self-correction ratio or a different accuracy percentage. This doesn't matter. What the teacher is seeking is something to alert and focus her attention on to the child's needs, not a summative measure of performance. The reason for doing a miscue analysis, rather than just depending on informal observations of the child's reading, is the way it deliberately focuses attention on the child and on the balance of skills within the child's strategies, and a series of such analyses over time can provide some sort of a profile, for that particular child, of her developing strategies. And the accuracy score indicates whether the child and the level of text difficulty are well matched.

Feedback: evaluating your performance and children's learning

When you evaluate a lesson, part of what you are doing is thinking about how well you put the material over and how well you managed the organisation and control of the children; part of what you are doing is judging how much you think the children understood and how much they gained from it. Since you are not going to blame the children for not learning, your estimate of their learning is an indirect indicator of your own performance! This provides you with feedback to help you develop your own performance better for future occasions.

I have separated this element from assessment of the children because the emphasis is tending to fall on what you did as a teacher and what you can learn from reflection that can help you develop your teaching skills in relation to planning, presentation, explanation and task design.

You need to ask yourself both what went right (and why) and what went wrong (and why). It is as important to understand why things went well as it is to understand why things went badly. Indeed, it is more important, because it gives you a positive model for the future! It might be kinder to yourself to put the questions in terms of 'What would I do again, and why?' and 'What would I do differently, and why?' The answers to these questions are likely to be found in your perception of the children's reception of your lesson. Were they attentive, interested, responsive? Could they answer your questions? Did they volunteer related information and observations? Were they able to do the work? Were they motivated? Did they understand the point of the lesson?

Feedforward: assessment of what children can do and need to learn next

The emphasis at this point in the cycle is on looking forward and on looking to the children's needs. You have to relate two factors, the requirements of the curriculum and the children's level of attainment, knowledge and understanding in relation to it. In the light of your underpinning knowledge of the subject matter and of the ways children learn, and your assessment of the children's current grasp, you determine what the next step should be. The curriculum determines the destination and the route, but your assessment of the children and where they are at determines the direction and size of each step along the way and how you set about taking it.

IMPLICATIONS FOR THE CLASSROOM

In discussing formative assessment, we have skipped between talking about individual needs, and whole-class needs. The same principles apply to both, but there can clearly be a conflict of interests. Not everybody needs the same things at the same time. Progressively throughout Key Stage 2, the gaps between different children's capabilities widen and so the potential need for differentiation in teaching and tasks becomes greater.

This is one reason why groups for the literacy hour should be based on reading ability. This will make it easier to match instruction and activities to the needs of the children. Small group work and individual work in the Literacy Hour provide opportunities for differentiated work. The rest of this chapter will deal with individual assessment within the classroom setting.

Assessment and the individual

The teacher in the classroom is the best person to make assessments. She can see the whole child, and as we have seen, reading, while a process and a skill, is also something that involves the whole child, emotions and attitudes, values and motivation, interests and beliefs, social identity and experience, as well as knowledge and abilities. As we have argued, testing oversimplifies and obfuscates. But as teachers we want to take into account the complex interconnectedness of the issues that affect reading.

Looking at the whole child

In Scotland it has been recognised that national tests could only provide limited diagnostic information and the Minister for Education responded to teachers' requests for a project to develop diagnostic assessment in the service of teaching. Hayward and Spencer, who helped to develop it, discuss (1998a) 'Taking a Closer Look at Reading' (The Scottish Council for Research in Education, 1995), which promotes the assessment of reading by helping teachers observe and reflect on the whole child in relation to reading and work with him or her to identify the appropriate 'next step'.

'Taking a Closer Look at Reading' is in three parts, together with a booklet of illustrative examples. The first part deals with learning to read and the need for diagnostic assessment as part of the teaching process. It draws particular attention to three areas: children's motivation, their previous experience and present abilities, and effective tasks and flexible teaching strategies.

The second part deals with diagnostic procedures and emphasises the teacher's professional judgement, based to a great extent on observing day-to-day classroom activities and noticing individuals' 'growth points'. In particular teachers are advised to observe how children interpret and tackle particular tasks, what their strategies are.

A major part of what the teacher aims to do is help the children become more reflectively alert about what they are doing and trying to achieve in reading tasks. The kinds of interpretative skills that the teacher uses are typically those used and developed in miscue analysis: what is being achieved successfully (from both the child's and the teacher's perspective); what is being attempted, possibly without complete success; and what skills the child needs to develop.

The third part deals with the intervention procedures to promote successful reading. The areas dealt with are:

- attitudes and motivation – in general and in relation to the particular task
- decoding skills – relating to both words and sentences
- pursuit of meaning – using prior knowledge and context in trying to make sense of what they are reading
- awareness of language use – imaginative responsiveness to the use of language, images and structures that convey meaning.

One of the key themes is that the children themselves play an important role in deciding what they think the 'next step' for them should be, what to read and for what purposes. They are to be partners in their own education. The children are to be engaged in discussing and thinking about their own reading strategies in ways intended to encourage their commitment to any proposed action, whether to do with graphophonics or using contextual skills for constructing meaning or whatever.

Children become involved in 'feedback discussion' about their own strengths and weaknesses and in self-assessment. Further, the kind of information that becomes available is more meaningful to parents and in primary–secondary school liaison.

Underpinning the 'Closer Look' approach is a belief, grounded in research, that teachers and children work better when they have a clear purpose in mind for each reading task and that skills tend to develop in a global, interactive way. Marie Clay's (1985) work on reading recovery suggested its rigorous but eclectic approach.

Perhaps one of the most interesting aspects of the development of the 'Closer Look' materials was the dropping, as a result of experience, of specific diagnostic tests because they were stressful for the children, thus giving unreliable results; because they emphasised what children could not do rather than what they could, and did not identify development needs; and because they tended to become an end in themselves, distorting the teachers' approach to the 'Closer Look'. Though it is early days, the approach has generally been found useful and practical by teachers in promoting effective practice.

CASE STUDY

A closer look at Lynne

Hayward and Spencer (1998b) provide some interesting, even moving, case studies in connection with the 'Closer Look' programme. Lynne, aged 7, confides to her teacher, 'I can't read but I would really like to be able to.' Recognising that Lynne is behind the rest of her new class, her teacher determined to find out what she thought about reading, and discovered she had some limiting concepts. Only reading scheme books were real reading, library books weren't. Lynne was frightened of being found out by other children. Though she wanted to learn, the only value she foresaw in it was to be able to read to her own baby when she grew up.

The programme the teacher determined on was, first, to build up Lynne's confidence by giving her opportunities to read to younger children and by listing all the things to do with reading that she was good at and providing her with a record of achievement for her reading. Secondly, she aimed to develop Lynne's enjoyment of reading by introducing her to library books and asking her to recommend books to younger children and by building in rewards for undertaking tasks like taping her favourite story and allowing other children to listen. The approach was, then, in the first instance, one of considering the whole child and building up her self-esteem rather than simply concentrating on skills.

Discussion points

1 Think of a backward reader you know: when trying to help, where do you start?
2 What is the right balance between working on self-esteem and on decoding skills when helping a backward reader?

CASE STUDY

A closer look at 'the next step'

In another case study, this time of a 9-year-old boy, the problems were different. He was keen enough, and had just begun taking books home to read. But he tended to read one word at a time and treat a line of print as if it were a sentence. (This was perhaps a carry-over from early reading texts where lines and sentences coincided.

continued...

For the same reason, some children put a full stop at the end of each line of their writing.) He did not seem to use meaning as a checking device or remember the stories very clearly. The teacher decided to concentrate on decoding and saw the most important 'next step' as being to work on the fluent articulation of his reading, and thought that paired reading might help. She seemed to be working on the reasonable assumption that if he could read and hear the sentences fluently, he would be able to make sense of them better and realise that this was what reading was all about.

Discussion points

1 Approaching this boy's problems, would you have started by tackling decoding or somewhere else?
2 Does fluent joined-up reading necessarily mean joined-up thinking about a text?

These examples indicate the kind of way that the teacher can assess a particular child's needs and adapt a programme specifically to meet those needs. The needs can be seen in a wider framework than simply the development of skills, essential though they are. The child's self-confidence, interest and commitment are also required. If the teacher is to be helpful in this kind of way, she needs to observe and record the child's reading with insight and involve the child in her own development.

Assessment and record keeping

As we have seen in the case of 'A Closer Look', assessment and record-keeping tie in with each other. You keep records of the assessments you have made and you use the records you have made to help you make assessment over longer periods. So what sorts of assessments and records do you make?

The Primary Language Record, developed in the UK and further developed in the USA, provides a model of holistic, long-term record-keeping, covering the whole of literacy development. It aims to identify children's strengths, treat mistakes as useful diagnostic information to inform teaching and to record positive development over time. The sort of evidence recorded includes parental and children's own perspectives as well as the teacher's.

The components of the Record include parental interviews, child–teacher conferencing records, narrative reports on the child's overall language performance, end-of-year comments from the child and parents, information for the next year's teacher and reading scales plotting dependence-to-independence, experiences and so on. The rating on the scales is based on teacher observation, not totally unlike the 'best-fit' level descriptors of the National Curriculum Attainment Targets. Preliminary studies on the Record in both the

UK and the USA have recently indicated that its scales can be scored reliably enough to make it possible to use the Record for summative, accountability purposes, as well as formative purposes.

Benefits claimed for this approach include the way it helps teachers become better observers of children, the way it can guide teaching and the way it educates teachers both in terms of understanding literacy development and in developing their diagnostic skills and attentiveness.

CASE STUDY

Accentuate the positive!

Falk (1998) cites the case of a 7-year-old bilingual boy with behaviour problems whose literacy record to date simply detailed what he could *not* do and concluded by saying that he had a negative self-concept. However, when his new teacher used the Record to track his progress, she began to see him differently. For example, although his decoding was weak, he had a good sense of story and was adept at using the pictures to gain meaning. The teacher exploited his positive abilities and interests and also used them to build up his sight vocabulary of key words.

Prompt questions in the Record, like 'What experiences and teaching have helped/would help development?', assisted in focusing the teacher's provision. Indeed, some of the personal comments about using the Record from teachers in New York manage to sound like religious testimonies from the newly converted!

Discussion points

1 Why is it easier to record what children can't do than what they can do?
2 Suggest some prompt questions for a Record to encourage helpful observations in this area.

Using the National Curriculum Level Descriptions

Vincent and Harrison (1998), reporting on a national pilot study in England and Wales exploring ways to operationalise the assessment of the Attainment Levels, note that our national tests have never quite resolved the tension between summative and formative requirements and that the government has not committed itself to developing new standardised group tests. They quote at length a scrupulous and conscientious teacher assessment that uses the Level Descriptions as criteria and ask 'why such accounts should be considered a less acceptable form of evidence . . . than the results of a standardized test' (or, for that matter, a government-sponsored non-standardised test like SATs). In the level descriptions we have a valuable criterion guide for helping us make descriptive assessments.

What the experience of 'A Closer Look', the Primary Language Record and Vincent and Harrison's work suggests is that a structured but open teacher-led assessment system has a great deal to recommend it. It is not only more helpful for teaching purposes than standardised and national tests, but it could, through using scales based on the National Curriculum Attainment Level Descriptions, be at least equally as valid and reliable a way of measuring attainment for accountability purposes as SATs.

Thinking about specifications for record-keeping

'Responsive' approaches that operate through things like portfolios and DARTs do not satisfy Horner's (1998) criterion of approaches that try to get directly at the reading act. 'Responsive' approaches tend to rely on evidence derived from speaking and writing. Such approaches need to be complemented by assessments like miscue analysis and running reading records that get more 'directly at the reading act'. A useful record will include 'direct', observational materials and keep comments on, and samples of, work of a more 'indirect' nature.

'Getting directly at the reading act'

Listening to readers and doing miscue analyses are about as near as we can come to getting directly at the reading act and the child's reading processes. But a further angle on the process is not just to diagnose the child's performance, but to ask the child herself about what she was attempting, what she found difficult and why. This sort of enquiry not only gives you new insights or confirms your own interpretations, but it engages the child in taking an interest in her own progress, performance and enjoyment. Encouraging this sort of reflectivity is a theme running through the 'new paradigm' initiatives and both the Primary Language Record and the 'Closer Look' materials.

You may manage a couple of miscue analyses a year for an average child – largely to confirm what you have observed in a more informal way in the ordinary course of listening to her read. The results may, however, throw up unexpected perceptions – most commonly, perhaps, about unexpected weaknesses in graphophonics that effective contextual guessing has tended to conceal.

With children who give you cause for concern, you may employ miscue analysis more often to determine what sort of help the child needs, what skills are letting her down. In any event, you should keep a record both of the analysis and also of your day-to-day observations about the skills the child is employing, and any other information you note about the child as a reader.

This sort of additional information will range from where the child is in the reading scheme and what things she enjoys, reads at home and talks about to response and performance in Literacy Hour activities and in any informal and standardised tests, if they are available. Some reading tests, like the Neale Analysis of Reading Ability and the New Macmillan Reading Analysis provide diagnostic information, and some, like the Macmillan Diagnostic Reading Pack also provide remedial packages to go along with them.

Periodically, you can review your observations, noting any significant patterns and developments. The advantage of making notes is threefold: because you are making notes, you tend to be more alert; you remember what you notice and put the information together into a picture, especially when you look back over a period of time; and you have the basis for reports for parents and for handing forward at the end of the year.

At the same time, it can be valuable to encourage children to keep a reading diary for themselves, to record the books they have read and what they liked or disliked about them, the other materials they read, for example, at home, about football or whatever, and to note down any observations they have about themselves as readers, for example, what *kinds* of things they like and dislike, whether they think they have changed or developed in their skills or their likes and dislikes. All this both provides you, as a teacher, with further insights on the children (for example, about what sorts of books to recommend to them next) and tends to promote the children's self-esteem and sense of themselves as developing readers.

Getting at reading through speech

Speech is ephemeral unless we tape-record it. And even in the tape-recorded form, it is not very accessible unless one transcribes it. And anyone who has tried transcribing speech finds all kinds of good reasons for not doing it again! So, for the most part, the assessments we make from speech are likely to be informal and impressionistic. In reading conferences and discussions about their reading with individuals, we will gather information we might summarise for our records or simply hold in the tablets of our memories. During discussions, of course, we are responding to the child and giving feedback, so we could say instant assessment is going directly into teaching intervention even as we converse!

A good deal of the reading-related speech going on in the classroom is going to be between children, either in book reports, or in discussions of texts or in DARTs discussions. As teachers, we are going to be variously overhearers and participants. In some small-group discussions, it is useful to have a tape-recorder, either simply to help focus and format the discussion, or for the children to work on a presentation of their discussion, as might occasionally happen with DARTs discussions. In either event, the recording will be accessible to you, as the teacher. Assessment of this may involve your feeling that you need to make certain inputs in future, or that you want to set the tasks in slightly different ways.

Getting at reading through writing

The advantages of written responses to reading is that they are easily accessible to you and that children can be encouraged, through framing and other means, to present an organised response. In discussing reading diaries, we have already broached this area. Additionally, all the kinds of written responses that have been discussed in Chapters 4, 5 and 6, from book reviews to poems to note-making for topic writing, are grist to the mill. What is important is to remember that the evidence about reading is mixed up with evidence about writing. Disentangle it as you may!

The teacher's need for confidence in making and using assessments

Harrison *et al.* (1998) comment that:

> many decades of externally administered tests of reading
> have made many teachers feel deskilled in the area of
> reading assessment, but we would argue that teachers . . .
> are potentially in the best position to make a contribution
> to assessment processes, and . . . to put the information . . . to
> good use.

What we need, in order to be able to help children better, is confidence in our own abilities to make assessments, an appropriate perception of the limitations of national and summative assessment for furthering educational processes, and a better picture of children's skills and strategies than traditional testing has provided. We have to take up SCAA's challenge (Horner, 1998): 'formative assessment . . . is for teachers to decide as part of their ongoing, day-to-day teaching'. What we need is the courage to 'use our loaves' in the kind of way that has happened in Scotland with the teacher-driven move to develop 'A Closer Look at Reading' and its teacher-led approach to formative assessment. What we need is courage to believe ourselves expert, and in particular, expert about our own children.

Summary

Assessment has two faces. One is concerned with public accountability and is concerned with making summative judgements, often through tests imposed from above. The other is formative. Formative assessment is that element in good classroom practice concerned with feedback and feedforward; it is about evaluating children's current knowledge, abilities and needs in order to determine the next step that needs to be taken in teaching. National policy has emphasised summative assessment at the expense of formative. National policy has had the effect of diminishing teachers in their own, as well as the public's eyes, and undermining their professional self-confidence.

Yet teachers are the people in the best position to know the whole child and be able to make informed formative assessments and act upon them. Further, their on-going assessments can contribute the most useful kind of information to summative assessments. What is needed is for teachers to operate systematic formative assessment procedures that feed into good practice in the classroom, using informed observation and monitoring strategies and keeping organised records in ways that provide profiles of development. To do this, teachers need to have professional self-confidence and the courage of their calling.

- Assessments can be summative, making categorical judgements of attainment at the end of a process, or they can be formative, designed diagnostically to determine children's needs and thus to feed information into planning for future teaching.

- Summative assessments can be used for labelling, as with exam results, and for accountability purposes, as with SATs.

- Formative assessment has more immediate classroom uses, in providing feedback and feedforward, determining what to teach next.

- Effective formative assessment, with its eye on individual development, implies diagnostic observation and record-keeping.

- Well-kept cumulative diagnostic records can have at least as much validity as summative assessments.

● Classroom teachers are the people in the best position to make formative assessments and maintain diagnostic records.

● Teachers need to regain confidence in themselves in this role.

Harrison, Colin and Salinger, Terry (eds) (1998) *Assessing Reading 1: Theory and Practice*, Routledge

Coles, Martin and Jenkins, Rhonda (eds) (1998) *Assessing Reading 2: Changing Practice in Classrooms*, Routledge
These books result from an international seminar on reading assessment, and provide a rich mine of the most recent thinking in the area.

Glossary

The technical terms used in this book are, I hope, explained in the text where they are first used. This glossary provides a reminder of the meanings, if needed. However, for the technical terms of grammar I refer you to *Rediscover Grammar with David Crystal* (David Crystal, 1988, Longman), and for the technical terms of poetry, I refer you to *A Linguistic Guide to English Poetry* (Geoffrey Leech, 1969, Longman), as including them here would make the glossary far too long!

affix	the generic term for prefixes and suffixes (q.v.)
alphabetic reading	decoding (q.v.) using alphabetic knowledge
'apprenticeship'	a 'language experience' approach (q.v.)to teaching, emphasising the close relationship between teacher and child in shared reading (q.v.)
'articulatory loop'	the mechanism for the retention of auditory memory (q.v.)
auditory memory	the ability of the short-term working memory to retain sound images (for longer than it can hold visual images)
autism	a condition characterised, among other things, by problems with empathy (q.v.) and with relating to other people
balanced development	combining bottom-up (q.v.) and top-down processes (q.v.) in reading, with bottom-up processes taking the leading role
blending	fluently combining individual phonemes into the sound of a word
bottom-up processing	the aspect of the reading process concerned with identifying the words on the page
bridging inferences	inferences that fill in gaps in a text by the application of common knowledge, e.g. in reading 'He got a cup but found the kettle was missing', we infer he wanted a hot drink.
chunking	the process of consolidating separate items into a single perceptual unit for recognition purposes, e.g. as you perceive MALT, but not LTMA, as a single unit
closed questions	questions with a definite right answer, asked to test children's knowledge (see also **open questions**)
cohesion	the effect of verbal links of meaning within and between sentences, e.g. in 'She got up and went shopping. Buying new clothes on a bright Spring morning always made her feel good', 'buying' relates back to 'shopping' and 'morning' relates back to 'got up', connecting up the meanings coherently within the text
conative	expressing desires and striving to satisfy them
consolidated alphabetic reading	the orthographic phase (q.v.) of reading in which spelling patterns are chunked (q.v.) as recognition units (q.v.)
content words	words that convey the substantive conceptual meanings in a sentence, e.g. nouns and verbs, adjectives and adverbs (see also **function words**)

context	the surrounding situation of meaning
criterion-referenced and norm-referenced testing	'criterion referenced' refers to fixed standards in tests, while 'norm-referenced' refers to comparative performance – how a child performs compared with the average for her age
cross-checking	the process of ensuring the different sources of information (q.v.) agree
cues	the clues a reader uses in identifying words and determining meanings
DARTS	Directed Activities Related to Texts – tasks to perform on passages of text
decoding	the process of identifying words by using alphabetic information to determine pronunciations
dual route	the two routes that operate in parallel in orthographic (q.v.) readers to identify words: directly from the spelling; and from the internalised pronunciation
dyslexia	a developmental processing impairment generally related to a phonological (q.v.) deficit
elaborated and restricted codes	styles of language use associated with differing patterns of social communication and control, marked by differing levels of explicitness
emotive meaning	meanings other than the literal, e.g. expressing feelings, attitudes and motives
empathy	feeling with someone else; emotional imagination
environmental print	words in the environment (labels, shop names, road signs, etc.) that children learn to recognise spontaneously even before attending school
flash cards	single-word cards used to teach sight recognition of words by rote, characteristic of look-and-say approaches (q.v.)
formative and summative assessments	formative assessments are designed to help the teacher know where children are at and what to teach next, and may be qualitative in nature, while summative assessments provide quantitative data at the end of a programme, and are useful for accountability purposes
framing	providing a structured set of written sentence or half-sentence prompts to help children negotiate a formal writing task
function words	words without much meaning in themselves but which qualify or indicate the relationships between content words in a sentence, e.g. articles, prepositions, conjunctions, etc., as in 'The cat sat **on the** mat'
genre	kind or category of written text, e.g. novel, biography, etc.
given and new	what is deemed to be known and what is deemed to be, as yet, unknown
global context	the wide context (q.v.) of overall meanings in a text, not restricted to the immediate phrase or sentence
glue ear	a common medical condition, impairing hearing, but readily treatable by the insertion of a grommet to drain fluid from the inner ear
graphemes	the written equivalent of a phoneme (q.v.) , e.g. a, ee, igh, eigh, p, ph
graphic knowledge	the ability to identify grammatically and semantically significant part-word units like prefixes, suffixes and inflections (q.v.)

graphophonics	the whole range of ways in which spelling-sound correspondences can be used to identify words, including phonics and rime analogy (q.v.)
guessing	the use of context to anticipate what a word should be, without actually reading the word
homographs	different words, spelled the same, but possibly pronounced differently, e.g. sow (noun), sow (verb)
homophones	different words, sounding the same, but possibly spelled differently, e.g. so, sew, sow (verb)
inferences	meanings, not explicit in a text, but derivable from it
inflection	the morphemic modification of word endings to indicate their meanings and grammatical agreements in a sentence, e.g. he si**ts**, a dog**'s** breakfast, it br**oke**
interrogation of text	seeking for answers in a text to questions the text has itself provoked, e.g. as with suspense, where we want to know what happens next
'language experience' approaches	approaches to the teaching of reading that emphasise the importance of motivation, contextual meaning, prediction (q.v.) and supportive adult help in shared reading (q.v.), while devaluing decoding (q.v.) skills
logographic learning	pre-alphabetic (q.v.) sight-word learning
look-and-say	an approach to the initial teaching of reading that emphasises the rote learning of a sight-word vocabulary (q.v.) to ensure successful reading of early texts
mental set	a readiness to operate in one kind of way, with an associated inflexibility with regard to a change of approach
miscue	an error or mistake in reading a word, resulting from processing or taking into account only a part of the information available
miscue analysis	a procedure for recording miscues (q.v.) verbatim and then interpreting them to determine what reading strategies are being attempted
morphemes, bound and free	morphemes are the minimal units in language that carry an element of meaning. A bound morpheme is one that cannot stand on its own, but has to be part of another word, e.g. '-ed', as in 'walked' and 'talked'; 'uni-' (as in unit, unicycle, universe), whereas 'free' and 'apricot' are free morphemes
morpho-syntactic awareness	the awareness associated with graphic knowledge (q.v.) and the morphemic and syntactic significance of certain spelling chunks, e.g. in distinguishing the occasions when the final 's' on a word is part of the stem (e.g. is), a plural marker (e.g. tins), a possessive (e.g. Tony's) or a third person singular verb (e.g. fills).
'normal' distribution	a statistical concept referring to the equal distribution of scores about a mode, producing a bell-shaped graph
onset	the consonant sounds that precede the vowel sound in a syllable (q.v.)
open questions	questions without a 'right' answer, and to which single-word answers are not appropriate, asked to stimulate thought and imagination or elicit personal experiences and responses (see also **closed questions**)

orthographic reading	reading by identifying words from fully processed recognition units (whole word or part word spelling chunks) (see also **consolidated alphabetic reading**)
over-learning	learning something so thoroughly that it becomes automatic or second-nature
parts of speech	categories of word function in a sentence, e.g. noun, verb, preposition, etc.
partial alphabetic reading	identifying words by decoding (q.v.) only a few of the letters and guessing the rest
peripety	from Aristotle: the unexpected turn of events or discovery at the climax of a story
phonemes	the minimal units of sound within words that are significant for distinguishing one word from another, e.g. 'fax' has four phonemes, but 'facts' has five
phonics	whether for reading or writing, the exploitation of letter–sound correspondences for working words out
phonological awareness	alertness to the component sounds within words, identified by research as significant in facilitating learning to read
phonological code	the way printed letters represent the sounds of words
phonological route	the processing path that identifies a printed word by translating it into an (internalised) pronunciation
post-modernist criticism	a school of literary criticism, concerned more with how texts mean than what they mean, more with the role of the reader than the writer, and more with socio-political origins than literary-moral significances
pragmatics	the aspect of semantics concerned with meanings and communication within a particular shared situation
pre-alphabetic reading	reading dependent on the sight recognition of words from some aspect of their appearance prior to the learning of the alphabet – also called 'logographic reading' (q.v.)
pre-conscious	area of normally unconscious activity that is accessible to conscious introspection if we try
prediction	the anticipation of a word, a meaning or future events from the preceding context (see also **guessing**)
prefixes	bolt-on word parts at the beginning of a word, e.g. **un**clear, **pre**pare, **re**peat
priming	the effect of context in facilitating predictions
proximity rule	the tendency to try to relate the things that are nearest at hand
pseudo-words	invented meaningless 'words' to test graphophonic or morphological skills, e.g. **gluph**; one **wug**, two ___?
reading process	the psychological processes of perceiving print and translating it into words, sentences and meanings
recognition units	spelling sequences, whole or part words, that are perceived and identified as complete units
referent	that which is referred to
referential meaning	literal meaning, what is referred to
register	language variety distinguished according to its use
response	the global reaction, cognitive, affective and attitudinal, to a text by a reader

rime	that part of a syllable (q.v.) that includes the vowel and any subsequent consonant sounds; the part that potentially could rhyme
rime analogy	using the rime spelling of a known word to help identify an unknown word, working on the assumption that identical rime spellings represent identical rime pronunciations
root	the etymological origin of a word, or (sometimes) the stem (q.v.) of a word
running reading records	a procedure not unlike miscue analysis (q.v.), designed by Marie Clay for use in the early years
SATs	Standard Assessment Tests – government-sponsored tests for accountability purposes
segmenting	the reverse of blending (q.v.): the separating out of a pronunciation into smaller units, e.g. syllables, onset and rimes, phonemes (q.v.)
self-correction	spontaneously correcting a miscue or mistake in reading as a result of reviewing the contextual or graphophonic information available
self-monitoring	the alertness to meaning and graphophonic information that permits and triggers self-correction (q.v.)
self-tutoring	the autodidactic learning of the better identification of words as the result of self-correction (q.v.)
semantic context	the context of meaning
semantic–pragmatic disorder	a condition characterised, in part, by an inability to distinguish between semantic and pragmatic meanings (q.v.) (i.e. meanings related to people's intentions in situations, as distinguished from literal meanings), possibly related to autism (q.v.) and problems with empathy (q.v.)
semantics	the study of meanings
shared reading	the procedure of an adult and child(ren) reading a text together, with the child progressively, over a number of readings of a particular text, taking over the reading from the adult
sight-word learning/recognition	learning to identify words on sight, without having to work them out. Some such learning is logographic (q.v.), with the words learned by rote. But later on, words that have been fully worked out a number of times also come to be recognised instantly as sight words
skewed distribution	a statistical concept, where the distribution curve is asymmetical (see **normal distribution**)
sounding-out routines	in phonic reading, the process of sounding out the letters and blending them into a pronunciation
sources of information	the reader has three ways of helping to identify the words in a text: (a) graphophonics, including sight recognition and decoding the print; (b) using semantic information to prime graphophonic perception, predict wording and check for meaningfulness; and (c) using syntactic information for priming, prediction and guiding semantic processes (q.v. most terms used here!)
stem	the morphemic core of a word (often a free morpheme (q.v.)) which may then have bound morphemes (q.v.) of various kinds added to it to develop the word's meaning and syntactic status,

e.g. **love** → **lov**able → un**lov**able → un**lov**ably. Questionably called a 'root' (q.v.) in the National Literacy Strategy.

stress   in pronunciation, the relative auditory prominence or accentuation of one syllable (q.v.) compared with adjacent syllables, creating rhythm in speech

sub-text   the meanings and motives that underlie overt expression, as with 'Come upstairs and see my etchings'

suffix   a word-part added after the stem (q.v.) of a complex word, determining meaning and part of speech of a word, e.g. crea**tion**, comfor**table**, sing**ing**

summative   see **formative**

syllable   that phonological unit in a word that centres on a vowel sound, together with its associated consonants

syntactic context   the grammatical situation of a word within a phrase or sentence which specifies the part of speech or agreement that is required, e.g. 'I (verb needed) it on to the (noun needed) very (adverb needed).'

syntax   the grammatical rules governing word order and agreements in constructing well-formed phrases and sentences, e.g. 'a red cart', not 'cart a red'

synthetic phonics   reading by phonic procedures, synthesising the word sound from the letter sounds by blending

tenor   that aspect of language style that indicates social function and purpose and expresses attitudes to the subject and the audience, e.g. in levels of formality

token word   'fish, fish, fish' constitutes three token-words, but only one type-word

top-down processing   that aspect of the reading process (q.v.) that is concerned with identifying and checking word recognition using information from the semantic and syntactic contexts (q.v.)

type word   see **token word**

whole-word teaching   teaching sight-word recognition (q.v.) without reference to the word's alphabetic composition

word-attack skills   graphophonic (q.v.) and other skills used for working out unknown words

working memory   the immediate, but short-duration, memory in which the significance of current sensory inputs is worked out, before processed material and meanings are consigned to longer-term memory

References I

ACADEMIC REFERENCES

Adams, Marilyn Jager (1990) *Beginning to Read: Thinking and Learning about Print*, MIT

Aristotle, trans. I. Bywater (1920) *On the Art of Poetry*, Oxford

Barnes, Douglas (1976) *From Communication to Curriculum*, Penguin

Beard, Roger (1987) *Developing Reading 3–13*, Hodder & Stoughton

Beard, Roger (ed.) (1993) *Teaching Literacy: Balancing Perspectives*, Hodder & Stoughton

Beard, Roger and Oakhill, Jane (1994) *Reading by Apprenticeship?* NFER

Benton, M. and Fox, G. (1985) *Teaching Literature: Nine to Fourteen*, Oxford

Bernstein, Basil (1971) *Class, Codes and Control*, Vol. I, Routledge & Kegan Paul

Bettelheim, Bruno (1978) *The Uses of Enchantment*, Penguin

Biddulph, Steve (1998) *Manhood*, Hawthorn Press

Bielby, Nicholas (1994) *Making Sense of Reading: The New Phonics and its Practical Implications*, Scholastic

Bielby, Nicholas (1998) *How To Teach Reading: A Balanced Approach*, Scholastic

Brooks, Greg, Gorman, Tom, Kendal, Lesley and Tate, Alison (1992) *What Teachers in Training are Taught about Reading*, NFER

Brown, J.A.C. (1964) *Freud and the Post-Freudians*, Penguin

Browne, Ann (1996) *Developing Language and Literacy 3–8*, Chapman

Brownjohn, Sandy (1980) *Does It Have To Rhyme?* Hodder & Stoughton

Brownjohn, Sandy (1982) *What Rhymes With 'Secret'?* Hodder & Stoughton

Brownjohn, Sandy (1989) *The Ability To Name Cats*, Hodder & Stoughton

Brownjohn, Sandy (1993a) *Poetry Express 2: O frabjous day!* Ginn

Brownjohn, Sandy (1993b) *Poetry Express 3: The World's Stage* Ginn

Bryant, Peter and Bradley, Lynette (1985) *Children's Reading Problems*, Blackwell

Bryant, Peter and Nunes, Terezinha (1999) 'Spelling and Grammar', in press

Bussis, A., Chittenden, E., Amarel, M. and Klausner, E. (1985) *Inquiry into Meaning*, Lawrence Erlbaum Associates, NJ

Byrne, Brian (1998) *The Foundation of Literacy: The Child's Acquisition of the Alphabetic Principle*, Psychology Press

Carter, Dennis (1998) *Teaching Poetry in the Primary School: Perspectives for a New Generation*, David Fulton

Chew, Jennifer (1997) 'Traditional Phonics: What it is and what it is not', *Journal of Research in Reading*, Vol. 20, No. 3

Chukovsky, K. (1963) *From Two to Five*, University of California

Clay, Marie M. (1985) *The Early Detection of Reading Difficulties*, Heinemann

Clay, Marie M. (1991) *Becoming Literate: The Construction of Inner Control*, Heinemann

Clegg, Alec (ed.) (1964) *The Excitement of Writing*, Chatto & Windus

Coles, Martin (1998) 'Assessing reading: Changing practice', in Coles, M. and Jenkins, R. (1998) op. cit.

Coles, M. and Jenkins, R. (1998) *Assessing Reading 2: Changing Practice in the Classroom*, Routledge

Cook, Elizabeth (1969) *The Ordinary and the Fabulous*, Cambridge

Crevola, C.A. and Hill, P.W. (1998) 'Evaluation of a whole-school approach to prevention and intervention in early literacy', *Journal of Education for Students Placed at Risk*, Vol. 3, No. 2, pp 133–57

DFE (1995) *The National Curriculum: Key Stages 1 and 2 (1995)* DFE

DfEE (1997) Circular 10/97 and DfEE (1998) Circular 4/98, *Teaching: High Status, High Standards*, DfEE

DfEE (1998) *The National Literacy Strategy Framework for Teaching*, DfEE

Dombey, H. and Moustafa, M. (1998) *Whole-to-Part Phonics: How Children Learn to Read and Spell*, Centre for Language in Primary Education

Donaldson, M. (1989) 'Sense and sensibility: Some thoughts on the teaching of literacy', Occasional Paper No. 3, Reading and Language Information Centre, University of Reading. Reprinted in Beard, R. (ed.) (1993) op. cit.

Downing, J. (1973) *Comparative Reading: Cross-National Studies of Behaviour and Processes in Reading and Writing*, Collier Macmillan

Egoff, S., Stubbs, G.T. and Ashley, L.F. (eds) (1969) *Only Connect: Reading in Children's Literature*, Oxford (Toronto)

Ehri, Linnea C. (1991) 'The development of reading and spelling in children: An overview', in Snowling, M. and Thomson, M.E. (eds) (1991) op. cit.

Ehri, Linnea C. (1995) 'Phases of development in learning to read words by sight', *Journal of Research in Reading*, Vol. 18, No. 2

Eliot, T.S. (1933) *The Use of Poetry and the Use of Criticism*, Faber

Erikson, Erik (1963) *Childhood and Society*, 2nd edition, Norton, NY

Ellis, A.W. (1993) *Reading, Writing and Dyslexia: A Cognitive Analysis*, 2nd edition, Lawrence Erlbaum Associates

Elkonin, D.B. (1973) 'USSR', in Downing, J. (1973) op. cit.

Falk, B. (1998) 'Using direct evidence to assess student progress: How the Primary Language Record supports teaching and learning', in Harrison, C. and Salinger, T. (1998) op. cit

Forster, E.M. (1962) *Aspects of the Novel*, Penguin

Frith, Uta (1985) 'Developmental Dyslexia', in Patterson, K.E. *et al.* (eds) (1985) op. cit.

Fry, Donald (1985) *Children Talking About Books: Seeing Themselves As Readers*, Open University

Funnell, Elaine and Stuart, Morag (eds) (1995) *Learning to Read*, Blackwell

Goswami, Usha (1991) 'Recent work on reading and spelling development', in Snowling, M. and Thomson, M.E. (1991) op. cit.

Goswami, Usha (1993a) 'Orthographic analogies and reading development', *The Psychologist*, July

Goswami, Usha (1993b) 'Towards an interactive analogy model of reading development: Decoding vowel graphemes in beginning reading', *Journal of Experimental Child Psychology*, 1994

Goswami, Usha (1995) 'Phonological development and reading by analogy: What is analogy and what is not?', *Journal of Research in Reading*, Vol. 18, No. 2

Goswami, Usha and Bryant, Peter (1990) *Phonological Skills and Learning to Read*, Lawrence Erlbaum Associates

Graham, J. and Kelly, A. (eds) (1998) *Reading Under Control*, David Fulton

Greenfield, Susan (1997) *The Human Brain*, Weidenfeld & Nicolson

HMI (1990) *The Teaching and Learning of Reading in Primary Schools*, DES

Halliday, M.A.K. (1969) 'Revelant models of language', *Educational Review*, Vol. 22, No. 1

Harding, D.W. (1962) 'Psychological processes in the reading of fiction', *British Journal of Aesthetics*, Vol. 2, No. 2, reprinted in Meek M. *et al.* (eds) (1977) op. cit.

Hardy, Barbara (1977) 'Narrative as a primary act of mind', in Meek M. *et al.* (eds) (1977) op. cit.

Harris, Margaret and Coltheart, Max (1986) *Language Processing in Children and Adults*, Routledge & Kegan Paul

Harrison, C., Bailey, M. and Dewar, A. (1998) 'Responsive reading assessment: Is post-modern assessment of reading possible?', in Harrison, C. and Salinger, T. (1998) op. cit.

Harrison, C. and Salinger, T. (1998) *Assessing Reading 1: Theory and Practice*, Routledge

Hatcher, P.J., Hulme, C. and Ellis, A.W. (1995) 'Helping to overcome early reading failure by combining the teaching of reading and phonological skills', in Funnell, E. and Stuart, M. (1995) op. cit.

Hayward, L. and Spencer, E. (1998a) 'Taking a closer look: A Scottish perspective on reading assessment', in Harrison, C. and Salinger, T. (1998) op. cit.

Hayward, L. and Spencer, E. (1998b) 'Taking a closer look at reading: a Scottish perspective', in Coles, M. and Jenkins, R. (1998) op. cit.

Horner, Sue (1998) 'Assessing reading and the English National Curriculum', in Harrison, C. and Salinger, T. (1998) op. cit.

Hughes, Ted (1967) *Poetry in the Making*, Faber

Hurry, J. (1995) 'What is so special about Reading Recovery?', *The Curriculum Journal*, Vol. 7, No. 1, pp 93–108

Jung, K. (1959) *The Archetypes and the Collective Unconscious*, Routledge

Kennedy, M.M., Birman, B.F. and Demaline, R.E. (1986) *The Effectiveness of Chapter 1 Services*, Office of Educational Research and Improvement, US Department of Education (Washington DC)

Kingman Report (1988) *Report of the Committee of Inquiry into the Teaching of English Language*, HMSO

Lawrence, D.H. (1925) 'Why the novel matters' and 'Morality and the novel' in Lawrence D.H. (1961) op. cit.

Lawrence, D.H. (1961) *Selected Literary Criticism*, Heinemann

Lewis, C.S. (1954) *English Poetry in the Sixteenth Century*, Oxford

Lewis, C.S. (1969) 'On three ways of writing for children' in Egoff, S. *et al* (eds) (1969) op. cit.

Lewis, M.M. (1963) *Language, Thought and Personality*, Harrap

Lewis, M.M. (1969) *Language and the Child*, NFER

Lunzer, E. and Gardner, K. (1984) *Learning from the Written Word*, Oliver & Boyd

Martin, T. and Leather, B. (1994) *Readers and Texts in the Primary Years*, Open University

McGaw, B., Long, M.G., Morgan, G. and Rosier, M.J. (1989) *Literacy and Numeracy in Australian Schools*, ACER Research Monograph No. 34, ACER (Hawthorn, Victoria)

Meek, M., Warlow, A. and Barton, G. (eds) (1977) *The Cool Web: The Pattern of Children's Reading*, Bodley

Millard, E. (1996) 'Some thoughts on why boys don't choose to read in school', an occasional paper, National Literacy Trust

Millard, E. (1997) *Differently Literate: Boys, Girls and the Schooling of Literacy*, Falmer

Minns, Hilary (1990) *Read It To Me Now!*, Virago

Murdoch, Iris (1970) *The Sovereignty of Good*, Routledge & Kegan Paul

Nunes, Terezinha (1998) *Developing Children's Minds Through Literacy and Numeracy*, Institute of Education

Nunes, T., Bryant, P. and Bindman, M. (1997) 'Morphological spelling strategies', *Developmental Psychology*, Vol. 33, No. 4

Oakhill, Jane and Garnham, Alan (1988) *Becoming a Skilled Reader*, Blackwell

Ogden, C.K. and Richards, I.A. (1923) *The Meaning of Meaning*, Routledge

Open University (1972) *Language in Education: A Source Book*, Open University

Palmer, Sue (1998) in English Association Newsletter No. 158

Patterson, K.E., Marshall, J.C. and Coltheart, M. (1985) *Surface Dyslexia*, Lawrence Erlbaum Associates

Pearson, P.D., Spalding, E. and Myers, M. (1998) 'Literacy assessment as part of new standards', in Coles, M. and Jenkins, R. (1998) op. cit.

Perera, K. (1984) *Children's Writing and Reading: Analysing Classroom Language*, Blackwell

Perera, K. (1993) 'The "good book": Linguistic aspects', in Beard, R. (ed.) (1993) op. cit.

Pickard, P.M. (1961) *I Could a Tale Unfold*, Tavistock

Piluski, J.J. (1994) 'Preventing reading failure: A review of five effective programmes', *The Reading Teacher*, 48, pp 15–19

Pinker, S. (1995) *The Language Instinct*, Penguin

Protherough, R. (1983) *Developing Response to Fiction*, Open University

Riley, J. (1996) *The Teaching of Reading: The Development of Literacy in the Early Years of School*, Paul Chapman Publishing

SCAA (1994) *English Draft Proposals*, DES

Scottish Council for Research in Education (1995) *Taking a Closer Look at Reading*, SCRE

Sedgwick, Fred (1997) *Read My Mind*, Routledge

Seymour, P.H.K. and Elder, L. (1985) 'Beginning reading without phonology', *Cognitive Neuropsychology*

Slavin, R.E., Madden, N.A., Dolan, N.J., Wasik, B.J., Ross, S.M., Smith, L.J. and Dianda, M. (1996) 'Success for all: A summary of research', *Journal for Students Placed at Risk*, Vol. 1, pp 41–76

Snowling, M. (1987) *Dyslexia*, Blackwell

Snowling, M. and Thomson, M.E. (eds) (1991) *Dyslexia: Integrating Theory and Practice*, Whurr

TGAT (1988) *Report of the Task Group on Assessment and Testing*, DES

Thomas, Huw (1998) *Reading and Responding to Fiction: Classroom Strategies for Developing Literacy*, Scholastic

Tolkien, J.R.R. (1964) *Tree and Leaf*, Allen & Unwin

Tucker, Nicholas (1981) *The Child and the Book*, Cambridge

Vincent, D. (1994) 'The assessment of reading', in Wray, D. and Medwell, J. (1994) op. cit.

Vincent, D. and Harrison, C. (1998) 'Curriculum-based assessment of reading in England and Wales: A national pilot study', in Harrison, C. and Salinger, T. (1998) op. cit.

Vygotsky, L.S. (1962) *Thought and Language*, MIT

Waterland, Liz (1985) *Read With Me: An Apprenticeship Approach to Reading*, Thimble Press

Wells, Gordon (1987) *The Meaning-Makers: Children Learning Language and Using Language to Learn*, Hodder & Stoughton

Whitehead, F. *et al.* (1977) *Children and their Books*, Macmillan

Winkworth, E. (1977) *User Education in Schools*, British Library Reseach and Development Department

Woodhead, Chris (1979) 'Teaching literature: the Oxford Educational Research Group Project', *Oxford Review of Education*, Vol. 5, No. 1

Wray, D. (1985) *Teaching Information Skills Through Project Work*, Hodder & Stoughton

Wray, D. (1994) 'Information handling: an important dimension to literacy', in Wray, D. and Medwell, J. (1994) op. cit.

Wray, D. and Leewin, M. (1997) *Extending Literacy: Children Reading and Writing Non-fiction*, Routledge

Wray, D. and Medwell, J. (1994) *Teaching Primary English: The State of the Art*, Routledge

References II

LITERARY REFERENCES, INCLUDING CHILDREN'S LITERATURE

Adams, Richard (1973) *Watership Down*, Penguin

Alexander, Lloyd (1973) *The Book of Three*, Collins

Bastable, T. (1977) *A Dictionary of Dinosaurs*, Pan/Piccolo

Bawden, Nina (1976) *Carrie's War*, Puffin

Collins Pathways (1996) *The Age of Dinosaurs*

Collins Pathways (1996) *Millie's Story*

Collins Pathways (1996) *The Pantomime Cat*

Dahl, Roald (1984) *The BFG*, Penguin

Dickens, Charles (1955) *Hard Times*, Oxford

Garfield, Leon (1988) *Shakespeare's Stories*, Gollancz

Godden, Rumer (1975) *The Diddakoi*, Puffin

Hardy, Thomas (1957) *Tess of the D'Urbevilles*, Macmillan

Harvey, A. (1993) *He Said, She Said, They Said*, Blackie

Heide, F.P. (1975) *The Shrinking of Treehorn*, Puffin

Hodgson-Burnett, F. (1951) *The Secret Garden*. Puffin

Kemp, Gene (1979) *The Turbulent Term of Tyke Tiler*, Puffin

Kerr, Judith (1974) *When Hitler Stole Pink Rabbit*, Collins Lions

Martin, Nancy (1998) *Introducing Wordsworth: Classic Poems for Literacy Teaching in KS2*, Wordsworth Trust

Maxwell, Gavin (1963) *Ring of Bright Water*, Allen Lane

McKee, D. (1980) *Not Now, Bernard*, Anderson Press

Milne, A.A. (1924) *When We Were Very Young*, Methuen

Morpurgo, Michael (1984) *Friend or Foe*, Magnet

Oxford Primary School Dictionary (1993) Oxford

Oxford Reading Tree (1986) *Teacher's Guide 1*, Oxford

Pearce, Philippa (1976) *Tom's Midnight Garden*, Puffin

Scholastic Literacy Centre (1993) Bentley, D. and Reid, D. (consultants), Scholastic

Sendak, Maurice (1970) *Where the Wild Things Are*, Puffin

Serraillier, Ian (1960) *The Silver Sword*, Puffin

Story Chest (1991) *Teacher's File*, Nelson

Story Chest (1991) *The Hungry Giant*, Nelson

Swindells, Robert (1982) *The Ice Palace*, Puffin

Swift, Jonathan (1991) *Gulliver's Travels*, Everyman

Tolkien, J.R.R. (1966) *The Hobbit*, Allen & Unwin

Van Der Loeff, A. Rutgers (1963) *Children on the Oregon Trail*, Puffin

Webb, Kay (ed.) (1979) *I Like This Poem*, Puffin

Westall, Robert (1977) *The Machinegunners*, Penguin

Westall, Robert (1989) *Blitz*, Harper Collins

Williamson, Henry (1965) *Tarka, the Otter*, Bodley

Poems referred to and/or quoted in Chapter 5 can be found in the following publications:

Alfred, Lord Tennyson, 'Morte d'Arthur', in Opie, I. and Opie, P. (1983) (eds) *The Oxford Book of Narrative Verse*, Oxford

Alfred, Lord Tennyson, 'The Eagle', in Mitchell, A. (ed.) (1993) *The Orchard Book of Poems*, Orchard, and in Philip, N. (ed.) (1990) *A New Treasury of Poetry*, Blackie

Auden, W. H., 'The Night Mail', in Webb, K. (ed.) (1979) op. cit.

Blake, William, 'The Tyger', in Mitchell, A. (ed.) (1993) *The Orchard Book of Poems*, Orchard, and in Philip, N. (ed.) (1990) *A New Treasury of Poetry*, Blackie

Chesterton, G.K. 'The Donkey', in Webb, K. (ed.) (1979) op. cit.

Eliot, T.S., 'Skimbleshanks: the Railway Cat', in Eliot, T.S. (1939) *Old Possum's Book of Practical Cats*, Faber

Gordon, George, Lord Byron, 'The Destruction of Sennacherib', in Heaney, S. and Hughes, T. (eds) (1982) *The Rattlebag*, Faber

Hughes, Ted, 'An Otter' in *Lupercal* (1960) Faber

Spender, Stephen, 'The Express', in Skelton, R. (ed.) (1964) *The Poetry of the Thirties*, Penguin

Stevenson, R.L., 'From the Window of a Railway Carriage' in Webb, K. (ed.) (1979) op. cit.

Wordsworth, William (1805–6) 'The Prelude', in *The Prelude: A Parallel Text*, Penguin, 1971

Index